THE GATHERING
PACIFIC STORM

THE GATHERING PACIFIC STORM

Emerging US-China Strategic Competition
in Defense Technological and Industrial Development

EDITED BY

Tai Ming Cheung and Thomas G. Mahnken

Rapid Communications in Conflict and Security Series
General Editor: Geoffrey R.H. Burn

CAMBRIA
PRESS

Amherst, New York

Requests for permission should be directed to:
permissions@cambriapress.com, or mailed to:
Cambria Press
University Corporate Centre,
100 Corporate Parkway, Suite 128
Amherst, New York 14226, U.S.A.

Cover Image: USS Zumwalt (DDG 1000). U.S. Navy photo/Released.

Library of Congress Cataloging-in-Publication Data on file.

ISBN: 9781604979459

TABLE OF CONTENTS

LIST OF FIGURES

List of Tables

THE GATHERING PACIFIC STORM

The Emergence of Direct US–China Defense Technological Competition

Tai Ming Cheung

The geostrategic relationship between the People's Republic of China and the United States has been defined as much by rivalry and distrust as by cooperation and friendship over the seven decades of its existence. The two countries were fierce adversaries between the 1950s and 1970s, and although relations warmed thereafter, they find themselves once again sliding into military strategic competition in the opening decades of the twenty-first century. The two governments have sought to downplay their strategic differences and emphasize their shared interests and the cooperative and interdependent nature of their broader bilateral relationship. Even in military-to-military ties, there has been a considerable thickening of exchanges ranging from high-level visits to regular consultations on a wide range of issues. The Chinese authorities have regarded the maintenance of healthy ties with the United States and avoidance of security entanglements as critical to China's overarching priority of economic development.

In reality, the Chinese defense establishment has been stepping up the development of its military capabilities since the late 1990s, especially in assets that can deter and deny access to US forces operating in the Asia-Pacific. Moreover, the People's Liberation Army (PLA) and defense industry are drawing up ambitious long-term defense science and technology development strategies and plans with the goal of leapfrogging to the global technology frontier within the next two to three decades.

The United States has portrayed its efforts since the end of the last decade to pivot to the Asia-Pacific as a return to a more traditional balancing of its global military power after the exceptional out-of-area wars in Afghanistan and Iraq after September 2001. US defense officials have also argued that their new operational concept of AirSea Battle was designed to counter worldwide anti-access threats to the United States and was not narrowly focused against China. However, in the past few years, the Pentagon has more explicitly identified China as one of the principal drivers behind renewed US efforts to rebuild its military technological capabilities and restore its overwhelming superiority. These efforts are being carried out through new research and development (R&D) initiatives such as the Third Offset Strategy and Defense Innovation Initiative.

While there are some similarities between this emerging US-China defense strategic competition and the Cold War, there are also significant differences. The US-Soviet confrontation was primarily an ideological, geostrategic, and militarized rivalry between two countries and supporting alliances that were largely sealed from each other. This twenty-first century rivalry takes place against a backdrop of globalized interdependence, the blurring of military and civilian boundaries, and the growing prominence of geo-economic determinants.

The chapters in this book offer an overview of how the US-China strategic military technological competition has emerged over the past decade. The first chapter introduces the competitive strategies analytical framework, which outlines some of the key considerations that need to be addressed in any examination of US-China military technological competition. Attention then turns to the US response to the steady erosion of its military technological superiority over China, which is set out in the Third Offset Strategy, and then Chinese views of this burgeoning competition. Case studies provide insights into the competition in the military domains of air, sea, space, and emerging technology. The remaining chapters examine the strategic and global implications of this intensification of US-China long-term military technological competition.

THE COMPETITIVE STRATEGIES FRAMEWORK

Although technological capabilities, economic resources, industrial policies, military postures, and geostrategic considerations are critical drivers of the technological competition between the United States and China, defining the evolving nature of their strategic interaction is central to the analysis. One especially relevant analytical approach is the competitive strategies framework addressed in chapter 1 by Thomas Mahnken.

As Mahnken explains, the notion of a competitive strategy refers to:

> the peacetime use of military power to shape a competitor's choices in ways that favor our objectives. That is, it is concerned with the development, acquisition, deployment, and exercising of forces, as opposed to their use in combat. A competitive strategy assumes that the choices that the competitors have to make are constrained. A competitive strategy seeks to identify and exploit these constraints.[1]

More specifically, the competitive strategy framework has a number of features pertinent to assessing the US-China interaction:

1. There is an assumption that interaction between competitors as they make strategic choices is in part because of the actions of the other party. This interaction may or may not be tightly coupled and depends on other factors such as the influence of domestic institutions, bureaucratic politics, and strategic culture.

2. The choices that competitors have open to them are constrained by economic, technological, human, political, alliance, and/or other factors. A competitive strategy seeks to identify and exploit these constraints through cost-imposition strategies. Some of these approaches include strategies of dissuasion.

3. Competitive interactions may play out over decades, which is very likely the case with the United States and China.

THE US RESPONSE TO ITS ERODING MILITARY TECHNOLOGICAL SUPERIORITY

The Pentagon launched the Third Offset Strategy and the Defense Innovation Initiative in 2014–2015 to address the erosion in US military technological superiority. These aim to identify and invest in innovative ways to regain and sustain US military dominance. An offset strategy is a type of peacetime competitive strategy that seeks to harness technological, doctrinal, and organizational innovation to negate a competitor's strengths, and generate and sustain strategic advantage. The first instance of an offset strategy in recent US history coincided with the Eisenhower administration's New Look strategy, which sought to use nuclear weapons to negate the Soviet Union's advantage in conventional forces in the early 1950s. The second, referred to at the time simply as the "Offset Strategy," coincided with the development of precision-guided munitions, sensors, stealth, and networking in the 1970s in response to the numerically superior Warsaw Pact threat to Western Europe. The "Third Offset Strategy," first unveiled by then-Secretary of Defense Chuck Hagel in 2014, seeks to develop new technologies and operational concepts in response to the development of so-called anti-access/area denial (A2/AD) capabilities by China, among others.[2]

The Third Offset Strategy and the Defense Innovation Initiative have a number of characteristics, in which China looms large as a "pacing threat":

1. *Conventional deterrence against great powers:* The central tenet of the US strategy is to develop a dominant conventional deterrent against Russia and China that reduces the chances of major military conflict with them.
2. *Asymmetric competition:* Avoidance of competition in quantitative arms races with potential adversaries. Focus is instead on development of technologically superior quality to compensate for the numerical superiority these rivals currently wield.
3. *Strategy based, technology oriented:* While technology is important, operational strategies and organizational constructs are also key elements in gaining advantages against numerically stronger opponents.
4. *Operational level of war:* The primary focus of the initiatives is in the operational planning and conduct of campaigns that consist of assigning missions, tasks, and resources to military organizations. The principal operational concerns of the US Department of Defense (DoD) are:
   a. the growing vulnerability of its global system of military bases, especially those that are close to major potential adversaries in the Asia-Pacific and Europe;
   b. the increasing ability of opponents to detect, track, and engage US aircraft carriers and other major surface warships at extended ranges from their coasts;
   c. the build-up of modern integrated air defense systems that are making it increasingly difficult for US and allied airpower to enter into contested opposition airspace; and
   d. the militarization of space that means it is no longer a sanctuary from military conflict.[3]

DoD officials have acknowledged that the origins of the Third Offset Strategy come from the threat posed by China. Speaking at a defense forum in November 2015, Deputy Secretary of Defense Robert Work disclosed that the DoD first began to think about the Third Offset Strategy in the early 2010s when Ashton Carter, Deputy Secretary of Defense at the time, established the Strategic Capabilities Office which "focused on the advanced capabilities that we were seeing in the Western Pacific."[4] The only country undertaking these developments was China.

Development of the Third Offset Strategy and Defense Innovation Initiative signals that the United States has taken its first steps in engaging China directly in defense technological competition. From a US defense acquisition perspective, these strategies are being operationalized in the Long-Range Research and Development Program Plan (LRDPP), modeled on an effort started in the 1970s when the United States successfully offset Soviet military numerical superiority with disruptive technological capabilities such as stealth and precision strike.[5]

Former US Undersecretary of Defense for Acquisition, Technology, and Logistics Frank Kendall, who was in overall charge of the LRDPP, provided a succinct assessment of the military technological threat posed by China at a Congressional hearing in January 2015 in providing the geostrategic context for the renewed innovation drive by the DoD:

> China has developed and fielded advanced weapons designed to defeat US power projection forces. Many more are in development. These systems include a range of capabilities but foremost among them are accurate and sophisticated cruise and ballistic missiles designed to attack high value assets; particularly the aircraft carriers and airfields that we depend upon for power projection. These missiles, fielded in large numbers and coupled with advanced electronic warfare systems, modern air-to-air missiles, extensive counter-space capabilities, improved undersea warfare capabilities, fifth-generation fighters, and offensive cyber weapons pose a serious and growing threat.[6]

A number of new and emerging high technologies, especially in the areas of artificial intelligence and autonomy, have been revealed as the initial focus of the Third Offset Strategy and Defense Innovation Initiative in order, as Robert Work argued, "to deter" against potential adversaries:[7]

- *Autonomous 'deep learning' machines and systems:* The Pentagon wants to develop these capabilities to improve its early warning and prediction of events.

- *Human-machine collaboration:* How machines can interface with humans to assist with decision making. One example is the development of highly advanced helmets for fighter pilots that fuse data from multiple systems.

- *Assisted-human operations:* Research is being targeted on how machines can help humans operate more effectively. The Defense Advanced Research Projects Agency, for example, has been developing an experimental "Iron Man" exoskeleton suit. This research is different from "enhanced human operations" that focus on modifying the human body and brain, and which Work claimed "our adversaries are pursuing, and it scares the crap out of us, frankly."[8]

- *Human-machine combat teaming:* Leveraging the unique advantages of people and machines, including robotics and artificial intelligence, into hybrid teams with the goal of delivering decisive advantages on the battlefield. This is already being applied through the teaming of human operators and unmanned systems such as the US Army's Apache helicopter and Gray Eagle unmanned aerial vehicle or the US Navy's P-8 reconnaissance aircraft and the MQ-4C Triton unmanned carrier-launched airborne surveillance and strike drone.

- *Network-enabled semi-autonomous weapons hardened for electronic and cyber-warfare environments:* Many of the US military's weapons and systems are semi-autonomous and connected to vulnerable networks. These will require modification and hardening to prevent being disabled by increasingly sophisticated electronic and cyber warfare attacks, much like protection against an electro-magnetic pulse attack during the Cold War. Work is taking place, for example, to make the Small Diameter Bomb operate without reliance on global positioning system information to direct it to its target.

CHINESE VIEWS OF US-CHINA DEFENSE TECHNOLOGICAL COMPETITION

Perceptions among Chinese defense and national security policymakers and planners that the United States is becoming a direct military competitor and potential adversary have been gaining ground over the past decade. Intensifying security frictions and competing interests have deepened strategic distrust between the two countries, although the Chinese, especially official, views are more circumspect. In a 2012 study of US-China strategic trust, Wang Jisi, an influential academic foreign policy adviser to the Chinese leadership, pointed out that "some high-ranking Chinese officials have openly stated that the United States is China's greatest national security threat. This perception is especially widely shared in China's defense and security establishments and in the Communist Party's ideological organizations."[9]

These views of the increasingly contested nature of US-China security relations and interests have yet to be reflected in publicly available authoritative Chinese strategic and military doctrines and policies. These have tended to be more guarded in their assessments of the United States because China's overarching strategic priority continues to be economic development, which can only be effectively carried out in a non-antagonistic security environment.

In discussing the regional security situation surrounding China, the 2015 Chinese defense white paper pointed out that, "as the world economic and strategic center of gravity is shifting ever more rapidly to the Asia-Pacific region, the United States carries on its 'rebalancing' strategy and enhances its military presence and its military alliances in this region."[10] The white paper is even more circumspect in not mentioning the United

States in its assessment of intensifying global defense technological competition and its implications for China's national security:

> The world revolution in military affairs is proceeding to a new stage. Long-range, precise, smart, stealthy, and unmanned weapons and equipment are becoming increasingly sophisticated. Outer space and cyber space have become new commanding heights in strategic competition among all parties. The form of war is accelerating its evolution to informationization. World major powers are actively adjusting their national security strategies and defense policies, and speeding up their military transformation and force restructuring. The aforementioned revolutionary changes in military technologies and the form of war have not only had a significant impact on the international political and military landscapes, but also posed new and severe challenges to China's military security.

While official Chinese documents and policies are silent as to whether China's military developments are in direct response to perceived US threats and actions, there is an emerging debate of these action-reaction dynamics among security analysts, scholars, and writers in institutions affiliated with the military, state, and Communist Party.[11] Chapter 2 by retired Senior Col. Fan Gaoyue, who is a leading Chinese analyst of U.S. military affairs, highlights the growing discussion on the Third Offset Strategy by Chinese analysts. Fan points out that Chinese military analysts have divergent views on the rationale and intentions behind the Third Offset Strategy. Some believe it is a trap to lure China into a contest in areas in which the United States has strong advantages, much like what happened to the Soviet Union in the 1980s. Another school of thought is that the Third Offset is a cover for US weaknesses. The official Chinese view is to take a wait-and-see attitude and continue to press ahead with China's development of asymmetric capabilities.

To support this pursuit of increasingly advanced military technological capabilities, the Chinese defense industry is undertaking major reforms, which are detailed in chapter 3 by Tai Ming Cheung, Eric Anderson, and

Fan Yang. These reforms include new long-term plans and institutional arrangements, an emphasis on turnkey technologies and civil-military integration, and capital market access. China's increased ability to forge an independent development path will make it more resistant to US competitive strategies. The authors argue that the accelerating pace and intensity of Chinese defense industry developments represent a long-term challenge to US military technological superiority.

US-CHINA MILITARY TECHNOLOGICAL STRATEGIC COMPETITION IN THE AIR, SEA, SPACE, AND EMERGING TECHNOLOGY DOMAINS

US-China military technological competition in the space and missile, military aviation, naval, and new and emerging technologies are examined in several chapters. Chapter 4 by Kevin Pollpeter looks at the missile, space, and counterspace domains and argues that China and the United States find themselves in a security dilemma characterized by a competition that could easily turn into an arms race. Both sides, especially their navies and air forces, have developed new operational concepts and are emphasizing joint, networked approaches to command and control, investment in technologies and new organizations to ensure the survivability of space capabilities, and development of counterspace capabilities to deny the other side the use of space.

The indicators of direct competition in the aviation and maritime spheres appear to be more mixed. In the examination of US-China strategic competition in military aviation in chapter 5, Michael Chase and Oriana Mastro look at three factors—resource allocations, targeted platform development, and airpower employment concepts—to determine the competition's nature and extent. They conclude that while China has been competing with the United States for several decades, it is not until recently that the United States has directly thought about and responded to China.

Chapter 6 by Bryan Clark and Jordan Wilson assesses US-China strategic competition in the maritime arena, where the dynamics seem similar to what has been taking place in aviation. China has been pursuing an asymmetric approach to counter the US Navy since the 1990s that started with investments in long-range radars and cruise and ballistic anti-ship missiles before proceeding to the current focus of a rapid buildup of navy, coast guard, and maritime militia components. The US Navy has primarily continued its investment in long-range, high-endurance "blue water" capabilities to project power far from US shores. Clark and Wilson believe that bilateral maritime strategic competition is on the increase, although it is still in the initial stages of development.

Daniel Alderman and Jonathan Ray in chapter 7 focus on US-China strategic competition in emerging technologies, especially artificial intelligence (AI). While they see rising competition in the defense and security domains, they point out that R&D in commercial emerging technologies in the two countries is becoming deeply integrated and provides mutual benefit to each country's consumer markets. They also offer a basic analytical framework to simplify assessment of the complex bilateral interactions between the two countries in AI and other emerging technologies.

Chapter 8 offers a Russian perspective on the Third Offset Strategy and its implications for Sino-Russian cooperation. Vasily Kashin points out new patterns of defense technological cooperation between Russia and China, which might be deepened and accelerated in response to the Third Offset Strategy. The first trend is the growing role of Russian companies as subcontractors in Chinese defense industrial R&D and production projects. A second trend is the start of major joint projects, such as joint development of a wide-bodied commercial airliner. The third trend is the start of significant imports of major Chinese components for Russian military platforms and systems. Overall, Kashin believes that Russia and China may be moving to a mutually dependent military industrial alliance.

In the concluding chapter, Thomas Mahnken and Tai Ming Cheung consider the implications of this defense technological competition on the grand and national security strategies of the U.S. and China towards each other over the long-term measured in decades. For China, which will be under the leadership of Xi Jinping at least until the early 2020s and likely much longer, it will be looking to accelerate its efforts to further narrow the defense technological gap with the United States as it places greater emphasis on national security priorities and seeks to elevate its global standing. While Beijing will watch closely how the United States proceeds with the rejuvenation of its defense technological innovation capabilities and how it is directed against China, the Chinese authorities will continue to focus on its own priorities and seek to not be drawn too closely into an action-reaction dynamic with a more advanced and wealthy competitor. For the U.S., strategic competition with China is now one of its foremost defense and national security priorities. In responding to China's increasing international activism, Mahnken and Cheung say that the U.S. should seek to devise a strategy focusing on asymmetric advantages in geography, alliances, technology, and doctrine to constrain Chinese advances. Such a strategy over time promises to influence Chinese actions by imposing hefty costs and increasing risks.

Notes

1. Octavian Manea, "Lessons from Previous Competitive Strategies: Interview with Thomas G. Mahnken," Small Wars Journal website, January 21, 2014, http://smallwarsjournal.com/jrnl/art/lessons-from-previous-competitive-strategies.
2. See, for example, Robert Martinage, *Toward a New Offset Strategy: Exploiting US Long-Term Advantages to Restore U.S. Global Power Projection Capability* (Washington, DC: Center for Strategic and Budgetary Assessments, 2014).
3. Ibid, 23–32.
4. Remarks by Robert Work on the Third Offset Strategy at the Reagan Defense Forum, November 7, 2015, http://www.defense.gov/News/Speeches/Speech-View/Article/628246/reagan-defense-forum-the-third-offset-strategy.
5. "DoD Seeks Future Technology via Development Plan," *DoD News*, December 3, 2014, http://www.defense.gov/News-Article-View/Article/603745.
6. Testimony of Frank Kendall before the US House Armed Services Committee, January 28, 2015.
7. Remarks by Work at Reagan Defense Forum. See also his speech at the CNAS Defense Forum, Washington, DC, December 14, 2015, http://www.defense.gov/News/Speeches/Speech-View/Article/634214/cnas-defense-forum.
8. Remarks by Work at Reagan Defense Forum.
9. Kenneth Lieberthal and Wang Jisi, *Addressing US–China Strategic Distrust* (Washington, DC: Brookings Institution, 2012), 13.
10. The State Council Information Office of the People's Republic of China, "China's Military Strategy," May 2015.
11. Michael Swaine, "Chinese Leadership and Elite Responses to the US Pacific Pivot," *China Leadership Monitor* no. 38, summer 2012.

Chapter 1

Frameworks for Examining Long-Term Strategic Competition Between Major Powers

Thomas Mahnken

The topic of how the United States can most effectively bring its strengths to bear in peacetime against great power competitors has received renewed attention in recent years.[1] Several trends have brought on the current interest in so-called competitive strategies. The rise of China, and particularly China's investment in weapons and doctrine aimed at blunting the ability of the United States to project power into the Western Pacific, is shifting the military balance in the region and potentially beyond in ways unfavorable to the United States. Russia's aggressive behavior in Ukraine, Syria, and beyond poses an additional set of challenges. Both China and Russia are pursuing capabilities that the United States has long identified as sources of concern. For example, the 2001 *Quadrennial Defense Review* listed a set of emerging strategic and operational challenges that demanded attention, including: protecting critical bases of operations, assuring information systems in the face of attack, projecting and sustaining US forces in distant anti-access or area-denial environments and defeating such threats, denying enemies sanctuary through persistent surveillance and high-volume precision firepower, and enhancing the survivability of space systems and supporting infrastructure.[2] In the decade and a half following the publication of the report, the military balance has shifted away from the United States in each of these areas.

Another motivation for exploring strategies for peacetime competition is domestic. The United States faces constraints upon its ability to respond to the changing military balance, including more than a decade and a half of focus on counterinsurgency and limited funding of the types of capabilities that would be of greatest relevance to deterring or countering great power competitors, despite bipartisan calls to do so.[3]

The premium for strategic thinking is increasing as the US margin of superiority is decreasing. As threats to the United States, our allies, and our interests grow, there is an increasing need to deter aggression and influence the options available to competitors. This chapter offers a framework for thinking about a family of long-term peacetime strategies. It begins by describing the concept of competitive strategies, as well as four approaches to competitive strategy: denial, cost imposition, attacking a competitor's strategy, and attacking a competitor's political system. It goes on to explore the criteria that strategists and policy makers should consider in formulating a competitive strategy. It concludes with some thoughts on how to evaluate the success of such a strategy.

THINKING ABOUT COMPETITIVE STRATEGIES

Even though the term "competitive strategies" entered into the US Department of Defense lexicon in the 1970s, the concept of long-term peacetime competition between great powers is quite old.[4] History contains a number of cases of such competitions, including those between Athens and Sparta in the third Century BC, France and Great Britain from the eighteenth to the nineteenth centuries, Germany and Great Britain in the nineteenth and twentieth centuries, the United States and Great Britain in the nineteenth and early twentieth century, the United States and Japan during the first half of the twentieth century, and the United States and the Soviet Union during the second half of the twentieth century.[5] Some, such as the Anglo-American rivalry, ended peacefully and amicably. Others, such as the Anglo-German competition, led to war. Still others, such as the US-Soviet competition, yielded conflicts on the periphery and an armed and sometimes uneasy peace between the central actors.

Similarly, the strategy of imposing costs upon a competitor in order to influence his decision-making calculus has long been a part of the repertoire of strategy in peacetime. Many of the protagonists in past long-term competitions pursued conscious strategies to impose costs upon their rivals in peacetime in furtherance of their objectives. For example, from 1898 to 1914, Great Britain developed and executed a naval modernization program that sought, among other things, to impose considerable costs upon Germany as it sought to respond.[6] During the Cold War, the United States pursued a number of strategies against the Soviet Union that were meant to impose costs of various kinds on Moscow, including the Army and Air Force's development of AirLand Battle beginning in the 1970s, the Navy's Maritime Strategy of the 1980s, the development of stealth aircraft, and the Strategic Defense Initiative.[7]

More recently, America's adversaries have pursued cost-imposing strategies against the United States. Al Qaeda's September 11, 2001, terrorist attacks, and the responses to them, resulted in considerable costs. Such costs go beyond the physical destruction of the attacks on the World Trade Center and the Pentagon and the disruption of the economic life of the nation, to include the subsequent costs of transportation security initiatives and the time and efficiency costs that flow from them. Cyberattacks on US government network that have triggered the development and deployment of increasing layers of security have similarly yielded considerable costs, to include that of developing and fielding cyber security as well as the efficiency losses associated with such security measures.

The development and diffusion of so-called anti-access/area-denial capabilities (which the Chinese refer to as "counter-intervention" capabilities) are imposing considerable costs as well. China's development and fielding of conventional ballistic missiles of sufficient range and accuracy to hold at risk US air bases in Japan and beyond will force the United States to harden and disperse its basing infrastructure.[8] Its development of anti-ship ballistic missiles such as the DF-21D and DF-26 is forcing the US Navy to invest in countermeasures and potentially new operational concepts.[9] And its development of anti-satellite weaponry will cause the United States to invest in capabilities to safeguard its space-based systems or find alternatives to them.

It is important to situate competitive strategies within the larger realm of strategy. At a fundamental level, strategy is strategy; any modifiers are less important than the noun they modify. Strategy has to do with how a state or other political actor arrays its resources in space and time in order to achieve its aims against a competitor.[10] In other words, strategy represents the way an actor seeks to achieve his political objectives against a competitor. The key features of any strategy are rationality (the existence of political objectives and a plan to achieve them) and interaction with a competitor who seeks at the very least to achieve different objectives, if not thwart our ability to achieve our aims.[11]

Context nonetheless influences the range of options available to statesmen and soldiers. Strategy in wartime is constrained by choices made or deferred in peacetime. That is, militaries in peacetime place bets against an uncertain future. It is only when war comes that soldiers and statesmen learn whether those bets have been wise ones, and then only possibly. Donald Rumsfeld was fundamentally correct in observing that a nation goes to war with the army it has, not the one it wishes it had. Particularly in short wars, states must fight with their existing militaries. In protracted wars, the material dimension of strategy becomes more important as states have the ability to innovate and adapt, to field new forces and develop new doctrine. The armies that won World War I looked considerably different—and fought much differently—than those that entered the war, to include the emergence of a new domain of warfare (air power) and the employment of new ways of war (such as chemical weapons). Similarly, the forces in the field in 1945 possessed capabilities that had not existed at the outbreak of World War II in 1939, to include, most dramatically, the atomic bomb.

Competitive strategies follow the logic of strategy, but in peacetime. Strategy in peace differs from that in war in several ways. First, competitive strategies can, and often do, involve the use of military assets, but focus on the latent use of force to deter or coerce rather than to defeat competitors. Peacetime strategy focuses on when and how we reveal our research, development, and acquisition of new capabilities; what we choose to acquire; when and how we deploy them; and how we train with them. As a result, peacetime strategy leads to tradeoffs that are not present in time of war. For example, governments face the decision as to whether to reveal military capabilities in order to deter or influence a competitor, or to conceal them in order to preserve their operational effectiveness in a future conflict. During the 1970s and 1980s, for example, low-observable aircraft were developed in a highly classified setting for use against the Soviet Union in a future war. However, senior American leaders elected to reveal the existence of stealth aircraft to, among other things, force the Soviets to invest considerable sums, and time, to counter them.[12]

Second, strategy in peacetime occurs with a greater sense of uncertainty than in war. As Sir Michael Howard famously wrote nearly half a century ago, planning in peacetime is akin to navigating a ship through a thick fog of peace.[13] Third, statesmen and soldiers operating in peacetime generally have a much lower tolerance for risk in peacetime than in war. As a result, they often shy away from actions that could be seen as provocative for fear of exacerbating tensions with a competitor. Finally, it takes longer to determine the effects of one's strategy in peacetime than in wartime. Whereas the impact of one's actions on the battlefield manifest themselves in hours, days, weeks or months, the impact of peacetime actions often does not become apparent for years or more.

Competitive strategies are generally pursued to achieve limited aims.[14] That is, they are meant to change a competitor's decision-making calculus and thus his strategic behavior. They do not seek the overthrow of an adversary. In this regard, the competitive strategy that the United States pursued against the Soviet Union succeeded beyond the wildest imaginations of even its most enthusiastic supporters.[15]

Bradford A. Lee has helpfully identified four families of competitive strategies that are distinct but not mutually exclusive: denial, cost imposition, attacking a competitor's strategy, and attacking a competitor's political system.

Strategies of denial seek to prevent a competitor from being able to translate its operational means into the political ends that it seeks. More specifically, they attempt to convince a competitor's leadership that it would be impossible to achieve its political objectives through military means. For such a strategy to work, the defender needs to possess the ability to demonstrate that an aggressor cannot achieve his aims at any acceptable cost.[16]

Historical examples of peacetime strategies of denial include NATO's strategy against the Warsaw Pact during the Cold War, which sought to use conventional forces backed by the threat of nuclear escalation to convince the Soviet leadership that it would be impossible to invade and occupy Western Europe.

Some states possess geography that is favorable to a strategy of denial. Switzerland scarcely has to worry about aggression on the part of neighbors, even if they were so inclined. With the right investment in capabilities, Taiwan could harden itself against Chinese coercion.[17] In other cases, geography is less favorable. The Baltic states, for example, lack the geographic depth to make a strategy of denial by itself a winning strategy.

Even for small states, however, trends in military technology, particularly the growth and spread of precision weaponry as well as supporting intelligence, surveillance and reconnaissance systems and command and control networks, increasingly favor a strategy of denial.[18] Modern anti-tank guided munitions (ATGMs); precision rockets, artillery, and mortars; surface-to-air missiles; and unmanned aerial vehicles (UAVs) provide a growing range of options for states to carry out a strategy of denial.

Whereas strategies of denial seek to convince a competitor that it cannot achieve its aims, strategies of cost-imposition seek to convince an adversary's leadership that the costs of doing so are disproportionately high and that accommodation would be a more attractive option. Cost-imposing strategies may seek to have any number of effects upon a competitor. They may, for example, seek to dissuade or deter a competitor from engaging in actions that are disruptive or threatening by convincing them that they are too costly, ineffective, or will prove counter-productive. They may alternatively seek to channel a competitor into engaging in activities that are inoffensive or wasteful. As I have argued elsewhere, states need to think about imposing costs across multiple dimensions: economic and political as well as military.[19]

Various forms of military cost imposition can be seen in the US Air Force's pursuit of manned penetrating bombers against Soviet air defenses during the Cold War. During the early Cold War, US bombers planned to operate at high altitude. Beginning in the late 1950s, however, the Strategic Air Command shifted to low-altitude attack tactics and eventually deployed aircraft, such as the FB-111 fighter-bomber and B-1 bomber, that were optimized for low-altitude attack as well as weapons, such as the *Hound Dog* air-to-surface missile (ASM) and Short Range Attack Missile (SRAM), that were designed to allow bombers to launch attacks outside the range of Soviet surface-to-air missiles (SAMs), as well as increasingly sophisticated electronic warfare suites. When, beginning in the late 1970s, the Soviets began responding to such moves by deploying aircraft and SAMs designed to shoot down low-altitude bombers and cruise missiles, the United States began deploying stealthy aircraft such as the F-117 attack aircraft and B-2 bomber. Throughout most of the period, the United States was able to dictate the scope and pace of the competition to the Soviets, forcing them to respond to our moves while we retained the initiative.

Such an approach inflicted a variety of costs upon the Soviet Union. First, the Air Force's pursuit of manned penetrating bombers inflicted monetary costs on the Soviet Union by forcing it to acquire air defenses against high-altitude bombers in the 1950s, low-altitude bombers beginning in the 1960s, stealthy bombers beginning in the 1980s, and electronic warfare throughout. Each of these moves made previous investments in air defense irrelevant or obsolete. According to one accounting, it cost the Soviet Union $120 billion to counter US manned penetrating bombers over the course of the Cold War. The United States also forced the Soviet Union to bear technological costs by forcing the Soviet aerospace industry to invest first in look-down/shoot down target acquisition systems to counter low-flying bombers and later counter-stealth technologies against low-observable aircraft.

The United States bomber program confronted the Soviet leadership with a series of tradeoffs. For example, resources allocated to the service responsible for the strategic air defense of the Soviet Union, *PVO Strany*, could not be allocated to other services or missions. Similarly, resources devoted to strategic air defense could not be devoted to offensive missions.

These included the deployment of more than 10,000 SAMs, tens of thousands of air defense artillery systems, and 15 varieties of air defense interceptors. In addition, the Soviet Union built the MiG-25 *Foxbat* air defense interceptor to counter the XB-70 *Valkyrie* bomber, which the United States never deployed.[20]

A third approach is to attack a competitor's strategy by inducing him to engage in strategically self-defeating behavior. For example, the development of AirLand Battle doctrine by the Army and Air Force in the 1970s and 1980s combined US technological advantages with deep understanding of Soviet strategic and operational predilections, to include the Soviet General Staff's need to choreograph operations and its concern over the security of the Soviet homeland, to shake the confidence of the Soviet leadership in its ability to carry out its preferred strategy. Similarly, China's development of A2/AD capabilities is an effort to shake the confidence of US decision makers in the approach to power projection that the United States has followed since the end of World War II.

Finally, strategies that attack a competitor's political system seek to exploit and influence factions within a competitor's political system.[21] For example, recent scholarship indicates that President Reagan's 1983 announcement of the Strategic Defense Initiative (SDI) triggered a debate within the Soviet leadership over the wisdom of competing with the United States in space weaponry, as well as the form that competition should take. David Hoffman, for example, suggests that the announcement of SDI ultimately set up a situation by which Soviet leaders who favored a high-technology competition with the United States in space arms initially carried the day, only to be discredited by their inability to field high-technology weapons. That is, SDI put in motion a chain of events that ultimately made the Soviet leadership aware that it could not compete with the United States in high-technology weaponry.[22]

CONSIDERATIONS FOR FORMULATING AND IMPLEMENTING A COST-IMPOSING STRATEGY

Five considerations should govern the development and implementation of a competitive strategy, such as that of cost imposition, in peacetime.

First, the strategy must be aimed at a concrete adversary with whom we interact. One cannot develop strategy against an abstraction. Rather, strategy, in peace and in war, needs to be aimed at a particular adversary. Indeed, an understanding of the competitor's aims, strengths, weaknesses, and proclivities is central to strategic effectiveness.

Second, in order to develop, implement, and monitor a strategy, one must possess sufficient information to allow us to assess its effectiveness, or at the least to safeguard against undesirable second-order effects. In this regard, the motto of the strategist should mirror that of the physician: first, do no harm.

Developing and implementing a competitive strategy is predicated upon at least a first-order understanding of our own enduring strengths and weaknesses, and those of the competitor. This is necessary to ensure at least a reasonable chance that one's actions will elicit the response that one seeks, or at least to narrow the range of potential competitor responses.

The information requirements of successful strategy should not be underestimated. During the Cold War, the United States national security bureaucracy, to include the intelligence community, was almost singularly focused on the Soviet Union. The US government and philanthropic foundations undertook a wide variety of programs to build intellectual capital regarding the Soviet Union.[23] The United States collected and translated Soviet military writings and made them widely available to the US officer corps.[24] Moreover, US intelligence organizations undertook a range of sometimes highly risky operations to gain deep insight into Soviet decision-making.[25] Despite all these efforts, it took decades for the United States to gain a deep and nuanced understanding of Soviet decision-making.

Today, there is no comparable effort to understand China or Russia, even though both are in many ways much more open than the Soviet Union was. For example, whereas Soviet writings about future warfare were often classified, Chinese doctrinal publications are available for purchase in bookstores in China and on the Internet. However, whereas the US government translated and disseminated Soviet writings on warfare, comparable Chinese doctrinal publications are not broadly available. As a result, discussion of Chinese doctrine is often limited to the small subset of defense analysts who are fluent in Mandarin. Even more egregious, given its previous investments, the United States drew down its stock of intellectual capital on the Russian military after the end of the Cold War. The result has been the emergence of dangerous blind spots, confusion of continuity for novelty, and repeated strategic surprise.

Third, an effective strategy should take into account (and even exploit) the basic but often overlooked fact that both sides in a competition possess constrained resources. Indeed, the fact of limited resources – monetary, human, and technological – and the costs associated with them is central to cost-imposing strategies. Specifically, cost-imposing strategies can most fruitfully be pursued when we have an understanding of those constraints as well as ways to exacerbate them. These may include bottlenecks within a state's defense sector as well as the tradeoff between defense and other forms of government spending.

We are painfully aware of the limitations under which we labor. At the same time, we tend to discount or ignore the constraints that others face in pursuing their aims. Good strategy takes advantage of them.

Similarly, effective strategy should take into account the basic fact that each side in a competition is not a unitary actor, but rather a collection of bureaucratic entities, each of which has its own preferences, proclivities, and culture that frequently leads to performance that diverges considerably from the optimal.

This insight applies to both sides. To be successful, a strategy must navigate one's own bureaucratic terrain before it has a hope of affecting a competitor's bureaucracy. Put another way, strategies that rely upon one's own military services doing things that they do not want to do are unlikely to succeed. Conversely, strategies that match the preferences and proclivities of one's own military to the competitor are more likely to be successful.

Fourth, such a strategy should exploit time, and make it a virtue. That is, it should consider not only *what* actions we should take, but also *when*, with the latter timed to achieve the maximum effect. Time costs are important, and may translate into deterrent effects. Cost-imposing strategies, in concert with strategies of denial, should seek to frustrate and delay competitors from achieving capabilities that are dangerous and disruptive. For example, the United States, our allies, and our friends might consider deploying anti-access capabilities of their own to frustrate Chinese attempts to project power.[26] An anti-access approach would, for example, help Taiwan deter Chinese coercion and aggression.[27]

Finally, such strategies should account for interaction. Strategy does not involve imposing one's will upon an inanimate object, but rather a thinking competitor that is pursuing its own aims. Competitors will respond to our moves, often at times and in ways that we may not expect. Indeed, they should be expected to seek to drive the competition in ways that favor them and disfavor us.

As a result, for planning purposes it is useful to think of a competition as an interactive three move sequence made up of our initial action, our competitor's responses to it, and our subsequent counter-action. Our initial action should seek to elicit a response from our adversary – to dissuade him from undesirable actions or channel his behavior in ways that are favorable to us. We should undertake that action with at least a first-order sense of how the competitor may (or perhaps must) respond. However, the actual nature and timing of the competitor's response will give us additional information about the competition and should make our subsequent counter-action even more effective. Indeed, that counter-action should take account, and advantage, of our competitor's response.

Conclusion: Assessing the Effectiveness of Competitive Strategies

There are several ways to measure the effectiveness of a competitive strategy over time. One way is by estimating the costs that it imposes on the competitor across the dimensions described above. A successful strategy should impose costs out of proportion with the expenditure required to do so. That is, it should exploit imbalances in our favor. Ultimately, it should impose costs on a competitor sufficient to affect his decision-making calculus and, over time, change his strategic behavior.

Another measure of effectiveness involves strategic options. A successful strategy should increase the range of options available to the initiator and constrain those available to the target. A successful strategy should make the most disruptive and dangerous options unattractive to a competitor while at the same time increasing the set of options open to us.

A final set of measures has to do with initiative. The side that is implementing a successful strategy should possess the initiative in the competition, controlling its pace and scope while forcing its competitor to react to it.

Viewed against these criteria, recent American strategic performance has been poor. In recent years the United States has found itself on the wrong side of cost-imposing strategies inflicted upon us by competitors ranging from Al Qaeda to Russia and China. Moreover, Russian and Chinese military modernization is constraining the strategic options open to the United States at the same time that they are gaining a larger set of options. And in a number of key areas, the United States has lost the initiative in the competition and is reacting to competitors' moves rather than setting the scope and pace of the competition.

The United States can, and should, do better. Analogies to the past are always imperfect, and those to the US-Soviet competition during the Cold War have limited value. Still, to the extent that the analogy holds, our current situation is more akin to that of the 1950s than the 1980s. That is, we are still in the early stages of formulating a strategy for the long term. To improve American strategic performance, the US national security community needs to devote effort to identifying our enduring strengths and weaknesses, and those of key competitors such as China.[28] We also need to develop an understanding of our ability to inflict costs, as well as competitors' sensitivity to them. Furthermore, the United States needs to develop approaches to use the levers at our disposal to impose costs upon competitors to seek to dissuade them from undesirable actions or channel their behavior in ways that are favorable to us.

Finally, we need to plan for an interactive competition. History shows that peacetime competitions last decades. Moreover, whether we realize it or not, China and Russia have been competing with the United States for some time. We can expect this to continue whether or not we consciously choose to pursue a competitive strategy. The ultimate issue for US policy makers is thus not whether to compete, but whether to do so consciously in a way that advances US interests. Both history and strategic logic both suggest that the formulation and implementation of a thoughtful long-term strategy can only improve US strategic performance.

Notes

1. See, for example, Thomas G. Mahnken, ed., *Competitive Strategies for the 21st Century: Theory, History, and Practice* (Palo Alto, CA: Stanford University Press, 2012); Thomas G. Mahnken, "Arms Races and Long-Term Competition" in *Strategy in Asia: The Past, Present, and Future of Regional Security,* ed. Thomas G. Mahnken and Dan Blumenthal (Palo Alto, CA: Stanford University Press, 2014); Thomas G. Mahnken, *Cost-Imposing Strategies: A Brief Primer* (Washington, DC: Center for a New American Security, 2014); Thomas G. Mahnken, "Competitive Strategies for Small States," in *Frontline Allies: War and Change in Central Europe* (Washington, DC: Center for European Policy Analysis, 2015); Eric Sayers, "Military Dissuasion: A Framework for Influencing PLA Procurement Trends," *Joint Force Quarterly* 58 (2010): 89–93; Col Kenneth P. Ekman, *Winning the Peace through Cost Imposition* (Washington, DC: Brookings Institution, 2014); Andrew F. Krepinevich and Robert C. Martinage, *Dissuasion Strategy* (Washington, DC: Center for Strategic and Budgetary Assessments, 2008).
2. *Quadrennial Defense Review Report* (Washington, DC: Department of Defense, 2001), 30. Also listed was the need to leverage information technology and innovative concepts to develop an interoperable, joint C4ISR (command, control, communications, computers, intelligence, surveillance, and reconnaissance) architecture and capability that includes a tailorable joint operational picture.
3. William J. Perry and John P. Abizaid, co-chairs, *Ensuring a Strong US Defense for the Future: The National Defense Panel Review of the 2014 Quadrennial Defense Review* (Washington, DC: US Institute of Peace, 2014); Stephen J. Hadley and William J. Perry, co-chairs, *The QDR in Perspective: Meeting America's National Security Needs in the 21st Century* (Washington, DC: US Institute of Peace, 2010).
4. Thomas C. Schelling, "The Strategy of Inflicting Costs," in *Issues in Defense Economics,* ed. Roland N. McKean (Cambridge, MA: National Bureau of Economic Research, 1967); Michael E. Porter, "The Competitive Advantage of Nations," *Harvard Business Review* (May-June 1990), 73–93; A. W. Marshall, "Long-Term Competition with the Soviets: A Framework for Strategic Analysis," R-862-PR (Santa Monica, CA: RAND Corporation, 1972); A. W. Marshall and James G. Roche, "Strategy for

Competing with the Soviets in the Military Sector of the Continuing Political-Military Competition," Department of Defense memorandum, July 1976. See also Gordon S. Barrass, "US Competitive Strategy during the Cold War" and Daniel I. Gouré, "Overview of the Competitive Strategies Initiative" in Mahnken, *Competitive Strategies for the 21st Century.*

5. See, for example, James Lacey, ed., *Great Strategic Rivalries from the Classical World to the Cold War* (Oxford: Oxford University Press, 2016).

6. See, for example, Matthew S. Seligmann, "The Anglo-German Naval Race, 1898–1914," in *Arms Races in International Politics,* ed. Thomas G. Mahnken, Joseph A. Maiolo, and David Stevenson (Oxford: Oxford University Press, 2016).

7. Thomas G. Mahnken, "The Reagan Administration's Strategy toward the Soviet Union," in *Successful Strategies: Triumphing in War and Peace from Antiquity to the Present,* ed. Williamson Murray and Richard Hart Sinnreich (Cambridge: Cambridge University Press, 2014), 403–431.

8. Toshi Yoshihara, "Chinese Missile Strategy and the US Naval Presence in Japan: The Operational View from Beijing," *Naval War College Review* 63, no. 3 (Summer 2010).

9. Andrew S. Erickson, *Chinese Anti-Ship Ballistic Missile Development: Drivers, Trajectories, and Strategic Implications* (Washington, DC: Jamestown Foundation, 2012).

10. For an overview of definitions of strategy, see Barry D. Watts, "Barriers to Acting Strategically: Why Strategy is So Difficult," in Mahnken, *Competitive Strategies for the 21st Century,* 47–50.

11. Bradford A. Lee, "Strategic Interaction: Theory and History for Practitioners" in Mahnken, *Competitive Strategies for the 21st Century,* 28–32.

12. See, for example, Thomas G. Mahnken, *Technology and the American Way of War Since 1945* (New York: Columbia University Press, 2008), 162–164.

13. Michael Howard, "Military Science in an Age of Peace," *Journal of the Royal United Services Institute for Defense Studies* 119, no. 1 (March 1974): 4.

14. As Clausewitz wrote, "War can be of two kinds, in the sense that either the objective is to *overthrow the enemy*—to render him politically helpless or militarily impotent, thus forcing him to sign whatever peace we please; or *merely to occupy some of his frontier districts* so that we can annex them or use them for bargaining at the peace negotiations. Transitions from one type to the other will of course recur in my treatment; but the fact that the aims of the two types are quite different must be

clear at all times, and their points of irreconcilability brought out." Carl von Clausewitz, *On War*, ed. and trans. Michael Howard and Peter Paret (Princeton, NJ: Princeton University Press, 1989), 69.

15. Mahnken, "The Reagan Administration's Strategy toward the Soviet Union," 419.

16. A. Wess Mitchell, "The Case for Deterrence by Denial," *The American Interest*, August 12, 2015, http://www.the-american-interest.com/2015/08/12/the-case-for-deterrence-by-denial/.

17. William S. Murray, "Revisiting Taiwan's Defense Strategy," *Naval War College Review* 61, no. 3 (Summer 2008), 13–38.

18. Thomas G. Mahnken, "Weapons: The Growth and Spread of the Precision Strike Regime," *Daedalus* 140, no. 3 (Summer 2011), 45–57; Barry D. Watts, *The Maturing Revolution in Military Affairs* (Washington, DC: Center for Strategic and Budgetary Assessments, 2011).

19. Mahnken, *Cost-Imposing Strategies.*

20. Mahnken, *Technology and the American Way of War Since 1945*, 163–164.

21. Lee, "Strategic Interaction," 32–43.

22. David E. Hoffman, *The Dead Hand* (New York: Doubleday, 2009).

23. David C. Engerman, *Know Your Enemy: The Rise and Fall of America's Soviet Experts* (Oxford: Oxford University Press, 2009).

24. During the 1960s and 1970s, the US Air Force translated and published a series of Soviet doctrinal works. See, for example, A. A. Sidorenko, *The Offensive: A Soviet View* (Washington, DC: US Government Printing Office, 1970).

25. Christopher Ford and David Rosenberg, *The Admirals' Advantage: US Navy Operational Intelligence in World War II and the Cold War* (Annapolis, MD: US Naval Institute Press, 2005).

26. Toshi Yoshihara, "Japan's Competitive Strategies at Sea: A Preliminary Assessment" in Mahnken, *Competitive Strategies for the 21st Century*, 219–235.

27. William S. Murray, "Revisiting Taiwan's Defense Strategy," 13–38.

28. On Chinese proclivities, see Michael Pillsbury, "The Sixteen Fears: China's Strategic Psychology," *Survival* 54, no. 5 (October-November 2012), 149–182.

CHAPTER 2

A CHINESE MILITARY PERSPECTIVE ON THE US THIRD OFFSET STRATEGY

Fan Gaoyue

Chinese defense analysts have widely divergent views on the rationale and intentions behind the US Third Offset Strategy. Some characterize it as a trap to induce China and Russia into an arms race or a hoax designed by the United States to cover its weaknesses. Others see it as a competitive strategy to seek technological superiority that will safeguard the security of the United States and its regional allies and partners. This chapter presents a Chinese perspective on the strategy and its motivations, and offers some possible Chinese responses as China upgrades its own defense technological capabilities.

THE BIRTH OF THE THIRD OFFSET STRATEGY

Amid the implementation of a "rebalancing" strategy, the US Department of Defense (DoD) put forward its Third Offset Strategy in the second half of 2014. In August of that year, US Deputy Secretary of Defense Robert Work mentioned the strategy for the first time in a speech he gave at the National Defense University. On September 3, US Secretary of Defense Chuck Hagel confirmed that the Third Offset Strategy was in the works while delivering a speech to the Southeastern New England Defense Industry Alliance in Newport, Rhode Island.

Near the end of October, the Center for Strategic and Budgetary Assessments (CSBA) released the report *Toward a New Offset Strategy: Exploiting US Long-term Advantages to Restore US Global Power Projection Capability.*[1] Following this, on November 15, Secretary Hagel issued a memorandum, "The Defense Innovation Initiative," to clarify the basic framework of the strategy.[2] Deputy Secretary Work was directed to oversee the initiative. Hagel formally announced the Third Offset Strategy while delivering a speech to the Reagan National Defense Forum that same day.

In a January 2015 speech entitled "The Third US Offset Strategy and Its Implications for Partners and Allies," Work spoke about some of the aims of the strategy: "So to maintain our warfighting edge, we're trying to address this erosion—our perceived erosion of technological superiority—with the Defense Innovation Initiative and the Third Offset Strategy."[3]

The CSBA report discusses how the Third Offset Strategy will leverage US capability advantages in unmanned systems and automation, extended-range and low observable air operations, undersea warfare, and complex system engineering and integration to form a global surveillance and strike (GSS) network, which will be balanced, resilient, responsive, and scalable to counter adversaries' capabilities.[4] Further, to implement the strategy and realize the GSS concept, the United States will restore its power projection capabilities and capacity, bolster conventional deterrence through a credible threat of denial and punishment, and impose costs upon prospective adversaries as part of a long-term competition.

The United States has had past success with offset strategies to address severe international security challenges. The first, President Eisenhower's "New Look" strategy, was implemented in the early 1950s. The second was adopted by Secretary of Defense Harold Brown in the mid-1970s. The United States took away three important lessons from these successes:

1. Asymmetric punishment can be an effective instrument of deterrence.

2. Technology can multiply the combat effectiveness of a force such that it offsets the numerical advantages of a larger but technically inferior force.

3. Technology advantages can be used to shape the competition, shifting it into areas where the US military can compete more effectively.

Not surprisingly, plans for the Third Offset Strategy raise concerns among other countries, including China.

CHINESE PERSPECTIVES ON THE THIRD OFFSET STRATEGY

Since 2014, Chinese think tanks and academic institutions have launched a large number of projects to study the Third Offset Strategy, and hundreds of papers have been published in newspapers and magazines such as the *PLA Daily, World Military Review,* and *International Strategic Studies.* The perspectives of these researchers can be summarized as follows: 1) the Third Offset Strategy is a trap designed by the United States to drag China and Russia into a military competition favorable to the United States; 2) The strategy is a hoax designed by the United States to cover its weakness and enhance its deterrence; or 3) the Third Offset Strategy is a competitive strategy to sustain and strengthen US military technological superiority over its adversaries and safeguard the security of the United States and its allies and partners.[5]

In my view, the Third Offset Strategy most likely reflects current US strategic anxieties, including:

1. the relative decline of US economic strength;
2. rapid transformation of the old world order to a new order;
3. China's ever-increasing confidence; and
4. Russia's resurgence and assertiveness.

The decline of US economic strength

With the dissolution of the Soviet Union in 1991, the United States became the only superpower in the world. Driven by its strong hegemonic desire, the United States became mired in the Afghanistan and Iraq wars, which seriously impaired its national power. A worldwide financial crisis beginning in 2008 also inflicted heavy losses on the US economy. During the same time, developing countries such as Brazil, Russia, India, and China became important engines of the world economy. In 2010, the GDP and trade volume of the "BRIC" countries accounted for 18 percent and 15 percent of the world respectively. The decline in its relative economic strength has surely produced anxieties for the United States.[6]

The rapid transformation of the old order to a new order

Rapid changes in the early part of the twenty-first century include a trend toward multi-polarization, perhaps leading to a bigger say for developing countries and greater equality and democracy in how international affairs are handled, instead of deference to one or a few large powers. Since sustaining its global leadership and strengthening its dominance in international affairs have remained the key strategic objectives of the United States, such shifts could be seen as threatening.

China's ever-increasing confidence

After the end of the Cold War, the United States launched several wars under the banner of "international anti-terrorism," and its hegemony reached an all-time high. At the same time, China focused on economic development, resulting in an increase in GDP of about 7 percent annually for three decades.[7] As a result, China's national comprehensive strength has grown rapidly, which has made the United States quite uneasy. As an official US document points out, "Over the long term, China's emergence as a regional power will have the potential to affect the US economy and our security in a variety of ways...the growth of China's military power must be accompanied by greater clarity of its strategic intentions in order to avoid causing friction in the region."[8] Concerns about China's assertiveness in the Asia-Pacific have led the United States to increase its military presence in the region, deploying 60 percent of its navy and air force there to hedge against or contain China.[9]

Russia's resurgence and new assertiveness
Relations between the United States and Russia are also increasingly tense. As the 2014 CSBA report pointed out,

> In Europe, Russia is resurgent and increasingly assertive in its near abroad...China and Russia have been trying to close the technology gap by pursuing and funding long-term, comprehensive military modernization programs. They are also developing anti-ship, anti-air, counter-space, cyber, electronic warfare, and special operations capabilities that appear designed to counter traditional US military advantages—in particular, our ability to project power to any region across the globe by surging aircraft, ships, troops, and supplies.[10]

A 2016 poll indicated that 80 percent of Russians hold negative attitudes toward the United States.[11] Russia has a larger nuclear arsenal and better defense technology than China, and it has engaged in increasingly provocative acts. For example, Russian fighter jets have flown very close to and over US warships, and its long-range bombers have been patrolling the EU-Russia border and beyond.

In his testimony on the fiscal year 2015 defense budget, Defense Secretary Chuck Hagel concluded:

We are entering an era where American dominance on the seas, in the skies, and in space—not to mention cyberspace—can no longer be taken for granted. And while the United States currently has a decisive military and technological edge over any potential adversary, our future superiority is not a given.[12]

Hagel's words clearly reflect US strategic anxieties. To ease these anxieties, the United States put forward the Third Offset Strategy to seek continuing military superiority over China and Russia and try to deter them from challenging US hegemony.

The essence of the Third Offset Strategy is to shift the competition to technological areas where the United States has fundamental long-term advantages to offset its prospective adversaries' anti-access/area denial (A2/AD) capabilities. The First Offset Strategy realized its objectives by employing the US nuclear advantage to offset the Soviet Union's conventional advantage. The Second Offset Strategy realized its objectives through competition on the quality of weapons and equipment; that is, by employing the US advantage of high-quality, precision-guided weapons to offset the Soviet Union's numerical advantage in weapons and personnel.

To implement its third strategy, the DoD has initiated a new Long-Range Research and Development Planning Program to compete for technological superiority in the following areas:

1. space technology that can be launched quickly, has good space situation awareness, and has on-orbit servicing capabilities;

2. undersea technology, including unmanned undersea vehicles, detection technologies, and undersea navigation and communication;

3. air dominance and strike technology, including rapid strike and hypersonic aircraft;

4. air and missile defense technology, including multi-target killing and directed energy; and

5. new concept weapons technology, including 3D printing, high-energy lasers, and electromagnetic guns.

While the Third Offset Strategy reflects traditional US strategic thinking of putting technology above everything else to seek absolute military superiority, it also demonstrates new developments in US strategic thinking, including new ideas about deterrence (deterrence by denial and punishment), combined operations, and nuclear strategy.

Deterrence

US conventional deterrence depends upon the threat to restore status quo ante through the direct application of force. The Third Offset Strategy places more emphasis on "deterrence by denial" and "deterrence by punishment," that is, to decrease an adversary's perception of the probability of achieving its war aims in the first place and to increase the anticipated costs of attempting to do so by threatening asymmetric retaliatory attacks.

Combined operations

The United States stressed allies' continuous participation in its operations in the past, but the Third Offset Strategy emphasizes the protection of US allies. So on the one hand, the United States demands that its military allies such as Japan and Australia play an important role in keeping a stable military balance. On the other hand, the United States is putting more emphasis on building its own global surveillance and strike capabilities and preventing an adversary's offensive operations by rapid strike once deterrence fails.

Nuclear strategy

Although the United States had stated that it would reduce its dependence on nuclear weapons, Secretary of Defense Hagel announced a comprehensive reform of the US nuclear enterprise, including large-scale combat readiness maintenance, construction, and development plans, to support the Third Offset Strategy.[13]

The combination of these new developments constitutes a new and compound deterrence strategy to deter China and Russia.[14]

The Third Offset Strategy is an innovation strategy that will expedite a "revolution in military affairs." It has been a usual practice of the United States to make use of its technological innovation advantages to offset the strategic advantages of its principal adversaries and seize the initiative. The First Offset Strategy in the 1950s made use of the US nuclear advantage in a "nuclear military revolution" to offset the Warsaw Pact conventional numerical advantage. The Second Offset Strategy in the 1970s made use of the US electronic technological advantage to launch an "information technology-based military revolution." Once again, the United States got the upper hand in military competition with the Soviet Union, by developing information-based "technological enablers" to raise the efficiency of weapon platforms.

The Third Offset Strategy is trying to offset the ever-increasing military capabilities of China and Russia by developing game-changing technology, building a culture of innovation, and fostering thinking about old problems in new ways. US innovation practices can be summarized in four breakthroughs:

1. Technological innovation: Science and technology (S&T) innovation represented by computer, artificial intelligence, and 3D printing technology to promote the development of new concept weapons such as directed-energy weapons, electromagnetic guns, automated unmanned weapon systems, smart weapons, and supersonic weapons.

2. Operational concept innovation: The introduction of new concepts such as operational cloud, undersea operations, and global surveillance and strike to consolidate information dominance.

3. Organizational form innovation: Building a leaner and more effective joint force by optimizing organizations and systems ushered

by new technology, operational concepts, and operational styles to generate a new type of operational force.

4. Defense management innovation: An emphasis on strategic planning and optimized resource allocation to support reform and innovation, ensure the reliability and flexibility of the national defense industry base, and promote DoD innovation and operational modes.[15]

The GSS Network

The Third Offset Strategy will require the United States to leverage its capability advantages in cyber and electronic warfare, unmanned systems and automation, extended-range and low-observable air operations, undersea warfare, and complex system engineering and integration to construct a balanced, resilient, responsive, and scalable global surveillance and strike network. According to the CSBA, "while many elements of the US military would have important roles to play in a future GSS network, it would rely disproportionately upon air and maritime forces in general and unmanned platforms in particular."[16]

By combining the multitude of geographically distributed platforms, the GSS network will eliminate obstacles and create favorable conditions for US power projection. Its most prominent characteristic, however, is that all the elements needed to address middle and high threat environments can operate effectively in a much lower threat environment.

To realize the GSS network, the CSBA recommended 13 near-to-midterm candidate implementation actions, including:

1. Hedging against the loss of space-based enablers;
2. Developing and demonstrating counter-space capabilities;
3. Expanding the geographic coverage of the undersea fleet;
4. Expanding undersea payload capability and flexibility;

5. Expanding geographic coverage provided by fixed and deployable undersea sensor networks;

6. Developing and fielding modern ground-, air-, and sea-deployed naval mines;

7. Reversing the active defense versus missile attack cost exchange ratio;

8. Developing and fielding new counter-sensor weapons;

9. Accelerating fielding of an automated aerial refueling capability;

10. Accelerating development and expanding procurement of the Long-Range Strike Bomber program;

11. Developing and fielding a penetrating high-altitude long-endurance intelligence, surveillance, and reconnaissance unmanned aerial vehicles as an analog to the RQ-4 Global Hawk for medium-high threat environments;

12. Developing and fielding penetrating air-refuelable, land-and-carrier-based unmanned combat air system platforms;

13. Developing expeditionary, ground-based, local A2/AD networks comprising short- to medium-range integrated air defense systems, coastal defense cruise missiles, defensive mines and unmanned underwater vehicles, and mobile surface-to-surface missiles.[17]

The US military has adjusted its budget allocations to concentrate investment in GSS network construction. For example, the US military will replace the manned tactical aviation forces of the Navy, Air Force, and Marine Corps with unmanned air operation systems. The Navy will reduce the acquisition of large surface warships and F-35 fighter jets. The Army will reduce the number of its combat brigade teams and its modernization programs, and the Marine Corps will cancel its acquisition of amphibious combat vehicles.[18]

DEVELOPMENT OF US DEFENSE TECHNOLOGICAL CAPABILITIES

As the 2014 CSBA report points out:

> The US military faces a period of fiscal austerity of uncertain duration. Meanwhile the United States simultaneously confronts a complex array of mounting security challenges around the world. The United States cannot afford to simply scale up the current mix of joint power projection capabilities. Indeed, owing to ballooning personnel costs, especially with respect to medical care and retirement, manpower levels will likely shrink over the coming decades.[19]

On May 14, 2015, the US Congress approved the FY2015 Defense Authorization Act, allotting $0.4 billion for the Defense Innovation Initiative. The defense budget grew from $580.6 billion in 2015 to $585 billion in 2016. However, continuing fiscal uncertainties mean that the US military will likely invest more resources in defense technology than in manpower because of ever-increasing personnel costs.

This is not a new trend. In the First Offset Strategy, the US Government looked to nuclear weapons, with an increase in the budget for nuclear weapon research and development from $1 billion in 1957 to $1.9 billion in 1961. The Second Offset Strategy guided the US military to invest most of its research and development budget in information-based "technological enablers." Its investment in computer systems (software and hardware) increased from $6 billion in 1981 to $38 billion in 1990.

However, the history of human warfare has demonstrated that weaponry is an important, but not decisive, factor of a war. The decisive factor is man, not weapons. If the United States invested more of the defense budget to military personnel development (both in military skills and fighting spirit), perhaps less money would be spent and better outcomes would be achieved.

The Third Offset Strategy will guide both US military technology development and the allocation of future defense budgets. Accordingly, the DoD has adopted a number of measures to support its implementation, including:

Creation of "a long-range research and development program" to clarify technological development strategies

Compared with the "long-range research and development program" of the 1970s, the new program focuses on five important technologies: space, undersea, air strike, air and missile defense, and emerging military and civil developments. The DoD set up five working groups to draft the program, prioritize the items, and provide reference for the FY2017 defense budget.

Improvement of the "Better Buying Power" program to establish effective and flexible acquisition systems

In 2010, Under Secretary of Defense Ashton Carter put forth the "Better Buying Power" (BBP 1.0) program to optimize acquisition process. In 2012, Under Secretary of Defense Frank Kendall initiated "Better Buying Power 2.0" to transform "best practices" into better decision-making. To support the Third Offset Strategy, Kendall issued "Better Buying Power 3.0" in September 2014 to ensure that the US military can satisfy future national security requirements through innovation and technological advances.

Promotion of national defense education and innovation programs to train innovative leaders

The DoD initiated the "21st Century National Defense Education and Innovation Program" and the "National Defense Education Program" to train next-generation leaders able to deal with future risk.

Improvement of wargaming systems

On February 9, 2015, Deputy Secretary of Defense Robert Work issued a memorandum to reinvigorate wargaming and prototyping, and to make them better strategic analysis instruments.

Creation of new operational concepts

The US strategic research community and defense think tanks are exploring and developing new operational concepts such as cross domain operations, cloud cyber operations, undersea operations, and global surveillance and strike. In response, "AirSea Battle" was renamed the "Joint Concept for Access and Maneuver in the Global Commons" in January of 2015, and the Mitchell Research Institute of the US Air Force Association initiated its new "Operational Cloud" concept.[20]

The DoD has invested heavily in the development of new defense technological capabilities. Generally speaking, information technology has become a mainstay in weapons and equipment innovation and development. Information technology development will cover THz frequency and materialize new detection and communication systems, leading to improved battlefield situation awareness, information transmission, missile defense, and urban operations. Highly secure cipher communication, super-parallel calculation, high differentiation, and counter-interference detection will become possible in the "quantum era."

The accelerating integration of information technology development with biology, recognition, and nanotechnology will initiate an important reform in information technology, pioneer new technological fields, and catalyze new concepts for weapons and equipment. At present, the US military has made breakthroughs in brain-computer interfaces for controlling small aerial vehicles and robots.[21] It is predicted that micro-nano weapons could be employed in battlefields by 2030.

Stealth technology is employed more widely and in multi-frequency spectrums. The US military has employed stealth technology in its newly developed weapons and equipment. However, future weapons and equipment need to be stealthy not only to radar, but also in multi-frequency spectrums. For example, the new generation of US nuclear submarines has adopted integrated stealth for radar, infrared, and sound to raise its survivability and operational capability so that it can detect, strike, and destroy enemy targets.[22]

Heavy investments are being made in unmanned system technology, and capacities are developing rapidly. In 2007, the DoD issued a 25-year plan and invested $12 billion to develop unmanned systems for the Army, Navy, and Air Force with a requirement that one-third of land vehicles and deep-strike aircraft be unmanned within 10 years. The US military has continued its procurement of unmanned aerial vehicles (UAVs) such as the Predator, Gray Eagle, and an updated Global Hawk.

There have been many notable achievements. The US Navy's X-47B accomplished the first-ever carrier touch-and-go aboard the CVN 77 and the first-ever carrier-based arrested landing; and the MQ-4C completed its flight test across the contiguous United States. The deep-ocean unmanned Upward Falling Payload program for distributed situational awareness was initiated. The critical design of the prototype of Anti-Submarine Warfare Continuous Trail Unmanned Vessel was approved, and the research and development of next-generation unmanned surface warships and mine sweeping equipment is underway. The Marine Corps could move ahead with a program to mount laser weapons and Stinger missiles on light combat vehicles such as the Joint Light Tactical Vehicle to protect vehicle crews and nearby warfighters by 2022. The Air Force has completed flight tests of the X-56A. The US Army, together with the DoD, is assessing the performance of RQ-7 Shadow.[23] It is predicted that the US military will have a large robot force able to be deployed onto the battlefield by around 2030.

New concept weapons and platform technologies, including directed-energy, electromagnetic launching, cross-domain, and virtual technology, are moving from the theoretical to the practical at an accelerated pace. In recent years, the US military has launched new concept equipment research programs such as the "submarine plane" and "flying Hummer," which cross traditional boundaries of land, sea, and air. Innovations such as these will provide important support for the US military's future cross-domain synergy operations.[24]

Breakthroughs in cutting-edge basic technology are sure to give rise to new developments in military technology, weapons, and equipment.

New materials will enormously enhance the functions of weapons and equipment. For example, graphene will bring a new functional revolution to military electronic equipment and achieve a big leap in the capabilities of supercomputers, military communications, and intelligence analysis. In 2003, the US National Science Board funded the creation of a National Nanotechnology Infrastructure Network and invested $70 billion in research support. In 2013, researchers at the University of California Los Angeles developed a graphene-based micro capacitor that can charge a cell phone or a car in seconds, 1,000 times faster than an ordinary battery.

New energy technologies will promote the innovative design of weapons and equipment. New battery designs integrating structure and function can effectively solve the weight and volume challenges of traditional energy storage and have the potential to be widely used in soldier systems, mini-unmanned systems, and vehicles. Solar cells can directly convert sunlight into electricity and provide low-cost and almost permanent power without pollution.

Advanced manufacturing technology will alter the make and maintenance pattern of weapons and equipment. 3D printing (additive manufacturing) technology has caught the attention of major countries, and the United States has been active in pushing the actual application of 3D printing. The US National Aeronautics and Space Administration manufactured its first tool in space with 3D printing technology in December 2014. The US Army's Expeditionary Mobile Lab can print out parts needed on the battlefield with a 3D printer. In the future, 3D printing technology will gradually be applied in the field, which would break the design trammel of traditional manufacturing and innovate a new pattern of research and development or even a new pattern of logistic supply and equipment maintenance.[25]

PROSPECTS FOR THE THIRD OFFSET STRATEGY

Tremendous changes have taken place in world strategic patterns, the global security environment, and international relations in the first decades of the twenty-first century. Can the Third Offset Strategy produce the outcomes the United States expects given these changes?

Although its previous two offset strategies achieved what the United States had expected, prospects for the success of the Third Offset Strategy seem less certain for a number of reasons.

The era is different

The nature of the world order has changed radically. In the 1950s and 1970s, the world was split into a more confrontational West and East competing for world hegemony. After the end of Cold War, the United States had no real rival to its superpower status. Although today's world order seems to be moving toward multi-polarity, the United States remains the Number One power. Relations between the major powers are more constructive and cooperative, and competition among them is no longer a "life-or-death struggle."

The threats faced by the United States are different

During the Cold War, the Soviet Union was the clear threat to the United States. In the twenty-first century, the United States faces multiple threats that can be categorized as traditional, irregular, catastrophic, and/or disruptive. Traditional threats are posed by states that employ recognized military capabilities and forces (such as armies, navies and air forces) in well-understood forms of military competition and conflict. Irregular threats come from state and non-state actors, who use unconventional methods (such as terrorism and insurgency) to counter the traditional advantages of stronger rivals or to erode US influence, patience, and political will. Catastrophic threats involve the acquisition, possession, and use of weapons of mass destruction (WMD) or methods producing WMD-like effects. Porous international borders, weak international controls, and easy access to information-related technologies facilitate these threats. Disruptive threats come from adversaries who develop and use disruptive breakthroughs (including advances in biotechnology, cyber operations, space, and directed-energy weapons) to negate current US advantages in key operational domains.[26] These threats are ambiguous and complex, with China and Russia as potential, rather than stated, adversaries.

The target country is different
The previous US offset strategies were aimed at the Soviet Union, but the Third Offset Strategy is aimed mainly at China and Russia, who are cooperative partners, or at most potential adversaries, of the United States.

The economic situation is different
From the 1960s through the 1980s, the US economy grew at about 4 percent per year, and its share of global GDP was 34.4 percent. The Soviet Union's GDP was only half of that of the United States.[27] However, the US share of global GDP has slipped to 23.4 percent ($15.685 trillion in 2014) as its rate of economic growth has slowed. China's GDP has grown to about two-thirds the size of the United States and Russia's GDP is about one-eighth of the United States.[28]

S&T levels are different
During the Cold War, the United States and the Soviet Union were at roughly the same S&T level. At present China significantly lags the United States in S&T in more than 20 of 33 industrial sectors. In core technologies such as commercial aircraft, semiconductors, biological machinery, specialized chemicals, and system software, China is behind the United States by 20 to 30 years. Russia is perhaps a little better off than China.[29]

Political objectives are different

During the Cold War, the United States and the Soviet Union clashed for world domination. With the end of the Cold War, the United States became the world leader, a position it has held for 25 years. The United States would like to maintain its global leadership. China wishes to realize its two "hundred-year" goals: 1) to build a moderately prosperous society by 2021, when the Chinese Communist Party celebrates its centenary; and 2) by 2049, when the People's Republic of China marks its centenary, to build a modern socialist country that is prosperous, strong, democratic, culturally advanced, and harmonious.[30] Russia's political objectives are to develop its economy and restore its great power status.

On balance, the Third Offset Strategy seems to be the same strategy applied to a quite different strategic environment and to different target countries (China, Russia, Iran, North Korea, Syria), which might lead to different outcomes. That is, it might turn a cooperative partner into a potential adversary or a real adversary instead of shifting the competition to areas advantageous to the United States and imposing costs on its rivals.

The US military still faces a constrained and uncertain defense budget. According to then Secretary of Defense Chuck Hagel, "[t]he continuation of sequestration could impose nearly $1 trillion in cuts to the defense budget over 10 years in a department that has already begun taking deep cuts over the last few years."[31] If something similar to sequestration went on under the Trump administration, the DoD might not have enough resources to implement the Third Offset Strategy.

The Third Offset Strategy may still have a role to play: it may help the US military obtain a larger budget for defense R&D programs and improve defense technological innovation and capabilities. It may also help the United States sustain, and in some areas expand, its technological superiority. It may well deter potential adversaries from challenging the United States; however, prospective adversaries might try to avoid a defense technological competition trap altogether.

POSSIBLE CHINESE RESPONSES

The Second Offset Strategy is generally credited with playing a role in the collapse of the Soviet Union's economy. China (and Russia) will have learned from studying the previous US offset strategies and will not follow "the track of an overturned cart." In the face of the pressures posed by the Third Offset Strategy, China will try to avoid being dragged into a defense technological competition trap and may adopt a policy of "you do your things in your way and I do my things in my way." That is, China will not adopt a tit-for-tat policy to compete with the United States in the development of defense technology but will adopt asymmetric methods to develop the defense technologies it needs most.

At present China is trying to realize its dream of great national rejuvenation, and its priorities are the two "hundred-year" strategic goals.

China's defense budget has stayed at the level of 1.25–1.5 percent of its GDP, which is low compared with the United States (3.5 percent), Russia (3.32 percent), and South Korea (2.79 percent). In the future, China probably will adjust its defense budget according to the threats and challenges it faces and the development of its economy. I believe that China will most likely invest resources in the development of defense technologies such as aerospace, cyberspace, unmanned systems, and undersea warfare to modernize its national defense and narrow the gap between the US and Chinese militaries in accordance with its economic strength and unique strategic requirements.

NOTES

1. Robert Martinage, *Toward a New Offset Strategy: Exploiting US Long-Term Advantages to Restore U.S. Global Power Projection Capability* (Washington, DC: Center for Strategic and Budgetary Assessments, 2014).

2. Office of the Secretary of Defense, "The Defense Innovation Initiative," memorandum, November 15, 2014, http://archive.defense.gov/pubs/OSD0 13411-14.pdf.

3. Robert Work, "The Third US Offset Strategy and its Implications for Partners and Allies" (speech, Willard Hotel, Washington, DC, January 28, 2015), https://www.defense.gov/News/Speeches/Speech-View/Article/606641/the-third-us-offset-strategy-and-its-implications-for-partners-and-allies/.

4. Martinage, *Toward a New Offset Strategy*, v.

5. International Military Branch, China Association for Military Science/ Department of Foreign Military Studies, *World Military Review,* no. 5 (2015); China International Strategy Association, *International Strategic Studies*, no. 2 (2015).

6. Tang Xiaohua and Dan Shijun, "Calm Thinking About the Third Offset Strategy: Reflection of Hegemonic Mentality and Strategic Anxiety," *World Military Review* 5 (2015): 21.

7. "Shuju jianbao: 1980–2014 nian Zhongguo ge niandu GDP ji zengzhanglü yi jian" 数据简报:1980–2014年中国各年度GDP及增长率一览, 2015年01月20日 22:16 来源: 中国经济网 [Data briefing: China's 1980–2014 annual GDP and growth rate], China Economic Net, January 20, 2015, http://intl.ce.cn/specials/zxxx/201501/20/t20150120_4389486.shtml.

8. US Department of Defense, "Sustaining US Global Leadership: Priorities for 21st Century Defense," January 2012, 2.

9. Tang Xiaohua and Dan Shijun, "Calm Thinking about the Third Offset Strategy," 22.

10. Martinage, *Toward a New Offset Strategy*, 2.

11. "Opinions in Russia," *Washington Post* infographic, http://apps.washingtonpost.com/g/page/world/opinions-in-russia/1620/; Michael Birnbaum, Russia's Anti-American Fever Goes Beyond the Soviet Era's," *Washington Post*, March 8, 2015, https://www.washingtonpost.com/world/

europe/russias-anti-us-sentiment-now-is-even-worse-than-it-was-in-soviet-union/2015/03/08/b7d534c4-c357-11e4-a188-8e4971d37a8d_story.html?hpid=z1&utm_term=.8c07896fd948.

12. Chuck Hagel, "'Defense Innovation Days' Opening Keynote (Southeastern New England Defense Industry Alliance)" (speech, Newport, Rhode Island, September 3, 2014), https://www.defense.gov/News/Speeches/Article/605602/.

13. "Secretary of Defense Hagel Announces Nuclear Force Reforms," US Department of Defense press release, November 14, 2014, http://www.afgsc.af.mil/News/Article-Display/Article/629418/secretary-of-defense-hagel-announces-nuclear-force-reforms/.

14. Tong Zhen and Zhang Maolin, "Contents and Prospect of the Third Offset Strategy," *World Military Review* 5 (2015): 25.

15. Ibid., 24.

16. Martinage, *Toward a New Offset Strategy*, 49–50.

17. Ibid., 63–64.

18. Tong Zhen and Zhang Maolin, "Contents and Prospect of the Third Offset Strategy," 25–26.

19. Martinage, *Toward a New Offset Strategy*, 16–17.

20. Li Jian and Lu Dehong, "The Third Offset Strategy: The US Competition Strategy to Seek Military Monopoly," *World Military Review* 5 (2015): 9–10.

21. China Strategic Culture Promotion Association, "Report on US Military Power 2013," July 2014, 29–30.

22. China National Defense Science and Technology Information Center, *Weapons and Equipment 2030* (Beijing: National Defense Industry Press, 2014), 11.

23. China Strategic Culture Promotion Association, "Report on US Military Power 2013," 29.

24. *Weapons and Equipment 2030*, 16.

25. Ibid., 17–18.

26. US Department of Defense, "The National Defense Strategy of the United States of America," March 2005, 2–3.

27. Zhen Bingxi, "21 shiji chu Meiguo jingji shili zoushi" 21世纪初美国经济实力走势 [Trends of US economic strength in the early 21st century], *Research on International Challenges*, October 19, 2000, http://www.cqvip.com/read/read.aspx?id=11790348; Tao Duanfang and Yi Fu, "Soviet GDP Left West Guessing Half a Century."

28. "Chen Baosen: Meiguo jingji shili rengran chaoqiang" 陈宝森: 美国经济实力仍然超强 [Chen Baosen: US economic strength still very strong], *Global Times,* July 21, 2011, http://finance.huanqiu.com/roll/2011-07/18 36446.html; "2014 nian shijie geguo zonghe guoli he jingji shili qian shi paihang bang qiye paiming" 2014年世界各国综合国力和经济实力前十排行榜企业排名 [Top ten list of world countries comprehensive national and economic strength in 2014], China Ranking Network, September 18, 2014, http://www.askci.com/news/data/2014/09/18/152256bids.shtml.

29. "Zhongguo de keji shili daodi yu Meiguo xiangcha duoshao" 中国的科技实力到底与美国相差多少 [What is the difference between China and US scientific and technological strength?], Sohu, April 7, 2016, http://mt.sohu.com/20160408/n443644742.shtml.

30. The State Council Information Office of the People's Republic of China, "China's Military Strategy," May 2015, 6.

31. Cheryl Pellerin, "Hagel Announces New Defense Innovation, Reform Efforts," *DoD News*, November 15, 2014, https://www.defense.gov/News/Article/Article/603658/.

CHAPTER 3

THE "CINDERELLA" TRANSFORMATION

THE CHINESE DEFENSE INDUSTRY'S MOVE FROM LAGGARD TO LEADER AND THE IMPLICATIONS FOR US-CHINA MILITARY TECHNOLOGICAL COMPETITION

Tai Ming Cheung, Eric Anderson, and Fan Yang

China's defense industry has undergone a far-reaching makeover over the past two decades that has seen its fortunes transformed. From a chronic money-losing relic of the central planning era, the defense industry today is highly profitable, with a bulging pipeline of new generations of weapons under development and in production. It is now embarking on the next stage of its quest to join the ranks of the world's leading defense industrial powers.

Under the proactive and engaged leadership of Xi Jinping, the Chinese defense science, technology, and industrial (DSTI) system is evolving from a predominantly absorptive development model into a platform designed to enable more original, higher-end innovation. Among the many attributes that will be required in this upgrade are a far more advanced research and development (R&D) base, an operating culture that is more tolerant of risk, greater market competition, and closer integration between the civilian and military segments of the national economy. The success of the Chinese DSTI system to transition from the lower to the higher rungs of the innovation ladder will be critical in China's efforts to close the technology and capabilities gap with the United States and compete effectively in the intensifying military technological contest between the two countries.

This chapter examines the transformation currently taking place within the Chinese DSTI system and what can be expected in the near, medium, and long term. The chapter uses an innovation systems framework to distinguish the multitude of factors that have played a role in the Chinese defense industry's improving performance. Five of these factors will be reviewed: 1) leadership support; 2) civil-military integration (CMI); 3) the formulation of new medium- and long-term plans and institutional arrangements targeting breakthroughs and more advanced research; 4) the restructuring of the defense research institute system; and 5) the leveraging of capital markets for defense investment. The chapter also assesses the Chinese defense industry's key weaknesses to determine how much of a barrier they will be to the reform effort. These include corporate monopolies, bureaucratic fragmentation, weak management mechanisms, obsolete pricing regimes, and corruption. The chapter concludes with a discussion of the implications of a more capable and innovative Chinese defense industry for its intensifying military technological competition with the United States.

KEY FACTORS BEHIND THE CHINESE DEFENSE INDUSTRY'S IMPROVING FORTUNES

Since the turn of the twenty-first century, the fortunes of the Chinese defense industry have improved drastically, with generational leaps in development and production in many areas. One useful way to examine the complexities behind this far-reaching transformation is to view the Chinese defense industry through the prism of an innovation ecosystem. The defense innovation system is engaged in highly complex, time-consuming, and resource-intensive work. Innovation does not occur in isolation but requires extensive interaction and inputs from many sources and should consequently be viewed from a broad-based and systemic perspective.

The Chinese defense industry has innovation attributes and capabilities that can be divided into "hard" and "soft" categories.[1] Hard innovation capabilities are input and infrastructure factors intended to advance technological and product development. Soft innovation capabilities are broader in scope and cover political, institutional, relational, social, ideational, and other factors that shape non-technological and process-related innovative activity.[2]

A diverse array of hard and soft innovation factors have played important roles in the far-reaching transformation of the Chinese defense innovation system. Hard factors include: 1) resource allocations; 2) research and development capabilities; 3) manufacturing capabilities; 4) access to foreign technology transfers; 5) shifting the main impetus for technology development from defense industry dominance or "technology push" to a more war-fighter-driven process, or "demand pull"; 6) effectiveness of the acquisition system; 6) doctrine and strategy; and 7) corporate drivers. Prominent soft factors include: 1) high-level leadership support; 2) forging of a new state regulatory oversight model; 3) cultivation of new institutional culture and governance norms; 4) construction of a modern regulatory and standards-based regime; 5) improvement of technology diffusion; and 6) the external threat environment.

These factors can be further categorized according to their role and impact in the remaking of the Chinese defense innovation system (figure 1). Five types can be distinguished: catalytic, input, process, institutional, and output.

1. Catalytic factors are the sparks that ignite major changes or disruptive innovation. The threat environment and high-level leadership support are two catalysts that have paved the way for far-reaching changes to occur in the Chinese DSTI system.

2. Input factors refer to material, financial, technological and other forms of contributions that flow into the system. Most of these inputs are externally sourced but can also be internal. Resource allocations, technology transfers, and CMI are important input factors.

3. Process factors are the procedures, routines, and interactions that enable the innovation system to operate smoothly. Important processes in the Chinese DSTI system include the workings of the acquisition system, technology-push versus demand-pull dynamics, and the drawing up and implementation of plans and programs.

4. Institutional factors are the structural and normative mechanisms, actors, and rules that anchor the innovation system and play a major role in its governance. They include the governance regime, standards, legal and administrative regulations, the role of corporations, and state and military agencies.

5. Output factors are responsible for determining the nature of the products and processes that come out of the innovation system. They include the production process, maintenance, the role of market forces such as marketing and sales considerations, and the influence of end-user demand.

This chapter looks at five factors in detail: 1) leadership support; 2) CMI; 3) the formulation of new plans and institutional arrangements targeting breakthroughs and more advanced research; 4) restructuring of the defense research institute system; and 5) leveraging of the capital markets for defense investment.

Figure 1. Key factors driving the Chinese defense innovation system.

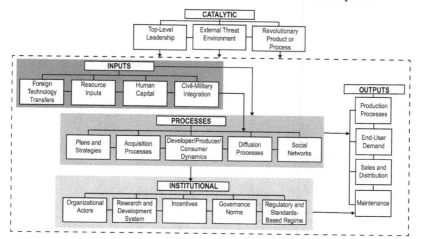

THE STATE OF THE CHINESE DEFENSE INDUSTRY

The Chinese defense industry in the mid-2010s is enjoying record revenues and profits. Driven by leadership concerns about mounting challenges to the country's external security environment and rapid advances in the global technological order, investment in research, development, and acquisition has soared, greater efforts are being made to acquire and absorb foreign technologies, and the existing defense innovation system is being remade.

This has resulted in significant improvements in technological, economic, and industrial performance. The country's ten major state-owned defense corporate groups, which together control the defense industry's six sectors, have enjoyed nearly double-digit annual growth in revenues and profits over the past decade (figure 2). Between 2004 and 2016, total profits of the big ten increased from RMB 15 billion to RMB 134 billion.[3]

Figure 2. Financial performance of the Chinese defense industry, 2004-2015.

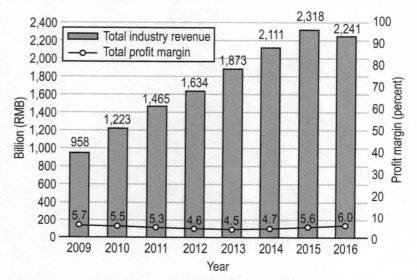

Source. Information obtained from annual reporting of the ten defense corporations. See also *China Civil-Military Integration Development Report 2015* (Beijing: National Defense University Press, 2015), 61.

The ordnance, space, electronics, and aviation industries were the most profitable sectors, whereas the shipbuilding industry has struggled because of a severe downturn in global shipbuilding. While the robust expansion of the defense industry is a bright spot amid the slowing growth in the rest of the Chinese economy, its prospects depend on continuing high levels of defense budget increases that also appear to be beginning to ease. The rate of increase for the 2017 defense budget was only 7 percent, the second year of single-digit growth and a likely marker of the end of double-digit budget increases dating back to the beginning of the 1990s.[4]

However, the official defense budget represents only one funding stream for the defense industry, which has access to funding and resources from a diversified array of sources. Funding for defense-related R&D, for example, comes primarily from other areas of the central government budget, most notably those allocated to the State Administration for Science, Technology, and Industry for National Defense (SASTIND), which is not included in the official defense budget. Moreover, around half of the defense industry's revenue and profits comes from civilian businesses; in some sectors like ordnance and nuclear this could be as high as 80–90 percent.[5] In addition, since 2013, the defense industry has been allowed to seek investment funding from capital markets that provide access to large pools of financial resources, including shareholder funds, bank loans, and bonds. These different sources will allow the defense industry to mitigate the impact of slowing official defense budget increases.

An important new trend is also becoming apparent in the performance of the shipbuilding industry. Until the mid-2000s, Chinese naval shipyards were heavily reliant on foreign, primarily Russian, technology transfers for their industrial development. The US Office of Naval Intelligence notes, however, that since the beginning of the 2010s, the PLA Navy's "surface production shifted to platforms using wholly Chinese designs and that were primarily equipped with Chinese weapons and sensors (though some engineering components and subsystems remain imported or license produced in country)," and considers some of these new systems "comparable in many respects to the most modern Western warships."[6] The space and missile industry has also been among the leaders in promoting technological self-reliance in the defense industry.

WEAKNESSES IN THE CHINESE DEFENSE INDUSTRY

The accelerating pace of output in the Chinese defense economy is taking place at the same time as it is confronted with deep-seated structural problems.[7] The principal constraints and weaknesses that the Chinese defense economy faces stem from its historical foundations and uncertain efforts to overcome the corrosive legacy of its difficult past history. The institutional and normative foundations and workings of the Chinese defense industry were copied from the former Soviet Union's command defense economy, and they continue to exert a powerful influence. The PLA and defense industrial regulatory authorities seek to replace this outdated top-down administrative management model with a more competitive and indirect regulatory regime, but there are strong vested interests that do not want to see major changes.

One of the biggest hurdles that PLA and civilian defense acquisition specialists point out is the defense industry's monopoly structure. Little competition exists because each of China's six defense industrial sectors is closed to outside competition and dominated by a select handful of state-owned defense corporations. Contracts are typically awarded through single sourcing mechanisms to these corporations. Competitive bidding and tendering only takes place for non-combat support equipment, such as logistics supplies.

A second weakness that has seriously handicapped the effectiveness of Chinese defense economy is its bureaucratic fragmentation. This is a common characteristic of the Chinese organizational system, but is especially virulent within the large and unwieldy defense sector.[8] This severe structural compartmentalization is a major obstacle to the development of innovative and advanced weapons capabilities because it requires consensus-based decision making that is carried out through extensive negotiations, bargaining, and exchanges.

A third major weakness is that the PLA continues to rely on outdated administrative tools to manage projects with defense contractors in the absence of an effective contract management system. The PLA did implement the use of contracts on a trial basis in the late 1980s with the introduction of a contract responsibility system.[9] These contracts are administrative in nature, however, and have little legal standing because of the lack of a developed legal framework within the defense industry. Consequently, contracts are vague and do not define contractual obligations or critical performance issues such as quality, pricing, or schedules. Contracts for complex weapons projects can be as short as one to two pages, according to analysts.[10]

A fourth serious weakness is the lack of a transparent pricing system for weapons and other military equipment, representing a lack of trust between the PLA and defense industry. The existing armament pricing framework is based on a "cost-plus" model that dates to the planning economy, in which contractors are allowed 5 percent profit margins on top of actual costs.[11] A number of drawbacks to this model hold back efficiency and innovation. One is that contractors are incentivized to push up costs, as this also drives up profits. Another is that contractors are not rewarded for finding ways to lower costs such as through more streamlined management or more cost-effective designs or manufacturing techniques.

To address this long-standing problem, the PLA, Ministry of Finance, and National Development and Reform Commission (NDRC) held a high-level meeting on armament pricing reform in 2009, which concluded that the outdated pricing system had seriously restricted weapons development and innovation.[12] At the beginning of 2014, the PLA General Armament Department (GAD) announced that it would conduct and expand upon pilot projects on equipment pricing.[13] These represent modest steps in the pricing reform process, but the PLA will continue to face fierce opposition from the defense industry on this issue.

A fifth impediment is corruption, which appears to have thrived with the defense industry's uncertain transition from centralized state planning to a more competitive and indirect management model.[14] PLA leaders have highlighted the RDA system as one of a number of high-risk areas in which corruption can flourish, along with the selection and promotion of officials, the enrollment of students in PLA-affiliated schools, funds management, and construction work.[15] The almost complete absence of public reporting on corruption in the defense industry and RDA system means that the extent of the problem is not known.

These are long-standing weaknesses, and previous efforts to overcome them have faced strong resistance with only marginal success. Will China's current military reforms and reforms to its DSTI system be different from past efforts? So far, as explored in the remainder of the chapter, the answer seems to be yes.

PREPARING FOR THE NEXT STAGE OF DEFENSE INDUSTRIAL ADVANCEMENT

Under Xi Jinping's leadership, China's DSTI system is evolving. Large hurdles remain, but the pace at which changes are being announced and implemented under the current administration exceed what has previously been seen. The chapter looks at five factors in this evolution in detail below.

HIGH-LEVEL LEADERSHIP SUPPORT

High-level and sustained support and guidance from Chinese Communist Party, state, and military leadership elites has been essential in the Chinese defense industry's transformation efforts. Leadership backing and intervention has been vital in addressing entrenched bureaucratic fragmentation, receiving adequate resource allocations, and tackling chronic project management problems. Without this leadership engagement, it is likely that much of the progress of the defense industry would not have happened.

Leadership is often involved through the establishment of leadership small groups and special committees. The committed involvement of the country's top leaders is especially critical, and Xi Jinping has taken a keen and active interest in DSTI issues. Between November 2012 and December 2016, Xi took part in more than 40 publicly reported events related to the PLA and defense science, technology, and industrial industries, which is considerably higher than his predecessors such as Hu Jintao (figure 3).

Figure 3. Reported visits to military and defense science and technology-related facilities made by Xi Jinping, November 2012–December 2017.

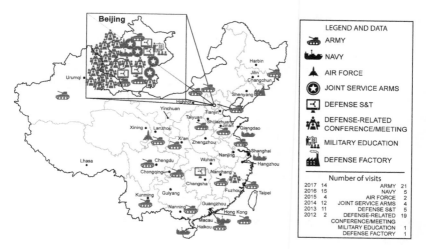

Activities that have signaled his interest in defense S&T issues include:

- Inspection of the aircraft carrier *Liaoning* and J-15 carrier fighter plant, Liaoning Province, September 2013: Within his first year as Central Military Commission (CMC) chairman, Xi made a high-profile visit to tour the *Liaoning* aircraft carrier in Dalian and to look at the progress in the development of the J-15 fighter aircraft at Shenyang Aircraft Corporation.

- Tour of National University of Defense Technology in Changsha, Hunan, November 2013: At the military's leading high-technology R&D establishment, Xi noted that the work of defense scientists and engineers should be "closely linked with real combat and army service."[16]

- Convening of a Politburo study session on military innovation, Beijing, August 2014: Xi pointed out that a global revolution in military science and technology affairs is currently taking place "at a speed so fast, in a scope so wide, at a level so deep, and with an impact so great that it has been rarely seen since the end of World War II." Xi said this represented both a challenge and opportunity, which required China's defense establishment "to vigorously promote military innovation."[17]

- Keynote speech at the All-Army Armament Conference, Beijing, December 2014: With the leaderships of the PLA's armament apparatus and defense industry in attendance, Xi affirmed the "historical achievement" in the PLA's weapons development, and urged accelerating the pace of construction.[18]

- Visit to the CMI high-tech exposition, October 2016: Xi's visit stressed high-level leadership support of CMI reform and was followed soon after by the announcement of a high-level CMI commission that Xi would head in February 2017.[19]

FORMULATING NEW LONG-TERM PLANS AND INSTITUTIONAL ARRANGEMENTS

The Xi Jinping administration signaled its intention to carry out a major overhaul of the defense industry as part of an ambitious national program of economic and military reforms at the Third Plenum of the 18th Party Congress in 2013. A flurry of activity since then by defense industrial decision-makers has produced new medium- and long-term defense industrial development strategies, plans, and institutional arrangements that represent a potential turning point in the defense industry's evolution from an innovation follower to an innovation leader.

The reform planning effort began in earnest in March 2014 when the CMC established a leading group on national defense and military reform. This group, headed by Xi Jinping, was key in the implementation of the PLA's most far-reaching structural reform in its history, which began in late 2015 and early 2016.[20] While these reforms were targeted at the PLA's central, regional, and service commands, they also had important implications for the armament management system. GAD was reorganized into the CMC Armament Development Department

(CADD) and given responsibility for the centralized unified management of the military armament system. The GAD's Science and Technology Committee was elevated to a commission reporting directly to the CMC leadership.[21]

In parallel, the state defense industrial bureaucracy formulated new strategies and plans for a significant transformation of the defense industry. One of these key plans is the 13th Defense Science, Technology, and Industry Five-Year Plan (13th Defense S&T FYP). Issued at the beginning of 2016, the plan sets out six key tasks on which to make significant progress by 2020. These are: 1) facilitating 'leapfrog' development of weapons and military equipment; 2) enhancing innovation capabilities in turnkey areas; 3) improving overall quality and efficiency; 4) optimizing the structure of the defense industry and vigorously promoting CMI; 5) accelerating the export of armaments and military equipment; and 6) supporting national economic and social construction.[22] Compared to its predecessor, the 13th Defense S&T FYP has a stronger focus on the development of high-technology weaponry and CMI and signals a significant shift from absorption and re-innovation to original innovation in the defense industry.

In a further signal of Chinese leaders' efforts to chart a long-term course for the country's defense S&T development, in June 2015 SASTIND announced the establishment of a Defense S&T Development Strategy Committee headed by its director, Xu Dazhe. It will conduct research and provide policy input to the country's leadership for long-term defense R&D over the next 20 to 30 years.[23] Remaining bureaucratic hurdles are still evident in other areas, however. SASTIND in 2015 announced that it was in the process of preparing a 2025 Defense Science and Technology Industry Plan and a 13th Five-Year Plan for Civil-Military Integration. Two years after their announcement, however, both plans appear to be stalled.[24]

TARGETING BREAKTHROUGHS IN TURNKEY TECHNOLOGICAL CAPABILITIES

Another trend in the Chinese national and defense S&T system in the Xi Jinping era is a stronger emphasis on making breakthroughs in core technological capabilities, also referred to as turnkey technological capabilities. Under this approach, Chinese plans and strategies to improve original innovation take an "asymmetric" approach in which key sectors and core technologies are prioritized for investment and development.[25]

China's S&T megaprojects are a manifestation of this trend. An original set of 16 megaprojects was announced in the 2006–2020 Medium- and Long-Term Science and Technology Development Plan, including high-end all-purpose chips, integrated circuit equipment, broadband mobile communication, high-grade numerical machinery, and nuclear power plants. Xi has announced that China would accelerate implementation of these megaprojects.[26] In 2015, a new round of megaprojects in conjunction with the 13th Five-Year Plan through a new program entitled "Science, Technology and Innovation 2030" was announced.[27] Projects selected for this program are said to "embody national strategic intentions" and include aero-engine and gas turbines, quantum communication, information network and cyber security, smart manufacturing and robotics, deep-space and deep-sea exploration, and key materials, among others.

Also in 2015, Chinese authorities announced a plan to establish large-scale, multi-disciplinary, national laboratories that would work in both civilian and defense-related fields. Support for the new laboratories reaches the top echelons of leadership, with Xi stating that national laboratories "are important vehicles in which developed countries seize the high ground in technological innovation."[28] These laboratories are viewed as critical platforms to accelerate fundamental and applied research that will enable China to reach the global frontier.[29] Details are still few, but if the national laboratories are successfully established, it will "represent a major transformation of China's R&D system."[30] In addition, SASTIND has called for the building of defense national laboratories and DSTI innovation centers to further support China's national defense S&T innovation system.[31]

INTENSIFYING EFFORTS TO REALIZE THE POTENTIAL OF CIVIL-MILITARY INTEGRATION

CMI has been promoted in China since the early 2000s but with little tangible success because of unclear strategy, ineffective implementation, and weak civil-military coordination. Despite a lack of progress, however, China sees CMI as essential in its drive for original innovation. Efforts to promote CMI have focused primarily on reforms of state-owned defense conglomerates and the implementation of policies, platforms, and other mechanisms to allow private sector technology to flow more smoothly into defense projects. The transfer of state-owned defense technology to the private sector is important to support China's "innovation-driven development" and the financing of China's defense industry.

Over the past few years, the Xi administration has made a renewed push to make CMI a viable policy tool. Key among these efforts was Xi's announcement in March 2015 elevating CMI to a national strategy. This was reaffirmed in a March 2016 meeting of the Politburo chaired by Xi during which the members approved a new document titled "Opinions on Integrated Development of Economic and National Defense Building" and approved CMI as a national strategy.[32] In January 2017, the Central Commission for Integrated Military and Civilian Development, a new coordinating body headed by Xi, was created to oversee CMI implementation efforts.[33] These developments are crucial to confronting the bureaucratic challenges and vested interests that have long stalled CMI progress.

SASTIND is a key organizer and implementer of China's CMI push and issued CMI Strategic Action Plans (SAP) in 2015 and 2016.[34] The SAPs are wide ranging and consist of goals and work objectives to implement CMI effectively. Categories include opening the defense industry to civilian participation, improving resource sharing between the civilian and defense sectors, promoting defense conversion, accelerating high-technology industrialization in the defense industry, and developing integrated industries.[35]

One clear signal of the change effected by CMI's upgraded status is the broadening of agencies engaged in the process that addresses the fragmented and marginalized nature of CMI implementation. For example, the NDRC in June 2014 restructured its Economic Mobilization Office into the Economic and National Defense Coordination Development Department that is responsible for CMI.[36] The involvement of NDRC is important as it is considered a heavyweight in economic policymaking and has significantly more bureaucratic clout and political influence than ministerial-level organs. Membership of a CMI inter-ministerial coordinating small group that meets annually is also expanding. Chaired by Minister of Industry and Information Technology Miao Wei, its membership has expanded to include important players such as the CADD, the CMC S&T Commission, and the Chinese Academy of Sciences.[37]

SUPPORTING HIGH-TECH DEFENSE INDUSTRIALIZATION

In conjunction with CMI efforts, China is currently engaged in a comprehensive effort to boost its advanced manufacturing capabilities in high-tech industries. A cornerstone of this effort is the "Made in China 2025" plan issued in May 2015, which outlines a strategy for China to comprehensively upgrade its industrial economy and achieve its goal of becoming a world-leading manufacturer by 2049.[38] As such, the plan prioritizes ten industrial sectors for policy and funding support, including CMI-related industries such as new generation information technology, automated machine tools and robotics, space and aviation equipment, maritime equipment and high-tech shipping, and new materials.

Close coordination took place between civilian and defense agencies in drafting Made in China 2025 to emphasize CMI priorities, and SASTIND continues to have a role in its implementation and evaluation. SASTIND Director Xu Dazhe sits as a representative on the State Strong Manufacturing Power Building Leading Small Group established by the State Council in 2015 and led by Vice Premier Ma Kai to oversee Made in China 2025.[39] This body directs the work of the Manufacturing Power Building Strategy Advisory Group, which is tasked with issuing a technical "green paper" every two years to update to the ten original sectors in the Made in China 2025 plan and also includes SASTIND representatives.[40]

RESTRUCTURING OF THE DEFENSE RESEARCH INSTITUTE SYSTEM

Reform of defense corporation research institutes (RIs) has long been anticipated in China's defense industry reforms, but there have only recently been signs of progress. The defense RIs are a core component of the R&D capabilities of China's defense firms. Their designation as "government-affiliated institutions" (事业单位), however, has meant that they are subject to state ownership restrictions and cannot be restructured into listed entities, creating a major bottleneck for the defense industry's ongoing efforts to securitize their assets on capital markets. Incentives to restructure the RIs are great, however, as they account for a large share of revenue in some sectors (for example, 30 percent of the profits of the China Shipbuilding Industry Corporation (CSIC) in 2014 came from its 28 RIs).[41]

In 2016, Chinese authorities began tackling defense RI reform and drafted a number of reform policies."[42] The space and missile conglomerates China Aerospace Science and Technology Corporation (CASC) and China Aerospace Science and Industry Corporation (CASIC), which have the largest number of RIs, are taking the lead in the implementation of the reforms.[43] Analysts argue that this will significantly promote innovation, facilitate CMI, and bring in more investment for defense R&D from the capital markets.

LEVERAGING CAPITAL MARKETS FOR DEFENSE INVESTMENT

CMI and the restructuring of defense RIs hint at a larger trend in China's defense industry. The defense industry is being opened to the capital markets, and the big ten state-owned defense corporations are seeking to take advantage of the lucrative financial opportunities that this may offer to better manage and leverage their assets. With firm order books, a pipeline full of new generations of equipment under development, and plenty of high-level leadership support, the defense industry is attracting interest from a proliferation of domestic investment vehicles that have appeared in the past couple of decades, and especially in the past few years.

In 2013, SASTIND began to permit firms to issue share placements using military assets as securitization.[44] CSIC became the first defense firm to undertake a private share placement in September 2013 and raised RMB 8.5 billion (US$1.4 billion) to acquire production facilities to manufacture warships. More than one-third of the funds were earmarked for the acquisition of medium- and large-sized surface warships, conventional submarines, and large landing ships, while almost another third was designated for arms trade-related undertakings and civil-military industrialization projects.[45] CSIC explained that the funds would "satisfy the development and manufacture of a new generation of weapons and equipment," adding that, "we need urgent large-scale technological improvements and need to expand our financing channels."[46]

All ten defense conglomerates have begun actively issuing public and private equity offerings and bond issuances, although to varying degrees (figures 4 and 5). Total equity and bond offerings between 2010 and June 2016 equaled RMB 419.16 billion ($62.87 billion), equivalent to 8.9 percent of the official Chinese defense budget over the same period, with equity deals and bond offerings accounting for almost equal portions of the total.[47] The shipbuilding industry is currently the most active defense industry in China's capital markets, raising 39 percent of the total among all defense industries and almost double the funds raised by the next closest industry, the aviation sector. The space, ordnance, nuclear, and electronics industries trail these two sectors but have still raised significant amounts of funding from the capital markets.

Figure 4. Total equity and bond offerings in China's state-owned defense companies by defense sector, 2010–June 2016.

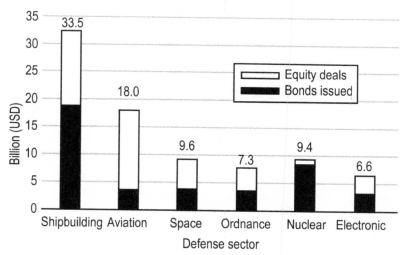

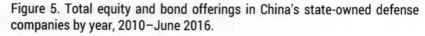

Figure 5. Total equity and bond offerings in China's state-owned defense companies by year, 2010–June 2016.

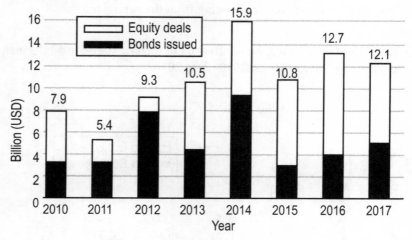

As of May 2017, the big ten defense companies had approximately 100 subsidiaries listed on China's stock exchanges, which accounted for almost 30 percent of total assets.[48] Analysts estimate that if China follows the United States, which has around 70 percent of defense industrial assets listed, Chinese firms could raise upwards of another RMB 1 trillion of funds. As an example of the magnitude and speed of growth at which the Chinese firms may grow, CASC plans to triple its asset securitization rate from its current 15 percent to 45 percent by the end of the 13th Five-Year Plan.[49] Other defense conglomerates can be expected to strive for similar growth.

IMPLICATIONS FOR US-CHINA MILITARY TECHNOLOGICAL COMPETITION

The prospects for the Chinese defense industry to successfully transition from an innovation follower to an original innovator that is able to engage in higher-end technological development appears encouraging because of the confluence of powerful factors in support of its efforts. Among these factors, proactive and engaged leadership support from Xi Jinping has been key in catalyzing reforms in fields that have long eluded military and defense industry planners and regulators, such as CMI and reform of defense research institutes. Some areas, such as the establishment of national laboratories, are still in planning stages, and it remains to be seen if they will push through entrenched interests in China's defense industry.

What are the implications for the intensifying military technological competition with the United States from a more capable and innovative Chinese defense industry? First, as the Chinese defense industry becomes more self-reliant and less dependent on foreign sources, China's path of defense technological development will become less subject to constraints imposed by foreign technology regulatory controls. Chinese analysts see this as key to countering the US Third Offset Strategy, which they see in part as an effort to lure the China to compete in areas in which the United States enjoys a decisive advantage.[50]

Second, as the pace and intensity of the Chinese defense industry's restructuring efforts quicken, the United States will find it has a narrowing window of opportunity to pursue the Third Offset Strategy and other related initiatives to maintain its strategic superiority before China is able to catch up in critical areas. The next 5–10 years could be a decisive period in shaping long-term US-China military technological competition. This viewpoint is shared by Chinese decision-makers, including Xi Jinping, who see China as engaged in a zero-sum global race for technological leadership in both the civilian and defense S&T domains.

China's efforts to move from an innovation follower to an original innovator take aim at the underpinnings of China's DSTI system. As such, tangible results in outputs from China's defense industry as a result of these reforms may not be immediately observable. For the United States to counter these reforms in China's defense industry, however, US military and defense industry planners will need to take countermeasures to strengthen the defense industrial base and DSTI system of the United States.

Notes

1. For an expanded discussion, see Tai Ming Cheung, "The Chinese Defense Economy's Long March from Imitation to Innovation," *Journal of Strategic Studies*, Vol. 34, No.3, June 2011.
2. Moses Abramovitz, "Catching Up, Forging Ahead, and Falling Behind," *Journal of Economic History* 46, no. 386 (1986).
3. Calculations for defense industry profits were aggregated from an IGCC database tracking financial performance of China's defense companies. Data for these transactions are compiled from numerous online sources for each of China's ten big defense conglomerates. Official announcements were referenced where possible.
4. "China's 2017 Defense Budget Rise to Slow Again," Reuters, March 4, 2017.
5. *China Civil-Military Integration Development Report 2015* (Beijing: National Defense University Press, 2015), 59.
6. US Office of Naval Intelligence, *The PLA Navy: New Capabilities and Missions for the 21st Century* (Washington, DC: Office of Naval Intelligence, 2015), 10, 12.
7. This section is based on the chapter "Weaknesses in China's Defense Industries," in Michael Chase et al., *China's Incomplete Military Transformation: Assessing the Weaknesses of the People's Liberation Army (PLA)* (Washington, DC: RAND, 2015).
8. Kenneth Lieberthal and Michel Oksenberg, *Policy Making in China: Leaders, Structures, and Processes* (Princeton, NJ: Princeton University Press, 1988), 35-42. See also Kenneth Lieberthal and David Lampton, eds., *Bureaucracy, Politics, and Decision Making in Post-Mao China* (Berkeley: University of California Press, 1992) and David Lampton, ed., *Policy Implementation in Post-Mao China* (Berkeley: University of California Press, 1987).
9. Tai Ming Cheung, *Fortifying China: The Struggle to Build a Modern Defense Economy* (Ithaca, NY: Cornell University Press, 2008) 83–85.
10. Interview with PLA acquisition specialist, Beijing, November 2011.
11. Mao Guohui, Introduction to the Military Armament Legal System, 158–159.

12. Zong Zhaodun and Zhao Bo, "Major Reform Considered in Work on the Prices of Our Army's Armaments," *Liberation Army Daily*, November 13, 2009.

13. "Armament Work: It Is the Right Time for Reform and Innovation," *Liberation Army Daily*, February 13, 2014.

14. Corruption is defined broadly in China as covering the improper behavior of state, party, or military officials, but the more common Western definition is the abuse of public office for personal gain in violation of rules.

15. "PLA Gets Tough on Duty Crimes," Xinhua, December 1, 2014.

16. "Xi Jinping Reviews Officials and Soldiers from National University of Defense Technology," Xinhua, November 2013, http://news.xinhuanet. com/politics/2013-11/06/c_118036424.htm.

17. "Xi Jinping Addresses Politburo 17th Collective Study Session, Emphasizes Need to Accurately Grasp New Trend in the World's Military Development, Advance with the Times to Vigorously Promote Military Innovation," Xinhua, August 30, 2014.

18. "Xi Jinping Attends PLA Armament Work Conference, Emphasizes Quickening the Building of an Armament System Commensurate with the Requirements of Performing Missions, Providing Strong Material and Technological Support for the Fulfillment of the Strong Army Dream," *China Military Industrial News*, December 6, 2014.

19. "Xi Jinping Visits Technology Exhibition, Urges Greater Integrated Military-Civilian Development," Xinhua, October 19, 2016.

20. "Zhongguo de keji shili daodi yu Meiguo xiangcha duoshao" 习主席和中央军委运筹设计深化国防和军队改革纪实 [Documentary of the design process of deepening defense and military reform by Xi Jinping and the CMC], Sina.com, December 30, 2015, http://news.sina.com.cn/o/2015-12-30/doc-ifxncyar6047368.shtml.

21. "Ministry of National Defense Holds News Conference on CMC Administrative Reform and Reorganization," *China Military Online*, January 11, 2016.

22. State Council, "2016 nian guofang keji gongye gongzuo huiyi zai Jing zhaokai" 2016年国防科技工业工作会议在京召开 [2016 national defense science, technology and industry working conference was held in Beijing], January 9, 2016, http://www.gov.cn/xinwen/2016-01/09/content_5031770.htm.

23. "Guofang keji gongye fazhan zhanlüe weiyuanhui chengli" 国防科技工业发展战略委员会成立[Defense S&T development strategy committee

established], Xinhua, June 4, 2015, http://news.xinhuanet.com/politics/2015-06/04/c_1115508987.htm.

24. "Jungong ban 2025 huzhiyuchu hangkong fadongji jiang cheng tupokou" 军工版2025呼之欲出 航空发动机将成突破口 [Defense 2025 is coming soon: Aero-engines may become the breakthrough], Xinhua, June 19, 2015, http://news.xinhuanet.com/fortune/2015-06/19/c_127931606.htm.

25. Chinese Communist Party Literature Research Office, *Xi Jinping guanyu keji chuangxin lunshu zhaobian* 习近平关于科技创新论述摘编 [Selection of Xi Jinping's comments on science, technology, and innovation] (Beijing: Central Party Literature Press, 2016), 41.

26. "Xi Jinping zhichu keji chuangxin de san da fangxiang" 习近平指出科技创新的三大方向 [Xi Jinping pointed out three directions for technological innovation], *People's Daily*, June 2, 2016, http://politics.people.com.cn/n1/2016/0602/c1001-28406379.html.

27. "China Plans Strategic S&T Breakthroughs," Xinhua, March 11, 2015, http://news.xinhuanet.com/english/2015-11/03/c_134780388.htm.

28. *Xi Jinping guanyu keji chuangxin lunshu zhaobian*, 50–51.

29. "Shisanwu guihua gangyao (quanwen)" 十三五规划纲要 (全文) [The 13th five-year plan], Xinhua, March 18, 2016, http://sh.xinhuanet.com/2016-03/18/c_135200400_2.htm.

30. "Zhongke yuanzhang: Jiang jian yi pi guojia shyanshi jiejue zhongda keji wenti" 中科院长：将建一批国家实验室解决重大科技问题 [CAS president: A number of national laboratories will be established targeting major science and technology issues], *Sina News*, February 4, 2016, http://mil.news.sina.com.cn/china/2016-02-04/doc-ifxpfhzk8866244.shtml.

31. "Guofang Kegong Ju duo cuo bingju jiakuai tuijin guofang kegongye xietong chuangxin" 国防科工局多措并举加快推进国防科技工业协同创新 [SASTIND takes measures to accelerate national defense science, technology and industry coordinated innovation], June 29, 2016, http://www.sastind.gov.cn/n112/n117/c6603042/content.html.

32. "Shenyi 'guanyu jingji jianshe he guofang jianshe ronghe fazhan de yijian'" 审议《关于经济建设和国防建设融合发展的意见》和《长江经济带发展规划纲要》[Consideration of 'opinions on integrated development of economic and national defense building' and 'outline for Yangtze economic belt development plan'], *People's Daily*, March 26, 2016, http://paper.people.com.cn/rmrb/html/2016-03/26/nw.D110000renmrb_20160326_2-01.htm.

33. "Xi to Head Civil-Military Integration Body," *Global Times*, January 22, 2017, http://www.globaltimes.cn/content/1030186.shtml.

34. State Administration for Science, Technology and Industry for National Defense, "Guofang Kegong Ju guanyu yinfa '2016 nian Guofang Kegong Ju junmin ronghe zhuangxiang xingdong jihua' de tongzhi" 国防科工局关于印发《2016年国防科工局军民融合专项行动计划》的通知 [SASTIND issues '2016 SASTIND civil-military integration special action plan'], February 28, 2016, http://www.sdgfxh.com/zcfg_detail/newsId= 213.html.

35. "SASTIND Issues '2016 SASTIND Civil-Military Integration Special Action Plan.'"

36. National Reform and Development Commission, "Chuangxin gongzuo fangfa, tuidong junmin ronghe" 创新工作方法，推动军民融合 [Innovation work methods, pushing forward civil-military integration], April 28, 2015, http://www.sdpc.gov.cn/gzdt/201504/t20150428_689846 .html.

37. Ministry of Industry and Information Technology, "Junmin ronghe yujun yumin wuqi zhuangbei keyan shengchan tixi jianshe buji xietiao xiaozu di liu ci huiyi zhaokai" 军民结合 寓军于民武器装备科研生产体系建设部际协调小组第六次会议召开 [6th meeting of inter-ministerial coordination group on construction of scientific research and production system for military armaments], April 5, 2017, http://www.miit.gov.cn/ n1146285/n1146347/n1147601/n1147604/c5559183/content.html.

38. Ministry of Industry and Information Technology, "'Zhongguo Zhizao 2015' jiedu zhi liu: zhizao qiangguo 'san buzou' zhanlüe" 《中国制造2025》解读之六：制造强国#三步走》战略 [Interpret 'Made in China 2025': 'Three-Step' strategy to become a manufacturing power], May 19, 2015, http://www.miit.gov.cn/n11293472/n11293832/n11294042 /n11481465/16595227.html.

39. "Guowuyuan bangong ting guanyu chengli guojia zhizao qiangguo jianshe lingdao xiaozu de tongzhi" 国务院办公厅关于成立国家制造强国建设领导小组的通知 [Office of state council on notice on establishment of state strong manufacturing power building leading small group], June 24, 2015, http://www.gov.cn/zhengce/content/2015 -06/24/content_9972.htm.

40. "Guojia zhizao qiangguo jianshe lingdao xiaozu chengli Ma Kai ren zuzhang" 国家制造强国建设领导小组成立 马凯任组长 [State manufacturing power building leading small group established with Ma Kai as chair], *Observer*, June 24, 2015, http://www.guancha.cn/politics/ 2015_06_24_324516.shtml.

41. "Jungong keyan yuansuo fenlei gaige wenjian huo jinqi luodi" 军工科研院所分类改革文件或近期落地 [Defense research institute reform may be implemented soon], Xinhua, January 15, 2016, http://news.xinhuanet.com/finance/2016-01/15/c_128631763.htm.

42. Ibid.

43. "Jungong yuansuo fenlei gaige ying tupo hangtian xi wang cheng" 军工院所分类改革迎突破 航天系望成"领头羊" [Reform of defense research institutes made breakthroughs, space sector may take the lead], *Shanghai Securities News*, February 4, 2016, http://www.cnstock.com/v_industry/sid_rdjj/201602/3703256.htm.

44. State Administration for Science, Technology and Industry for National Defense, "Guofang Kegong Ju guanyu yinfa guofang keji gongye guding zichan touzi xiangmu guanli guiding de tongzhi" 国防科工局关于印发国防科技工业固定资产投资项目管理规定的通知 [SASTIND issues notice on rules for defense S&T and industry fixed assets investment program management], August 27, 2013, http://www.opt.ac.cn/jg/glbm/kjyglb/xagjsjgglwj/201309/W020140328373812704712.pdf.

45. "Zhonaguo zhonggong 84.8 yi ding zeng yu'an chulu kaichuang zhongda jungong zichan zhuru xianhe" 中国重工84.8亿定增预案出炉 开创重大军工资产注入先河 [CSIC releases plan for 8.48 billion set, creates precedent for defense asset injection], *Shanghai Securities News*, September 11, 2013, http://finance.sina.com.cn/stock/s/20130911/023716724295.shtml.

46. "China Navy Plots Course to Stock Market," *Financial Times*, September 11, 2013, https://next.ft.com/content/4f27d80a-1abb-11e3-a605-00144feab7de.

47. Calculations for public and private equity offerings and bonds were aggregated from an IGCC database collecting capital market transactions of China's defense companies. Data for these transactions are compiled from numerous online sources for each of China's ten big defense conglomerates from 2010 to June 2016. Official announcements were referenced where possible. Data primarily reflects only capital market transactions of the parent companies. Also, data for Chinese domestic capital transactions is believed to be complete, but Hong Kong and overseas transactions may have missing data. Bonds do not distinguish between public bonds and interagency bonds, and for private placement deals still being finalized, details such as investor and deal size are subject to change.

48. "Jungong zichan zhengquanhua yuqi" 军工资产证券化预期 [Military industrial asset securitization expectations], *Sina News*, May 27, 2017, http://finance.sina.com.cn/roll/2017-05-27/doc-ifyfqvmh9208949.shtml.

49. "Junmin ronghe zheme huo ni zhidao zenme shuli hexin gainian gu ma?" 军民融合这么火 你知道怎么梳理核心概念股吗? [CMI is trending, do you know how to sort out core stocks?], *Securities Times*, April 5, 2016, http://finance.sina.com.cn/stock/t/2016-04-05/doc-ifxqxqmf4052133.shtml.

50. Zhao Yang and Liu Na, "The Best Way of Predicting the Future Is to Create the Future: An Analysis of the Technical Background of the United States' High-Profile Presentation of the Third Offset Strategy," *Liberation Army Daily*, May 6, 2016.

CHAPTER 4

THE US-CHINA RECONNAISSANCE-STRIKE COMPETITION

THE SECURITY DILEMMA, MISSILES, SPACE, AND COUNTERSPACE

Kevin Pollpeter

Asia is in the midst of a geopolitical transition driven by the rise of China. China's growing economic and military power has led to its increased presence not only in Asia, but also globally. China's increasing assertiveness over territorial disputes and an increasing sense on the part of Chinese interlocutors that China needs strategic space has created concerns both within Asia and the United States that China seeks to become the hegemon of Asia.

This chapter examines competitive strategies between China and the United States in the fields of missiles, space, and counterspace through the lens of the security dilemma. Of particular focus is the PLA's development of anti-ship missile (ASM), space, and counterspace technologies and the response of the US Navy and the US Air Force to these developments. The chapter argues that through the development of ASM, space, and counterspace technologies, China is following a strategy of denial intended to convince the United States that it is impossible to achieve its objectives through military means. Through this strategy of denial, China is pursuing a de facto cost imposition strategy that threatens the United States' highly capable, but expensive weapon systems with relatively less expensive countermeasures.

The chapter finds that China's pursuit of these competitive strategies has placed the two countries in the beginning stages of an arms competition in space, counterspace, and missile technologies that shows signs of turning into an arms race. Deputy Secretary of Defense Robert Work has called this dynamic an "emerging guided munitions salvo competition."[1] I expand upon the notion by also including the use of space-based C4ISR (command, control, communications, computers, intelligence, surveillance, and reconnaissance) and counterspace technologies to provide a more well-rounded analysis that I call the "reconnaissance-strike competition."

China's development of long-range ASMs has the potential to usher in a new stage of naval warfare in which missile power replaces a doctrine of air power followed by the United States as the determining factor in naval warfare. In doing so, missile power places an even greater emphasis on long-range reconnaissance and the role of space technologies as an enabler of missile operations. The growing importance of space has also spurred the development of counterspace weapons to degrade an adversary's space-based C4ISR capabilities and an increased effort to ensure the survivability of space assets and the ability to reconstitute space-based architectures. As a result, future naval warfare will be decided by two main factors: weapon range and C4ISR capabilities.

China's emphasis on missile-centric naval warfare imposes operational and budgetary costs on the US military. Operationally, the US Navy has had to change its surface fleet concept of operations from land attack to naval warfighting with a focus on long-range ASM and counter-C4ISR capabilities. The US Air Force, which once regarded space as a sanctuary, is now developing a concept of operations to "fight through" attacks on space assets. In terms of budget, in an era of static or shrinking defense budgets, the need to develop technologies to carry out these new concepts of operations requires a reprioritization of Department of Defense funding that will inevitably take away from other priorities. Finally, this arms competition has the potential to destabilize the military dynamic between the United States and China. The development of long-range strike weapons and their critical reliance on C4ISR gives an advantage to those who strike first. Thus, both adversaries may feel compelled to strike first rather than risk losing their offensive capacity.

THE US-CHINA RECONNAISSANCE-STRIKE COMPETITION

The US-China reconnaissance-strike competition is seen in an emerging competition in missiles and space technologies. This competition represents a move away from platform-centric warfare to missile-centric warfare, its concomitant C4ISR requirements, and space warfare. The change to more missile-centric operations is resulting in weapons range, not just firepower, becoming the dominant force in naval warfare.[2] Because missiles are increasing in range, reconnaissance and the means to defeat reconnaissance are also more critical and will result in naval battles being decided by both weapons range and the effectiveness of reconnaissance.[3]

As evidence of this changing nature of warfare, China has been developing what the Center for Strategic and Budgetary Assessments calls "the world's most sophisticated arsenals of anti-ship cruise missiles (ASCMs)." These missiles "can be launched from mobile ground launchers, aircraft, ships, and submarines" and "are complemented by multiple types of ballistic missiles."[4] Specifically, Chinese ballistic missiles, launched from within China's well-protected borders, can conduct precision strikes against both fixed and moving targets as far away as Guam. Moreover, many Chinese ASCM can be fired from distances that are well beyond the range of US ASCM. China is also developing hypersonic weapons, which, if deployed, can close in on targets at speeds of at least Mach 5.

At the same time that China has been developing large numbers of missiles, the United States has been involved in two counterinsurgency campaigns that have emphasized the use of ground forces while its missile defense efforts have been spent on developing expensive systems designed to defend against small numbers of missiles fired by Iran or North Korea and not against the large numbers of missiles fielded by China.[5] This dynamic is changing, with the US military now responding to Chinese military modernization with new technologies and concepts of operations.

In order to carry out its missile-centric approach, the PLA has developed a new concept of operations called "system versus system" warfare that takes information as the core and moves the PLA away from a platform-centric approach to military operations. Recognizing the importance of information systems, the PLA seeks to further integrate information technologies with weapon systems and to be able to deny an adversary the use of its own information technology. Under this concept, warfighting is a contest between networks of systems, and the operation of every system and subsystem affects the performance of the entire system. Together the synergistic qualities of this system-of-systems configuration can yield a result greater than the sum of its parts, enabling joint operations through the use of networked information systems that provide each operational element with a real-time Common Operating Picture of the battlefield and allows units to be more flexible and adaptive.[6]

As a result, missiles and space technologies have begun to play a central role in Chinese military modernization efforts. Missiles provide the PLA a capability to accurately strike targets far from China's shores. But in doing so, the PLA has come to realize what the US military has realized for some time: long-range power projection requires space-based C4ISR. Space-based C4ISR can provide remote sensing to identify targets and conduct battle damage assessments, navigation to guide precision munitions, and communication to connect and integrate the actions of multiple services. In addition, China is developing a full range of counterspace technologies to defeat the ability of the US military to conduct its own long-range precision strikes.

The emerging US-China reconnaissance-strike competition is thus characterized by an action-reaction dynamic in which both sides are now developing new concepts of operations, establishing new organizations to lead space operations, investing in long-range ASMs, developing an operationally responsive space capability to ensure access to space and utilization of space-based capabilities, and counter-space capabilities to deny each other the use of space. These developments will be examined in detail in the next sections.

PROGRESS IN CHINA'S RECONNAISSANCE-STRIKE COMPLEX

Progress in China's Space Program

For the purposes of examining China's reconnaissance-strike complex, China's military space program can be divided into three technological and two mission areas. Technologically, China's space program can be divided into launch vehicles, satellites, and counterspace. In regards to missions, China's launch vehicles and satellites are intended to provide an operationally responsive space force whereas counterspace technologies are intended to deny space capabilities to adversaries. Moreover, the PLA has created a new organization, the Strategic Support Force, to conduct space operations.

Operationally Responsive Space

Operationally responsive space is a US concept that includes the capability to launch a variety of satellites into all orbits and the ability to rapidly reconstitute or plus up satellite constellations. The second capability is satellites that enable the PLA to achieve its mission objectives while also ensuring survivability.

Launch Capabilities

China is developing a new generation of liquid-fueled launch vehicles that can launch bigger and more capable satellites as well as smaller, solid-fueled, road-mobile launch vehicles that can conduct launches within shorter timelines. The new generation of liquid-fueled rockets is divided into light, medium, and heavy-lift versions that are able to send 1 to 25 metric ton payloads into low Earth orbit and 1 to 14 metric ton payloads into geosynchronous orbit.[7] With the addition of this capacity, China will be able to launch heavier satellites, such as larger remote sensing satellites with better imagery resolutions.

China has also developed two solid-fueled rockets that provide launch capabilities at the lower end of the lift spectrum. Although not as powerful as liquid-fueled rockets, solid-fueled rockets do not need to be fueled before launch and can be more easily transported by ground vehicles, enhancing responsiveness and survivability. The first of these solid-fuel rockets is the Long March 11. Reportedly based on the DF-31 ICBM, the LM-11 can carry a payload of 700 kilograms into orbit.[8] The second of China's solid-fueled rockets is the Kuaizhou launch vehicle. The Kuaizhou is reported to be based on the DF-21 medium range ballistic missile and is advertised as being capable of launching 300 kg into orbit with just four hours of preparation.[9]

Satellites

The second thrust of China's operationally responsive space effort is the development of an increasingly larger number of satellites with diverse capabilities (table 1). By 2020, China plans to have a global, 24-hour, all-weather Earth remote sensing system. To meet this goal, China has launched a number of new remote sensing satellites since 2000 to fulfill a variety of missions. These include satellites with a variety of resolutions that can provide both highly detailed imagery at the sub-meter level and imagery that is less detailed but can provide views of wider swaths of territory. This also includes satellites with synthetic aperture radar payloads to image targets in inclement weather and at night as well as electronic intelligence satellites to monitor the electronic emissions of ships. China is also developing a constellation of navigation satellites. By 2020, China also plans to have established a global satellite navigation system that can provide positioning accuracies of one meter with the assistance of ground stations.

Table 1. Selected Chinese Remote Sensing Satellites.

Satellite	Payloads	Resolutions	Number Operational (December 31, 2015)
Yaogan	EO, SAR, ELINT	EO=1m, SAR=1.5m	29
Gaofen	EO, Staring camera	EO= <1m-2m, 800m Staring camera=50m	5
Haiyang	EO and color scanners	EO=250m	1
Huanjing	EO	30m	3
Jilin	EO	0.72m	4
Tianhui	Stereoscopic	5m	3

Sources. Data from "Yaogan," Dragon in Space, http://www.dragoninspace.com/earth-observation/yaogan.aspx; Rui C. Barbosa, "Long March 3B lofts Gaofen-4 to Close Out 2015," nasaspaceflight.com, December 28, 2015, http://www.nasaspaceflight.com/2015/12/long-march-3b-gaofen-4-close-2015/; "China's Ocean Satellites" (中国海洋卫星), Aerospace China (中国航天), No. 372 (April 2009), 10–11; Wang Qiao, Wu Chuanqing, and Li Qing, "Environment Satellite 1 and Its Application in Environmental Monitoring," Journal of Remote Sensing 1 (2010): 104; Rui C. Barbosa, "China launches Jilin-1 mission via Long March 2D," nasaspaceflight.com, October 7, 2015, http://www.nasaspaceflight.com/2015/10/china-launches-jilin-1-mission-long-march-2d/.

Counterspace

China is developing a wide range of counterspace technologies that are designed to threaten satellites and support infrastructure from the ground to geosynchronous orbit (table 2). China's most prominent counterspace technologies appear to be direct ascent kinetic kill vehicles (KKV). First made apparent in a 2007 anti-satellite test, China has since conducted five tests that either directly or indirectly through ballistic missile defense tests sought to refine China's direct ascent capabilities. This included a 2014 test that released a warhead that flew to an altitude of 30,000 km. By doing so, China appears to be developing technologies to threaten satellites in higher Earth orbits, such as GPS and communications satellites.

In addition to direct ascent tests, China has also performed close proximity operations where one satellite has bumped into another and has conducted tests of robotic arms technologies in which one satellite equipped with a robotic arm closed with and grappled another satellite. Ostensibly done to test technologies for China's human spaceflight program, both tests also demonstrate the ability to get near a satellite to achieve effects on it.[10]

China has also been developing directed energy weapons such as lasers that can temporarily or permanently blind the imagers on remote sensing satellites or damage other satellite components.[11]

China has conducted cyber operations against US space facilities. These include a 2012 attack against the Jet Propulsion Laboratory that is assessed to have enabled the perpetrator to achieve full control over JPL networks and a 2014 attack against the National Oceanic and Atmospheric Administration that resulted in a two-day outage of meteorological coverage.[12]

Table 2. Chinese Counterspace Operations and Tests and Tests with Counterspace Implications.

Year	Technology
	Directed Energy
2006	Chinese laser paints US satellite
	Kinetic Energy
2007	China destroys FY-1C meteorological satellite with direct-ascent KKV
2010	China conducts mid-course ballistic missile defense test
2013	China conducts direct ascent KKV test to GEO
2013	China conducts mid-course ballistic missile defense test
2014	China conducts direct ascent KKV test
2015	KKV test of unknown purpose
	Co-orbital
2010	Two Shijian satellites involved in close proximity operation
2013	Three satellites involved in close proximity operation to test space debris removal and robotic arm technologies
	Cyber
2012	Cyber attack against Jet Propulsion Laboratory
2014	Cyber attack against National Oceanic and Atmospheric Administration

Finally, China is assessed to be able to jam satellite communications and GPS signals. China has acquired foreign and indigenous jammers that give it "the capability to jam common satellite communications bands and GPS receivers."[13]

Organizational Reform

The PLA created the Space Strategic Force (SSF) on December 31, 2015 to, in part, lead its space force. Although little official information on the SSF exists, its purpose is to enable the PLA to better coordinate the use of space-based C4ISR. This includes leading China's space launch centers, satellite control centers, and at least some of the PLA's intelligence organizations.

THE US MILITARY'S RESPONSE TO CHINA'S SPACE PROGRAM DEVELOPMENT

As the world's leading space power, the US military maintains a lead over China in space technologies even though the gap between the two countries has diminished rapidly. To improve the survivability of its space architecture, the US government is increasing the budget for space protection activities by $5 billion dollars over the next five years, including $2 billion for space control.[14] Moreover, it has developed a five-part strategy that involves enhancing the resiliency of satellites, developing counterspace technologies, improving space battle management and command and control (BMC2), partnering with allies, and capitalizing on the use of commercial space capabilities.

Enhanced Resiliency

In order to enhance resiliency, the DoD goal is to "[move] toward more resilient systems and system architectures, and pursu[e] a multi-layered approach to deter attacks on space systems" that are intended to make US satellites "hard to find, hard to catch, hard to hit, hard to kill."[15] This includes the use of "different orbits, mobility, deception, and distributed architectures" such as breaking up capabilities across a larger number of smaller satellites instead of concentrating them into a smaller number of larger satellites.[16]

Counterspace

The United States is reluctant to reveal its intentions or capabilities regarding what it calls "threat suppression" and no information is available on what, if any, technologies are being developed. The United States has, however, developed a number of counterspace and counterspace-related technologies in the past that provide the United States with a latent counterspace capability. In 1985, the United States destroyed a retired satellite with a missile launched from an F-15 fighter. The United States again demonstrated direct-ascent technologies in 2008 when it used a modified SM-3 missile interceptor to destroy an errant satellite. In 1997, the United States tested the Mid Infrared Advanced Chemical Laser against a satellite, simulating both inadvertent lasing and a hostile attack. The United States has also tested co-orbital capabilities. In 2005 the United States launched the XSS-11 satellite to test on-orbit servicing and maintenance, which provided the United States with an inherent co-orbital counterspace capability.[17]

Improved Battle Management and Command and Control
A third structural change is improving space BMC2 to allow the US military to "fight through" attacks on its space assets. This reform includes both organizational and technological change. Organizationally, the US military created the Joint Interagency Combined Space Operations Center (JICSpOC) in October 2015 (now called the National Space Defense Center). JICSpOC was created to test how the US military can provide space-based support to warfighters while under attack. The goal of JICSpOC was to clarify mission responsibilities between the military and the intelligence community in order to determine "who does what and how in the event of attacks on US satellites." Although the military and the intelligence community retain separate legal and command authorities, the goal of the organization is for the two entities "to be so closely bound together operationally that they do not stand alone."[18]

Technologically, the US Air Force is improving BMC2 systems with the "Air Force Space Surveillance System S-Band Radar" also known as the "Space Fence." The Space Fence will improve space situational awareness by increasing the number of objects able to be detected in space from 20,000 to 200,000 with "better accuracy, timeliness, and precision" and improve its capabilities from merely detecting objects to "simultaneously detect[ing], track[ing], and characteriz[ing] objects within its field of view."[19]

Commercial Capabilities

The Department of Defense is also reaching out to commercial space providers to increase redundancy and responsiveness. Here the DoD is relying on the combination of low-cost rockets provided by new entrants into the launch business and smaller, but increasingly capable, small and microsatellites being developed by the so-called new space companies. For some time, the Pentagon has been using commercial providers for satellite communications and remote sensing, but its plan is to further increase their use. For example, the DoD plans to increasingly use commercial remote sensing providers such as Planet. Planet will use a planned constellation of 150 cubesats, each with a mass of just 4 kg, to continuously image the earth with resolutions of 4–5 meters, providing a near real-time catalog of changes on the earth surface.[20]

International Partnerships

The United States is also partnering with other countries to add redundancy and resiliency. Japan and the United States, for example, have agreed to "strengthen the resilience and interoperability of critical space systems," focusing on "space-based positioning, navigation, and timing; enhanced space situational awareness; use of space for maritime domain awareness; research and development in space technologies; and use of hosted payloads."[21]

CHINA'S PROGRESS IN CONVENTIONAL MISSILE TECHNOLOGIES

China has a large inventory of ground, air, surface, and subsurface launched ballistic and cruise missiles (table 3). The PLA fields the world's first anti-ship ballistic missile, the DF-21D with a range of 1,500–2,000 km, giving the PLA the ability to attack ships east of Taiwan. The PLA has also developed the DF-26, which is reported to include a naval attack variant. With a range of 3,500–4,000 km, the DF-26 can be used to strike targets as far as Guam.[22]

The PLA is also developing a wide variety of ASCMs. Cruise missiles have several advantages over ballistic missiles. They are cheaper, can be launched from a variety of platforms, and can strike targets from different angles of attack. In addition, their small radar signature and their ability to fly at low altitudes allow them to more easily evade air defense radars.[23]

The Chinese military regards ASCMs "as an increasingly potent means of shaping the outcome of military conflicts."[24] According to the US-China Economic and Security Review Commission, "Taken together, the variety of platforms the PLA Navy has equipped with ASCMs provides China with a multilayered area denial capability in its near seas and beyond."[25] For example, "each of the PLA Navy's major surface combatants is equipped with ASCMs" while over half the PLAN's submarine force is capable of firing ASCMs, and by 2020 it is projected that the vast majority of PLAN submarines will be equipped with ASCMs.[26]

Table 3. PLA Anti-ship Missiles.

Designator	Launch platform	Top speed	Approximate range
YJ-83	Air and surface	Subsonic	185+
YJ-82	Subsurface	Subsonic	37
YJ-81	Air	Subsonic	50
YJ-8A	Surface	Subsonic	42
YJ-62	Ground and surface	Subsonic	277
YJ-18	Surface and subsurface	Supersonic	537
YJ-12	Air	Supersonic	400
SS-N-27	Subsurface	Supersonic	222
SS-N-22	Surface	Supersonic	120
DF-21D	Ground	Supersonic	1,500
DF-26	Ground	Supersonic	3,000

Source. "China's New YJ-18 Antiship Cruise Missile: Capabilities and Implications for US Forces in the Western Pacific" (p. 5) by Michael Pilger, 2015, US-China Economic and Security Review Commission Staff Research Report.

Hypersonics

China is also developing hypersonic weapons that can travel at least five times the speed of sound. China has conducted seven tests of a hypersonic glide vehicle called the Wu-14.[27] The Wu-14 is launched on a ballistic missile and then glides to its intended target at hypersonic speeds. China is also testing scramjet technologies that would power missiles to hypersonic speeds. Scramjets are slower than boost-glide vehicles and have shorter ranges, but are less expensive and more maneuverable.[28]

Hypersonic weapons offer two advantages over ballistic and cruise missiles. Unlike conventional ballistic missile warheads which may follow a traditional ballistic reentry to the target, hypersonic vehicles can better evade missile defenses through maneuver and approaching their target from lower altitudes. A second feature is their speed. Unlike cruise missiles, which can travel at supersonic speeds, warheads approaching at hypersonic speeds greatly reduce the attack response time of defenders, especially if they must deal with multiple, simultaneous threats.

THE US CHALLENGE AND RESPONSE

China's development of ballistic missiles, cruise missiles, and hypersonic weapons presents a number of challenges to the US military. These include insufficient numbers of ASCM-capable ships, missiles and missile interceptors, an inability to target supersonic missiles, the shorter ranges of US missiles, and a cost ratio that favors offensive systems. In other words, China currently possesses sufficient numbers of ballistic and cruise missiles to overwhelm US defenses, which is aided by China's inventory of supersonic cruise missiles and ballistic missile warhead penetration aids. China's lead in the number of ASCM-capable ships and ASMs allows it to win a war of attrition between surface ships. Finally, the cost ratio between offensive missile acquisition and the acquisition of missile defense systems lies in favor of missile acquisition, which means that the US Navy is on the losing end of an offense-defense arms competition in terms of both capabilities and cost.

Missile Inventory Deficit and Missile Defense Inadequacy

The US military faces a deficit of both missile interceptors and ASCMs in relation to the ballistic missile and cruise missile inventories possessed by the Chinese military. Moreover, current US missile defense systems lack the technological sophistication to adequately counter China's high speed, maneuverable missiles. As one analysis concludes, US "[theater missile] defenses [against ballistic missiles] lack the speed, accuracy, firing rates, and total interceptor inventories to cope with large numbers of sophisticated missiles equipped with countermeasures."[29]

ASCMs, for example, present numerous challenges to ships. Because they skim at just several meters above the water surface, they not only fly below air defense radars, they also fly below the minimum vertical range of air defense missiles. Moreover, some Chinese ASCMs can close in on their target at supersonic speeds and make 10g turns to evade defenses. Should they evade US air defense missiles, the Vulcan Phalanx 20 mm cannon point defense system deployed on US Navy ships cannot effectively track missiles performing evasive maneuvers at supersonic speeds.[30]

The US military is also outgunned by the PLA when it comes to numbers of ASCMs and ASCM-capable ships, giving the PLA the ability to suffer more losses yet still come out victorious. According to a 2012 study, in a conflict between the US and Chinese navies, the 50 ASCM-capable ships from the US Pacific Fleet would most likely face 85 ASCM-capable PLAN ships.[31] According to a 2010 study, the US Pacific Fleet possesses 280 Harpoon ASCM, or just 40 percent of the PLAN inventory. Further limiting the availability of ASCMs is the requirement of US ships to divide their duties between defensive missions to protect aircraft carriers and offensive missions to sink PLAN ships.[32] Based on these numbers, Gormley, Erickson, and Yuan conclude that in some situations a single US carrier strike group would be outmatched 7 to 1 in ASCMs launched by surface ships.[33]

As a result, by employing a "complex integrated attack" involving salvos of ballistic missiles and cruise missiles in conjunction with decoys and other penetration aids in a combination of low and high attacks approaching from different angles, Chinese attacks can overwhelm missile defenses.[34] Moreover, because of the limited number of missile interceptors and because successfully countering a missile attack requires multiple shots at each incoming missile, US forces may not only be unable to engage each missile involved in a full-on Chinese attack, but may also simply run out of ammunition before they have had a chance to engage all incoming threats.

Missile Range Deficit

US efforts at missile defense are further complicated by the relatively short range of US air and missile defenses when compared to the range of Chinese missiles. Chinese ballistic missiles can be fired from well within Chinese territory, out of range of most US attack platforms and well protected with air defense systems. (figure 6).[35]

Figure 6. Anti-ship missiles, approximate range (in kilometers).

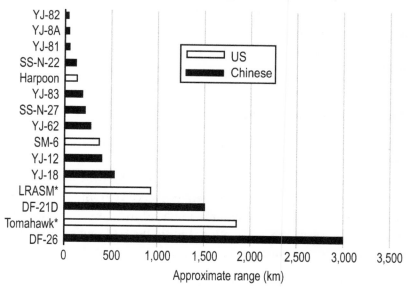

*Under development

Cost-Ratio Deficit

The final challenge is cost. The DoD is keenly aware that in this competition it has been on the losing side of the offense-defense cost ratio. As the former Commander of Northern Command, Admiral Bill Gortney, has stated, "when it comes to ballistic missile defense, we are on the wrong side of the cost curve. We're shooting down not very expensive rockets with very expensive rockets..."[36]

Although there is no direct evidence that China is explicitly following a strategy of imposing financial costs on the United States, the effect of China's emphasis on long-range ASM will force the DoD to make difficult choices regarding future funding allocations. The budgets for the Navy and Air Force since 2011 have remained stagnant or decreased. If this situation continues, increased allocations to defeat the long-range ASM threat will necessarily force reductions in other areas. As a result, declining or stagnant budgets will make it even more difficult to reduce the deficit in the number of ships and ASM between the US Navy and the PLA Navy.

THE US MILITARY RESPONSE

The Department of Defense has recognized these challenges posed by China's missile developments and has begun to address them. The first step taken by the US Navy has been to redress its doctrine for its surface fleet. Formed by its warfighting experience since 2001, the US Navy has been focused on land attack and maritime security missions, not naval warfare. As a result, the warfighting skills of the US Navy's surface fleet necessary to engage surface and subsurface combatants has atrophied.

The US Navy's surface fleet's new concept of operations to address this deficiency, "distributed lethality," has the goal of making "every ship a shooter."[37] It re-emphasizes offensive action and increasing surface force lethality in order "to provide more strike options to joint-force commanders, provide another method to seize the initiative, and add battlespace complexity to an adversary's calculus." A second part of this doctrine is to disperse naval assets in order to provide "a more complex targeting problem while creating more favorable conditions to project power where required."

The US Navy has already taken a number of steps to carry out this plan, modifying existing weapons to provide near-term offensive and defensive operations and developing new, potentially revolutionary weapons for the long term. First, the US military is modifying existing weapons to meet the disparity in ranges between Chinese and US ASCMs. The US Navy has modified the SM-6 missile, originally designed for defense against aircraft and cruise missiles, to have maritime strike and ballistic missile defense capabilities.[38] With this modification, US Navy ships will have two types of interceptors, and thus increased numbers, able to defend against ballistic missile attacks: the SM-3 to strike missiles during their mid-course phase and the SM-6 as a terminal phase defense system. The modification of the SM-6 missile to have a maritime strike capability provides additional flexibility, and its 370 km range and speed of Mach 3.5 will allow it to strike targets at greater ranges and speeds than the Harpoon ASCM.[39] Although not an ideal anti-ship missile due to its small warhead, the modified SM-3 provides an interim capability that the US Navy lacks. In addition to the modification of the SM-6, the US Navy also requested $434 million in its FY17 budget to modify 245 Tomahawk land attack cruise missiles to have a maritime attack capability. This upgrade will allow the US Navy to target ships at ranges up to 1,852 km, well beyond current Chinese ASCM range.[40]

Second, the US Navy is developing new missile defense technologies. Recognizing the limitations of its point defense system against cruise missiles, the US Navy is working to replace its Vulcan Phalanx 20 mm cannons with the SeaRAM, an anti-ship missile defense system that uses missiles instead of cannon to intercept incoming cruise missiles. Unlike the Vulcan Phalanx, the SeaRAM can intercept high performance, supersonic cruise missiles.[41]

The United States is also developing a number of potentially revolutionary missile defense systems. These include lasers, electromagnetic rail guns (EMRG) that use electromagnetic pulses to fire projectiles at speeds up to Mach 6 and ranges up to 177 km,[42] and hyper velocity projectiles (HVP), which use the same projectile as rail guns but are fired from traditional powder guns, such as the 5-inch and 155 mm guns found on US naval ships, to reach speeds up to Mach 3.[43]

Laser, EMRG, and HVP all help the US Navy solve its inventory deficit and cost ratio challenge. Lasers can be fired at a cost of less than $1 per shot and can be fired indefinitely as long as the ship can generate electricity. EMRG projectiles and HVP can be stored by the hundreds on ships at a unit cost of $26,000, compared to the multi-million dollar SM-3 and SM-6 missiles, of which only several hundred are owned by the entire US Navy.[44] Although still early in their development stage and facing difficulties in making them fully operational, such weapon systems hold great promise. According to Ronald O'Rourke of the Congressional Research Service, "Any one of these new weapon technologies, if successfully developed and deployed, might be regarded as a 'game changer' for defending Navy surface ships against enemy missiles. If two or three of them are successfully developed and deployed, the result might be considered not just a game changer, but a revolution."[45]

COMPETITIVE STRATEGIES, THE SECURITY DILEMMA, AND THE RECONNAISSANCE-STRIKE ARMS COMPETITION

China's development of long-range ASM also has operational consequences. Here, a more missile-centric approach to operations conforms to the findings of retired Navy Captain Wayne P. Hughes. Hughes, in his study *Fleet Tactics and Coastal Combat*, lists a number of tactical trends and constants based on historical evidence. Hughes finds that "the absolute and effective ranges of weapons have increased" and that "effective weapon range has come to dominate mere weight of firepower." He also concludes that "speed of a weapons platform is now subordinate to the speed of weapon delivery and that "[s]peed of delivery is governed by scouting and C2 processes as well as the sheer velocity of weapons." This has resulted in "weapon range and lethality...increase[ing] the size of the no man's land between the fleets." Furthermore, Hughes's conclusion that the "[g]rowth in weapon range and lethality has likewise led to an increase in land-sea interactions" seems to have presaged the use of ASBMs.[46]

Hughes also finds that the trend in naval warfare is for tactical surprise to increase and for the "first application of effective firepower" to be "the foremost tactical aim."[47] As Hughes writes, "It is wrong for the tactician merely to maintain an offensive frame of mind, thinking of nothing more than getting in the first attack. Naval forces must execute the first effective attack—the one after which the enemy can neither recover nor counterpunch successfully."[48] Most conventional analysis of a war between China and the United States, however, assumes that the PLA, with its emphasis on first strikes, will fire the first salvo, indicating that the PLAN's superiority in ship numbers and ASMs would be magnified even further.

Moreover, Hughes's conclusions conform to the expressed desire of the US and Chinese militaries to target C4ISR systems. Indeed, China's numerical superiority in ASM and ASM-capable ships has generated increased motivation in the US military to develop counter-C4ISR capabilities so that it can defeat the ASM threat before the missiles are fired. As Admiral Gortny has stated, "we need to look at the entire kill chain...of these ballistic missiles and try and through kinetic or non-kinetic means, and through deterrence, keep them on the rail."[49] As a result, counter-C4ISR, most likely including counterspace, will become a critical, if not the most critical aspect of future missile defense, leading to Hughes' conclusion that "reconnaissance from space will lead to battles in space."[50]

But the targeting of C4ISR systems can be destabilizing. According to Robert Jervis, "[w]hen weapons are highly vulnerable, they must be employed before they are attacked."[51] As a result, this aspect of reconnaissance-strike competition may be the most escalatory. As noted previously, owing to the fragile nature of space assets, space warfare is offense dominant. Seeing a need "to use it or lose it," either side or both sides may decide that whoever strikes first, wins. This may include strikes against space-based C4ISR assets and, for the US military, strikes against targets in China. These types of attacks could generate reprisals and further escalate the conflict.

The US Navy must also increase the number of ships. As the sides become more equal in capabilities, attrition will become more of a factor as ship losses could be expected to increase. In addition, because "the consequences of surprise become more serious,"[52] the potential for a strong first strike would also suggest that having enough ships to withstand the first battle would be paramount. Here again, however, stagnant US defense budgets will limit the ability of the US Navy to increase the number of ships.

None of this, of course, is predetermined. Other factors besides missile range and numbers would affect the battle. This includes the quality of personnel, sensor payload effectiveness, and the ability to integrate BMC2 systems. In particular, C4ISR appears to be a critical limiting factor for the PLA. According to the Office of Naval Intelligence, "Modern navies must be able to effectively build a picture of all activities occurring in the air and sea. For China, this provides a formidable challenge. Just to characterize activities in the 'near seas,' China must build a picture covering nearly 875,000 square nautical miles of water- and air-space.[53] The National Air and Space Intelligence Center adds, "One key dependency inherent to missile warfare is targeting: effective and timely target selection is an absolutely critical part of the kill chain."[54] In addition, the DoD concludes that it is "unclear whether China has the capability to collect accurate targeting information and pass it to launch platforms in time for successful strikes in sea areas beyond the first island chain."[55] Despite these doubts, however, China has made remarkable progress in this field and the idea that they will continue to improve their ability to locate, track, and target US ships cannot be dismissed.

CONCLUSION

Examination of the reconnaissance-strike dynamic between the US and Chinese militaries provides ample evidence that the US-China relationship has entered a critical, new phase where the need to "win the guided munition salvo competition" will dominate military modernization efforts. This emerging competition may revolutionize naval warfare, not only by deemphasizing air power but also through the development of new types of missile defenses. It may also usher in a new era where space is considered a domain that must be denied to an adversary. Both of these developments will add destabilizing factors that could lead a conflict to rapidly escalate.

Although it is apparent that a competition exists in long-range ASM and its concomitant reconnaissance and counter-reconnaissance capabilities, it is not yet apparent that this competition has turned into an arms race. According to the competitive strategies construct, competition is an interactive three-move sequence made up of an initial action, the response to it, and then a subsequent counter-action. As a result, we must wait to examine China's counter-reaction to the US reaction to assess whether the competition has begun to spiral. Unfortunately, it appears that the forces that have generated this competition are stronger than those that may impede it.

NOTES

1. Robert Work, "China Aerospace Studies Institute" (speech, RAND Corporation, Arlington, VA, June 22, 2015), http://www.defense.gov/ News/Speeches/Speech-View/Article/606683/china-aerospace-studies-institute.

2. Wayne P. Hughes, *Fleet Tactics and Coastal Combat* (Annapolis, MD: Naval Institute Press, 2000), 17.

3. Ibid., 721.

4. Mark Gunziger and Bryan Clark, *Winning the Salvo Competition: Rebalancing America's Air and Missile Defenses* (Washington, DC: Center for Strategic and Budgetary Assessment), 1.

5. Ibid.

6. PLA Academy of Military Science Military Strategy Research Department, *Zhanlüe xue (2013 nian ban)* 战略学 (2013年半) [The science of military strategy 2013] (Beijing: Military Science Press, 2013), 125.

7. Zhang Feng, "Zhongguo de changzheng wu hao yunzai huojian" 中国的长征五号运载火箭 [China's long march 5 launch vehicle], *Satellite Application* (卫星应用), 2012/5, 29.

8. "Changzheng shiyi hao" 长征十一号 [Long march 11], China Academy of Launch Vehicle Technology, May 12, 2016, http://www.calt.com/n4 82/n498/c4962/content.html.

9. "Guanchazhe wang Zhuhai hangzhan qianxian: feitian yi hao huojian yinfa guanzhu 4 xiaoshi ji ke" 观察者网珠海航展前线:飞天一号火箭引发关注 4小时即可"飞天" [Guancha net on the frontlines of the Zhuhai airshow: Feitian-1 triggers attention that it can launch in four hours], http://m.guancha.cn/military-affairs/2014_11_12_285792.

10. Brian Weeden, "Dancing in the Dark: The Orbital Rendezvous of SJ-12 and SJ-06F," *Space Review*, August 30, 2010, http://www.thespacereview.com/ article/1689/1; Kevin Pollpeter, "China's Space Robotic Arm Programs," *SITC News Analysis,* October 2013, http://igcc.ucsd.edu/assets/001/505 021.pdf.

11. Elaine M. Grossman, "Top Commander: Chinese Interference with US Satellites Uncertain," *World Politics Review,* October 18, 2006.

12. "NASA Cybersecurity: An Examination of the Agency's Information Security," statement of Paul K. Martin, Inspector General, National Aeronautics and Space Administration, February 29, 2012, 5; Mary Pat Fla-

herty, Jason Samenow, and Lisa Rein, "Chinese Hack US Weather Systems, Satellite Network," *Washington Post*, November 12, 2014.

13. Office of the US Secretary of Defense, *Annual Report to Congress: Military and Security Developments Involving the People's Republic of China 2011* (Washington, DC: US Department of Defense, 2012), 37.

14. Christian Davenport, "A Fight to Protect 'The Most Valuable Real Estate in Space'," *Washington Post*, May 9, 2016, https://www.washingtonpost.com/business/economy/a-fight-to-protect-the-most-valuable-real-estate-in-space/2016/05/09/df590af2-1144-11e6-8967-7ac733c56f12_story.html.

15. Office of the Undersecretary of Defense (Comptroller) Chief Financial Officer, *Defense Budget Overview: United States Department of Defense Fiscal Year 2017 Budget Request* (Washington, DC: US Department of Defense, 2016), 2–3.

16. Robert Work, "Satellite Industries Association" (speech, Washington, D.C., March 7, 2016).

17. "XSS-11 Points to Fixing Satellites on Orbit," Spacetoday.org, http://www.spacetoday.org/Satellites/XSS_11/XSS_11.html.

18. Colin Clark, "SecDef: JICSPOC Means 'One Room, One Floor' For Intel and Military," *Breaking Defense*, May 12, 2016, http://breakingdefense.com/2016/05/secdef-jicspoc-means-one-room-one-floor-for-intel-military/; Mike Gruss, "DoD, Intelligence Agencies Investing $16M in JICSpOC," *Space News*, September 11, 2015, http://spacenews.com/dod-intelligence-agencies-investing-16m-in-jicspoc/.

19. "Space Fence," http://www.lockheedmartin.com/us/products/space-fence.html.

20. See www.planet.com.

21. The White House Office of the Press Secretary, "FACT SHEET: US-Japan Cooperation for a More Prosperous and Stable World," April 28, 2015, https://obamawhitehouse.archives.gov/the-press-office/2015/04/28/fact-sheet-us-japan-cooperation-more-prosperous-and-stable-world.

22. Jordan Wilson, "China's Expanding Ability to Conduct Conventional Missile Strikes on Guam," US-China Economic and Security Review Commission Staff Research Report, May 10, 2016, 4. https://www.uscc.gov/sites/default/files/Research/Staff%20Report_China's%20Expanding%20Ability%20to%20Conduct%20Conventional%20Missile%20Strikes%20on%20Guam.pdf.

23. Dennis M. Gormley, Andrew S. Erickson, and Jingdong Yuan, *A Low-Visibility Force Multiplier: Assessing China's Cruise Missile Ambitions* (Washington, DC: National Defense University Press, 2014), xvii, 1–2.

24. Ibid., 100.
25. *2015 Report to Congress of the US-China Economic and Security Review Commission* (Washington, DC: US Government Printing Office, 2015), 355, 356.
26. Ibid., 355, 356.
27. Xi Zhu, "China Successfully Completes Seventh Test of Hypersonic Glider with Top Speed Reaching over 12,000 km/h," *People's Daily Online*, April 29, 2016, http://en.people.cn/n3/2016/0429/c90000-9051194.html.
28. *2015 Report to Congress*, 362–363.
29. Vitaliy O. Pradun, "From Bottle Rockets to Lightning Bolts," *Naval War College Review* 64, no. 2 (2010): 29–30.
30. Ibid., 22–23.
31. Dylan B. Ross and Jimmy A. Harmon, *New Navy Fighting Machine in the South China Sea* (master's thesis, Naval Postgraduate School, June 2012), 24.
32. Gormley, Erickson, and Yuan, *A Low-Visibility Force Multiplier*, 79.
33. Ibid.
34. Gormley, Erickson, and Yuan, *A Low-Visibility Force Multiplier*, xx.
35. Pradun, "From Bottle Rockets to Lightning Bolts," 25.
36. "Department of Defense Press Briefing by Admiral Gortney in the Pentagon Briefing Room," April 7, 2015, http://www.defense.gov/News/News-Transcripts/Transcript-View/Article/607034/department-of-defense-press-briefing-by-admiral-gortney-in-the-pentagon-briefin.
37. William J. Parker, "Is 'Distributed Lethality' the Future of Naval Surface Warfare?" EastWest.ngo, March 15, 2016, https://www.eastwest.ngo/idea/distributed-lethality.
38. Sydney J. Freedberg, Jr., "SM-6 Can Now Kill Both Cruise AND Ballistic Missiles," *Breaking Defense*, August 4, 2015, http://breakingdefense.com/2015/08/sm-6-can-now-kill-both-cruise-and-ballistic-missiles/.
39. Sam LaGrone, "SECDEF Carter Confirms Navy Developing Supersonic Anti-Ship Missile for Cruisers, Destroyers," *USNI News*, February 9, 2016, https://news.usni.org/2016/02/04/secdef-carter-confirms-navy-developing-supersonic-anti-ship-missile-for-cruisers-destroyers.
40. Sam LaGrone, "WEST: US Navy Anti-Ship Tomahawk Set for Surface Ships, Subs Starting in 2021," *USNI News*, February 19, 2016, https://news.usni.org/2016/02/18/west-u-s-navy-anti-ship-tomahawk-set-for-surface-ships-subs-starting-in-2021.
41. Andrew Tarantola, "SeaRAM Outfits the Navy's Favorite Gatling Gun with Homing Missiles," Gizmodo, September 24, 2014, http://gizmodo.

com/searam-outfits-the-navys-favorite-gatling-gun-with-homi-163685 3982.

42. Christian Davenport, "The Pentagon's Electromagnetic 'Rail Gun' Makes its Public Debut," *Washington Post*, February 6, 2015, https://www. washingtonpost.com/news/checkpoint/wp/2015/02/06/the-pentagons-electromagnetic-rail-gun-makes-its-public-debut/; "Electromagnetic Railgun," Office of Naval Research, http://www.onr.navy.mil/media-center/fact-sheets/electromagnetic-railgun.aspx.

43. Robert Work, "China Aerospace Studies Institute."

44. Ronald O' Rourke, *Navy Lasers, Railgun, and Hypervelocity Projectile: Background and Issues for Congress*, Congressional Research Service report, May 27, 2016, 4.

45. Ibid., 1.

46. Hughes, *Fleet Tactics and Coastal Combat*, 745–756.

47. Ibid., 749, 753.

48. Ibid., 860–861.

49. "Department of Defense Press Briefing by Admiral Gortney."

50. Hughes, *Fleet Tactics and Coastal Combat*, 745–756.

51. Robert Jervis, "Cooperation under the Security Dilemma," *World Politics* 30, no. 2 (1978): 196.

52. Hughes, *Fleet Tactics and Coastal Combat*, 753.

53. US Office of Naval Intelligence, *The PLA Navy: New Capabilities and Missions for the 21st Century* (Washington, DC: Office of Naval Intelligence, 2015), 24.

54. Lee Fuell, "Broad Trends in Chinese Air Force and Missile Modernization," testimony for the US-China Economic and Security Review Commission hearing on China's Military Modernization and Implications for the United States, January 30, 2014.

55. Office of the US Secretary of Defense, *Annual Report to Congress: Military and Security Developments Involving the People's Republic of China 2015* (Washington, DC: US Department of Defense, 2015), 35.

CHAPTER 5

LONG-TERM STRATEGIC COMPETITION BETWEEN THE UNITED STATES AND CHINA IN MILITARY AVIATION

Michael Chase and Oriana Skylar Mastro

Security competition between China and the United States in the Asia-Pacific region has been heating up over the past few years. This tension has manifested itself in a myriad of ways, including dangerous air encounters. In September 2015, a CNN reporter on a US Navy P-8 surveillance aircraft flying over the South China Sea released footage of the Chinese navy warning the US plane to "please go away" to "avoid a misunderstanding" as it flew in the vicinity of China's new man-made islands.[1] In May 2016, Chinese J-11 fighter jets intercepted a US Navy EP-3E Aries aircraft conducting a routine patrol mission in international airspace over the

South China Sea.[2] In June 2016, the Pentagon expressed its concern about another unsafe intercept, this time involving a Chinese fighter approaching at a "high rate of speed" as it intercepted a US Air Force RC-135 flying over the East China Sea.[3] In February 2017, a US Navy P-3C flying a routine mission near the Scarborough Shoal had to change course to avoid a potentially "unsafe" encounter with a Chinese KJ-200.[4] Most recently, in May 2017, two Su-30 Chinese fighter jets flew within 150 feet of the US Air Force WC-135, a radiation detection plane, flying over the East China Sea.[5]

The United States has responded to increased tensions in a number of ways to regain and sustain US dominance in airpower in the region. In March 2016, the United States and the Philippines announced the reopening of four Philippine air bases to the US military to reinforce rotational deployments near the South China Sea.[6] In addition, in June 2016, the United States sent a temporary detachment of US Navy EA-18G Growler electronic attack aircraft to the Philippines for bilateral training and to "support routine operations that enhance regional maritime domain awareness and assure access to the air and maritime domains in accordance with international law."[7] After Pyongyang's failed missile test in February 2017, the US Air Force deployed four B-1B Lancer heavy strategic bombers to Guam to strengthen its deterrence and global strike capabilities in the region.[8]

Military aviation has become a fundamental component of both countries' ability to achieve their regional aspirations. Xi Jinping often refers to the People's Liberation Army Air Force (PLAAF) as a strategic force to indicate its crucial role in overall national security and military strategy.[9] The state of military aviation determines the PLAAF's ability to contribute to offensive and defensive operations, through providing strategic warning, air attack, anti-air, missile defense, airborne operations, and strategic airlift.[10] US official statements echo this sentiment. Military aviation is the backbone of each of the US Air Force (USAF) core missions of air and space superiority; intelligence, surveillance, and reconnaissance; rapid global mobility; global strike; and command and control.[11]

Given the bilateral tensions and importance of airpower to national defense, has long-term peacetime strategic competition between the United States and China in the military aviation sector emerged? Specifically, what is the degree to which each country is engaging in a cost-imposing strategy to further their objectives at the other's expense and how successful are attempts to influence each other's decision-making calculus through such a competitive strategy? As Thomas Mahnken lays out in Chapter 1, competitive strategies in peacetime focus on "when and how we reveal our research, development, and acquisition of new capabilities; what we choose to acquire; when and how we deploy them; and how we train with them." This chapter builds on this framework by evaluating US and Chinese military aviation with respect to three factors that capture the degree and nature of strategic competition—resource allocation, targeted platform development, and airpower employment concepts. We argue that while China has been competing with the United States for decades, the China factor has only recently begun to drive US decisions.

THE US FACTOR IN CHINESE MILITARY AVIATION

Although the PLAAF was once an antiquated force relegated primarily to territorial air defense and support to other services, over the past decade it has emerged as an increasingly capable service with a broader set of missions and responsibilities. Chinese authors often refer to the PLAAF as a "strategic air force."[12] The PLAAF is also gaining bureaucratic stature, an important development given the traditional dominance of the army. Indeed, in 2004, the PLAAF commander became a member of China's powerful Central Military Commission (CMC).[13] That year, the PLAAF also received its own service-specific strategy, under which it is responsible for "integrated air and space, and simultaneous offensive and defensive operations."

The ongoing reorganization of the PLA appears poised to elevate the PLAAF's stature further, and its modernization is closely linked to the realization of Xi Jinping's concept of the "Dream of a Strong Army." For Chinese strategists, the US military represents a model to emulate in certain respects, but they also see US military power—and US airpower in particular—as a major threat to China's security. This has motivated Beijing to increase the level of resources devoted to defense (including countering US military intervention), modernize its armed forces (including its military aviation capabilities), and develop new approaches to employing its forces (including airpower within the context of joint campaigns). This section evaluates Chinese resource allocation, platform development, and airpower concepts, and concludes that China's focus on countering the United States has increasingly become a factor in these decisions over the past ten years.

RESOURCE ALLOCATION

China's defense spending has increased dramatically in real terms over the past 20 years. Although the rate of growth in the defense budget appears to be decreasing along with China's slowing economic growth, the PLA's budget enables it to make progress toward its objectives of modernizing its hardware, strengthening the quality of personnel, and improving its training and readiness. China does not publicly release information about the breakdown of its annual defense budget by service, or about the costs of specific programs, which makes it difficult, if not impossible, to come up with precise figures for its spending on the military aviation capabilities most relevant to this chapter. Nonetheless, the new capabilities China has been developing and deploying in recent years make it clear that airpower must be a high priority, along with other areas such as missiles, space, and naval capabilities.

Platform Development

The PLAAF is currently the largest air force in Asia and the third largest globally, according to the US Department of Defense's 2017 report on Chinese military power (current PLAAF force structure is shown in table 4). The trend is toward a larger percentage of modern aircraft. Today, a little more than one-third of the PLAAF's fighter aircraft (approximately 600) are fourth-generation fighters, including Su-27s, Su-30s, J-10s, J-11As, and J-11B fighters. Based on current modernization trends, however, the PLAAF "probably will become a majority fourth-generation force within the next several years."[14] Overall, DoD analysts assess that the PLAAF "continues to modernize and is closing the gap rapidly with Western air forces across a broad spectrum of capabilities." They judge that the PLAAF's modernization "is gradually eroding the significant technical advantage held by the United States."[15]

Table 4. PLAAF Force Structure, 2017.

Type	Number
Total aircraft (excluding UAVs)	About 2,700
Fighter aircraft	1,700 (includes about 600 fourth-generation fighters)
Bombers and attack aircraft	400
Transports	475
Special mission aircraft	115

Source. Annual Report on Military and Security Developments Involving the People's Republic of China 2017, 2017, Washington, DC: US Department of Defense.

From China's perspective, the development of advanced hardware is an important component of the PLAAF's attempts to transform itself into a "strategic air force." For China, this is about both copying from, and being prepared to counter, US capabilities. For example, Chinese strategists explicitly highlight the USAF as an inspiration for the development of

China's own air and space capabilities, including in areas such as stealth aircraft, unmanned systems, information technology, airborne warning and control, early warning systems, and strategic transport capability.[16] China's strategic objectives indicate that the PLAAF needs to be prepared to counter US military intervention, deal with less powerful rivals along its periphery, and protect China's interests in more distant locations through activities such as military operations other than war. Given this context, some, but not all, of the PLAAF's platform development can be seen as focused on competition with the United States. Based on sources such as China's official media, the assessments of regional observers, and US Department of Defense reports, the military aviation programs that appear to be the highest priorities for China include stealth fighters, large transport aircraft, UAVs, and strategic bombers.

J-20 and J-31 Stealth Fighters

China is emphasizing fighter modernization, with a particular focus on stealth fighters. As the US Department of Defense reports, "China has been pursuing fifth-generation fighter capabilities since at least 2009 and is the only country other than the United States to have two concurrent stealth fighter programs. China seeks to develop these advanced aircraft to improve its regional power projection capabilities and to strengthen its ability to strike regional airbases and facilities." This prioritization is due at least in part to Chinese assessments of the role of USAF stealth aircraft in recent conflicts. As the US Department of Defense points out,

> The PLAAF has observed foreign military employment of stealth aircraft and views this technology as a core capability in its trans-formation from a predominantly territorial air force to one capable of conducting both offensive and defensive operations. PLAAF leaders believe stealth aircraft provide an offensive operational advantage that denies an adversary the time to mobilize and to conduct defensive operations.[17]

This analysis has clearly informed China's development of stealth fighters.

Additionally, China's focus on stealth fighters tracks with the writings of PLAAF officers, as for many years Chinese strategists have argued that the PLAAF must emphasize domestic development of advanced fighters, including stealth aircraft. In addition, the PLAAF is not only working on modern platforms, but also focusing on improving other capabilities, such as radar systems and air-to-air missiles.

Y-20 Large Transport Aircraft

Chinese observers note the PLAAF's lack of adequate "strategic projection" capabilities. In particular, they lament a shortage of modern large transport aircraft, as the PLAAF currently depends on a small number of aging Il-76s imported from Russia. Although the PLAAF has employed its Il-76 transports domestically in disaster relief operations, and internationally in the 2011 evacuation of Chinese citizens from Libya, the search for the missing Malaysian Airlines flight MH370, and to provide humanitarian assistance following the 2015 earthquake in Nepal, Chinese strategists acknowledge that these aging planes cannot meet China's current strategic airlift needs, much less future requirements.[18]

Chinese writers argue that the PLAAF must develop and deploy a domestically produced large transport aircraft, a capability they regard as essential to ensuring the success of the PLAAF's attempt to become a modern "strategic air force." Accordingly, PLAAF analysts highlight the importance of the Y-20, China's first domestically developed large transport aircraft. In particular, Chinese experts have highlighted the Y-20's importance for missions such as responding to emergency situations and ensuring the safety of Chinese citizens abroad. They also note that it is essential for domestic and international disaster relief operations. Transporting airborne troops, which in the Chinese military are part of the PLAAF, could be another important mission.

Underscoring the emphasis China attaches to the development of a large transport aircraft, one Chinese commentator stated that the strategic importance of the Y-20 is greater than that of stealth aircraft and even China's first aircraft carrier, and a PLAAF pilot recruitment video released in 2015 prominently featured two developmental platforms: the J-20 stealth fighter and the Y-20 large transport aircraft.[19] In addition, Chinese commentators assess that the Y-20 will help China with the development of other platforms, most notably reconnaissance, aerial refueling, and airborne early warning planes.

UAVs

Unmanned systems are emerging as an increasingly important area for the Chinese military, as reflected by displays of UAVs at air shows, official media reports highlighting the inclusion of UAVs in military parades and exercises, and the plethora of photos of different UAV and UCAV systems that have appeared on Chinese websites over the past few years. PLAAF officers and other Chinese analysts argue that China should continue to develop advanced UAVs to perform a wide range of missions, and that at least some of these should incorporate stealth technology. As the DoD notes, "In addition to manned fighter aircraft, the PLAAF also views stealth technology as integral to unmanned aircraft, specifically those with an air-to-ground role, as this technology would improve that system's ability to penetrate heavily protected targets."[20]

Strategic Bombers

Although the PLA Rocket Force (PLARF) provides most of China's long-range conventional precision-strike capabilities, the PLAAF also plays an important role in this area. As the US Department of Defense notes, "The PLAAF already employs the H-6K bomber with the capability to carry six LACMs, a platform that will give the PLA a standoff offensive air capability with precision-guided munitions."[21] PLA media reports have highlighted China's bomber capabilities. One recent report that referred to the H-6K bomber as the "ace of the PLA air force" highlighted improvements such as "upgraded fuel economy and range," "improved ground attack capability," and the "latest electronic equipment."[22]

The PLAAF's growing emphasis on offensive operations and long-range strike capabilities indicates that it will continue to focus on increasing its role in this mission area. Indeed, PLAAF strategists appear to regard long-range bombers as key to strengthening the PLAAF's strategic deterrence and long-range strike capabilities. In September 2016, then PLAAF Commander Ma Xiaotian publicly confirmed China's plans to develop and deploy a new strategic bomber. DoD analysts assess that this new strategic bomber "will have additional capabilities with full-spectrum upgrades over the current bomber fleet, and will employ many fifth-generation technologies in their design."[23] Additionally, as the DoD notes: "There have also been Chinese publications indicating China intends to build a long-range 'strategic' stealth bomber. These media reports and Chinese writings suggest China might eventually develop a nuclear bomber capability."[24] It is certainly possible the PLAAF will have a nuclear deterrence and strike mission in the future, whether for strategic reasons (such as to contribute to nuclear force survivability and offer greater flexibility) or because the PLAAF concludes it is in its interests bureaucratically.

Employment Concepts

Chinese military writings reflect considerable deliberation on the types of campaigns the PLA would need to execute in future conflict scenarios. The reason for this is straightforward: Chinese military analysts assess that the Party leadership may call on them to use force in support of China's policy goals. For example, the 2013 edition of the *Science of Military Strategy* notes that even though the probability of a "large-scale, high-intensity defensive war" resulting from a "hegemonic nation" attacking China to delay or otherwise interrupt its rise is very low, there is a higher likelihood the PLA will face another type of conflict. In particular, the authors of this volume assess that a war over Taiwan, possibly involving US military intervention, is a greater danger and one the PLA must remain focused on as it continues to modernize.

Additionally, the authors assess the growing risk of a conflict over one of China's maritime territorial disputes.[25]

Although the PLA discusses many types of campaigns that could apply to one or more of these conflict scenarios in its professional literature, this chapter focuses on the subset of those campaigns in which airpower would figure prominently, and military aviation capabilities would play a considerable role in determining the outcome. These include the following PLA campaigns:

- *Conventional missile attack campaign.* China's "conventional missile attack campaign" would involve a "series of conventional missile attacks" aimed at the enemy's "important targets."[26] The PLARF would take the lead role in this campaign, but PLAAF and PLA Navy (PLAN) units could also play important roles. Such a campaign could be executed as a stand-alone for coercive purposes or to help China seize air, sea, and information superiority in support of other campaigns such as the "joint blockade campaign" or "joint island landing campaign."[27]

- *Joint blockade campaign.* The PLA's "joint blockade campaign" is a "protracted campaign" undertaken to "sever enemy economic and military connections" with the outside world and thereby compel the enemy to submit to China's demands.[28] Although the target is left unspecified, the campaign is clearly most relevant to Taiwan. PLA literature suggests that this campaign is envisioned as including conventional air and missile strikes and information and electronic attacks against the enemy to shatter its ability to resist the blockade.

- *Joint island landing campaign.* The "joint island landing campaign" is designed to "seize and occupy a whole island or important target." To successfully accomplish this objective, the PLA must also achieve numerous intermediate campaign goals, such as sea-crossing, destruction of the enemy's defenses, and securing a beachhead.[29] As with the blockade campaign, the obvious target is Taiwan.

- *Coral island and reef offensive campaign.* The PLA's "coral island and reef offensive campaign" involves operations aimed at the seizure of coral island and reef areas, and is presumably the campaign the PLA sees as relevant to potential conflicts with rival maritime territorial claimants, such as against the Philippines or Vietnam in the South China Sea.[30]

- *Joint anti-air raid campaign.* The key campaign that involves defense of the Chinese homeland from air and missile strikes is the PLA's "anti-air raid campaign." This is a joint campaign that aims to defend China against enemy air raids, but it is far from purely defensive as it seeks not only to defeat incoming attacks over or near Chinese territory, but also to strike at their source through Chinese air and missile attacks against enemy air bases or aircraft carriers.[31] The 2006 edition of the *Science of Campaigns* states, "the practice of recent local wars demonstrates that air raids have already become the enemy's main means of achieving strategic and campaign goals, and in the future it will be one of the greatest threats the PLA faces in the organization and implementation of joint operations."[32]

Because US military intervention could threaten the PLA's ability to accomplish its objectives in a number of scenarios, PLA publications make it clear that in order to achieve its objectives, the PLA must be prepared to deter, or, if necessary, counter US military intervention. The United States is not the only factor driving China's approach to the modernization of the PLAAF, as it has a broader set of missions, but it is clear that China's assessment of US airpower is an important factor in the development of Chinese military aviation.

THE CHINA FACTOR IN US MILITARY AVIATION

Airpower is critical to the US ability to maintain its military dominance in Asia, and the United States Air Forces is its most important employer with its 48 fighter and 9 heavy bomber squadrons, and approximately 800 aircraft.[33] To that end, the United States has focused on enhancing its conventional deterrent against China and on new operational strategies and organizational constructs to combat its eroding superiority. During the 1990s and 2000s, the rise of China did not greatly influence US decisions in the military aviation sector primarily because US global air superiority remained relatively unchallenged. However, China has narrowed the gap in its ability to deploy airpower, with an air-to-air capability now estimated to be about 70 percent of that of the United States.[34] These developments compelled the DoD to focus more heavily on the challenges of Chinese military modernization and required responses. This section evaluates US resource allocation, platform development, and airpower concepts and concludes that China has increasingly become a factor in these decisions over the past ten years.

Resource Allocation

While DoD does not maintain records on the amount of resources specifically devoted to the Asia-Pacific, indicators suggest the China factor is undoubtedly influencing resource allocation in the air domain. The USAF Force Structure Changes February 2012 document states that the USAF will shape its force to ensure that it is "adaptable and capable of deterring aggression and providing a stabilizing presence, especially in the highest priority areas and missions in the Asia-Pacific region."[35] The 2014 Quadrennial Defense Review (QDR) also pointed, albeit indirectly, to China when it states "the Department's investments in combat aircraft, including fighters and long-range strike, survivable persistent surveillance, resilient architectures, and undersea warfare will increase the Joint Force's ability to counter A2/AD challenges."[36]

Over the past four years, the total number of USAF military personnel deployed in the Pacific Air Forces' (PACAF) area of responsibility (AOR) has more than doubled, and the total number of fighter and attack aircraft in the AOR has increased from approximately 266 in May 2011 to 340 in October 2015 (tables 5, 6, and 7).[37] The United States also expanded the locations to which it deploys particular aircraft. For example, the USAF began to move bombers into the AOR in March 2004—there is now a continuous bomber mission at Andersen Air Force Base in Guam, with regular rotations of B-1, B-52 and B-2 squadrons.[38] PACAF A-10s flew the first air contingent to the Philippines to fly joint maritime patrols in the South China Sea.[39] This suggests one of US strengths vis-à-vis China is the ability to leverage allies and partners to improve competitiveness in military aviation.

Table 5. US Military and Civilian Personnel, 2011–2017 in the Asia-Pacific.

	Total military and civilian personnel (approximate)
May 2011	37,453
May 2012	37,469
May 2013	37,082
May 2014	36,952
Oct 2015	~45,000
Dec 2016	82,126
Sept 2017	87,961

Source. Data from USAF Almanacs published annually in *Air Force Magazine* each May. Oct. 2015 figure from US Air Force, "Pacific Air Forces Fact Sheet," US Pacific Air Forces, October 2015. 2016 and 2017 figures from Active Duty Master File, RCCPDS, APF Civilian Master, CTS Deployment File (as of November 2016), Civilian Deployment, https://www.dmdc.osd.mil/appj/dwp/dwp_reports.jsp.

Table 6. US Military Personnel Deployed, 2011–2017 in the Asia-Pacific.

	Military personnel deployed
Sept 2011	12,797
Sept 2012	12,639
Sept 2013	12,557
Sept 2014	12,121
Sept 2015	24,469
Dec 2016	67,142
Sept 2017	73,338

Source. Data from US Department of Defense, Defense Manpower Data Center database, https://www.dmdc.osd.mil/appj/dwp/dwp_reports.jsp. 2016 and 2017 figures from Active Duty Master File, https://www.dmdc.osd.mil/appj/dwp/dwp_reports.jsp.

Table 7. USAF Fighter and Attack Aircraft, 2011–2015 in the Asia-Pacific.

	Total fighter and attack aircraft (approximate)
May 2011	266
May 2012	263
May 2013	263
May 2014	261
Oct 2015	~340

Source. Data from US Air Force, "Pacific Air Forces Fact Sheet," US Air Force Association, "2011 USAF Almanac," p. 61; "2012 USAF Almanac," pp. 66–67; "2013 USAF Almanac," pp. 63–64; "2014 USAF Almanac," p. 29.

Platform Development

From 1996 to 2015, the US military experienced significant cuts, with heavy bombers and fighter aircraft suffering the greatest reductions at 29 and 37 percent respectively. However, improvements were made with a fifth-generation fighter capable of penetrating highly defended airspaces

(F-22), the introduction of UAVs for ISR (intelligence, surveillance, and reconnaissance) and attack purposes, and widespread use of precision munitions. There is no indication that China was a dominant factor in any of these decisions. The requirements of the wars in Iraq and Afghanistan coupled with budget constraints drove the size and development of aviation. The prioritization of military systems optimized for low-intensity conflict at the expense of systems needed for high-intensity conflict is further evidence of the absence of the China factor in US military aviation during most of the 1990s and early 2000s.[40]

However, over the past few years, the strategic and operational focus has shifted to give the China factor prime of place. The Third Offset Strategy, announced by then Secretary of Defense Hagel in November 2014, strives to develop disruptive technologies that will ensure US superiority, even as potential adversaries continue to modernize their militaries—a clear reference to China.[41] US military leaders realized that the United States was losing its technological edge and Chinese cruise and ballistic missile development in particular has increased the vulnerability of US platforms and basing.[42] The 2014 QDR demonstrated that US thinkers had begun to think about the developments in military aviation needed to fight in potentially contested airspace and address the challenges of a near-peer competitor. The QDR stated the intention to "modernize next-generation Air Force combat equipment—including fighters and bombers—particularly against advancing modern air defense systems."[43] The QDR specifically mentions three platforms that are a part of general modernization efforts, but are likely to be prioritized due to the China factor as well: the multi-role, fifth-generation F-35 fighter, which will provide improved survivability; a new, stealthy, long-range strike aircraft, "to maintain the ability to operate from long ranges, carry substantial payloads, and operate in and around contested airspace"; and the KC-46A next-generation tanker/cargo aircraft "to enable efficient and rapid long-range deployments."[44]

The F-35 Lightning II is a US fifth-generation, single-engine, multi-role fighter aircraft developed with eight other nations and meant to replace the F-16, A-10, and F/A-18 in US military service. All three variants have a primary mission of ground attack and a secondary mission of air-to-air combat, and all versions use a variety of techniques to reduce the aircraft's radar cross-section and enable safe operation within high-threat environments.[45] The USAF is slated to receive 1,763 F-35As, with production running until at least 2038.[46] The USAF justified its development initially with respect to Eurocentric threats—Russian-made SA-10s or SA-20s. [47] Some observers now also focus on the F-35's virtue as a stealthy multi-role fighter as an effective counter against China's A2/AD strategy;[48] however, other strategists argue that the F-35's short range renders it unfit to counter China's military and air force modernization in the long distances of the Pacific Theater.[49] From the data available, it is unclear whether improved Chinese capabilities added support to the program, or emerging threats were used mainly as bureaucratic tools to ensure continued funding for the program.

The KC-46 Pegasus is a multi-mission aerial refueling tanker and cargo aircraft intended to replace the aging USAF KC-135 Stratotanker and is expected to reach initial operating capability in 2017. The aircraft can deliver more fuel at all ranges, operate from shorter runways, and carry three times as many cargo pallets, twice as many passengers, and more than 30 percent more aeromedical evacuation patients than its predecessor.[50] The primary motivation behind the KC-46 was to replace the aging KC-135 with a dual-role aircraft that could provide cargo and passenger transport as well as multi-role tanking capability.[51] Others have noted that a renewed US focus on Asia, where distances between airfields were greater, called for aircraft that could enable other US air assets to operate at extended ranges.[52] Moreover, China's growing A2/AD capabilities "threaten to deprive the joint force of forward bases in the region...the combined risks of an aging fleet, A2/AD challenges, and high-intensity air warfare in contested environments combine to present a compelling case for tanker modernization."[53]

The B-21, formerly known as the Long-Range Strike Bomber (LRS-B), is a US bomber aircraft currently under development. It is designed to strike the most highly defended targets around the globe in extremely high-threat environments. The USAF plans to buy 100 B-21 aircraft to replace its B-52 and B-1 fleets, due to retire in the mid-2040s. Initial operating capability is expected for the new aircraft by the mid-2020s.[54] While not directly mentioned, the LRS-B is partly a response to the challenges posed by Chinese military modernization.[55] It "is intended to form a core element of the USAF's ability to operate in highly contested airspace against a peer or near-peer competitor."[56] Others began to acknowledge that a new Asia-centered set of strategic priorities "which, on the surface, would seem [to] indicate some rationale for something like this [bomber]."[57]

The Air Force also plans to procure air-to-surface missiles, such as the Joint Air-to-Surface Standoff Missile (JASSM), that will allow both fighter and bomber aircraft to engage a wide range of targets effectively even when the enemy's air defenses have not been fully suppressed.[58] The perceived need for standoff munitions has increased in recent years as A2/AD environments have become more prolific.[59] Some analysts have noted the potential ability of the JASSM-ER to penetrate deep into Chinese territory, thereby obviating the need for risky, manned bomber operations.[60] The need to conduct operations from a safe standoff distance also drives UAV development, which is increasingly focused on heavier strike payloads, standoff jamming and electronic warfare, and, potentially, aerial refueling and offensive or defensive counter-air missions.[61]

AIRPOWER EMPLOYMENT CONCEPTS

Flexibility and innovation in airpower employment concepts is one area where the United States has begun to cater to its strengths at the expense of Chinese weaknesses. The United States can no longer plan to respond to contingencies with rapid deployments of large numbers of fighters to bases and aircraft carriers close to China followed by the establishment of air superiority necessary to allow the heavy use of ISR and tankers close to the enemy without complications.[62] Of the four competitive strategies Bradford Lee identifies—denial, cost imposition, attacking a competitor's strategy, and attacking a competitor's political system—US attempts to maintain its air superiority have largely rested on cost imposition and denial.[63] Specifically, the United States has developed operational concepts such as AirSea Battle and improved base resiliency initiatives to show China its A2/AD strategy will be of limited effectiveness in wartime and the costs of its employment prohibitively high.

AirSea Battle

AirSea Battle (ASB) is an operational concept designed in 2010 to ensure access and maintain freedom of action in the global commons due to adversaries' A2/AD capabilities, now known due to its expanded joint nature as the Joint Concept for Access and Maneuver in the Global Commons, or JAM-GC. It is predicated on Networked, Integrated, and Attack-in-depth (NIA) operations that aim to disrupt the adversary's C4ISR, destroy the adversary's A2/AD platforms and weapons systems, and defeat an enemy's employed weapons and formation. If the ASB concept is executed properly, it should ensure that US forward deployments are able to continue to gain access and freedom of maneuver in any operational environment and thus maintain the ability to project power wherever our core interests necessitate. Although the Pentagon does not explicitly name any adversaries in its unclassified ASB review, China is a likely target given its sophisticated A2/AD capabilities.

Base Resiliency Initiatives

Given the centrality of airpower for the US ability to project power in the Western Pacific, the PLA has prioritizing the development of asymmetric capabilities to target US air superiority where it is at its weakest: on the ground. The United States has begun to increase active and passive defenses at its regional bases in the region as a result. US Patriot Advanced Capability-3 (PAC-3) missiles, which have been deployed to Okinawa, Japan, and Terminal High-Altitude Area Defense (THAAD) missiles, which have been deployed to the Andersen and Osan Air Force bases, are examples of such systems. The DoD has promised to invest in airfield repair capabilities as well as to procure fuel bladders to ensure survivability of supplies necessary to sustain operations. The QDR also called for the capability to disperse land-based forces to other bases and operating sites and operate and maintain front-line combat aircraft from austere bases with only a small amount of logistical and support personnel and equipment.[64] PACAF is also honing its resiliency strategy as part of the "Pacific Airpower Resiliency Initiative." This plan envisions improvements like bolstered defensive systems and the presence of Rapid Engineer Deployable Heavy Operation Repair Squadron Engineers (RED HORSE) Airfield Operations at theater bases.[65]

STRATEGIC COMPETITION IN MILITARY AVIATION: IMPLICATIONS AND RECOMMENDATIONS

Of the four types of competitive strategies—denial, cost imposition, inducing the opponent to engage in self-defeating behavior, and attacking the competitor's political system—the United States is largely focused on cost imposition whereas China is employing a strategy of all four. In this way, US-China strategic competition in military aviation is asymmetric. The United States is in the beginning stages of the competition, while China has been focused on this area for over two decades. Moreover, the asymmetry of capabilities and interests highlights a critical point: the Cold War defense technological competition between the Soviet Union and the United States fails to provide a template for the emerging US-China competition. Any conflict will occur where China is fighting close to home, and therefore does not face the same logistical challenges the United States does. This can also be leveraged as strength, however. While China enjoys the advantage of fighting close to home, the United States has the ability to project power all over the globe, partly due to its network of alliances and partnerships, which China lacks even regionally.

Another critical difference from the Cold War era is that neither the United States nor China will have the luxury of focusing all of its attention and resources on competing with the other side. This also means that strategies to induce the other side to engage in self-defeating behavior are unlikely to be effective. The United States has to worry about problems in other parts of the world. One of these is Russia, another potential major power adversary that poses a threat to US allies and has demonstrated a willingness to use different levels of unconventional and conventional capabilities to advance its interests in destabilizing ways. Additionally, Washington will not be able to ignore challenges from less-capable regional powers, most notably Iran and North Korea. Finally, non-state actors like ISIS and other regional security challenges like the civil war in Syria will continue to place demands on US military aviation.

Likewise, China will not be able to focus solely on competition with the United States and its allies and partners. As China's economic and security interests become increasingly global, the PLAAF will also need to be prepared to carry out missions at greater distances from China's borders, such as humanitarian assistance and disaster relief operations or non-combatant evacuation operations.

RECOMMENDATIONS

Given the long timelines associated with procurement, development, and acquisition, the United States will need to plan in anticipation of the next steps China will take in response to its own actions. There are a number of areas in which the United States should invest to cater to its own strengths and exploit China's weaknesses. Recent assessments by US strategists suggest that long-range bombers, long-range air- and sea-launched cruise missiles, aerial refueling aircraft, and long-range, long-dwell ISR platforms will play important roles in any future US concept of operations for power projection.[66]

Given China's geographic advantage, the United States should be primarily concerned with projecting power effectively from far distances, outside China's threat ring. This requires not only new capabilities like tankers, ISR UAVs, and improved standoff weapons, but also new deployment and operational concepts. The base resiliency and AirSea Battle concepts discussed here were first attempts of strategists to address the A2/AD challenge, not the last. Innovation will likely be focused on how to employ US platforms and increase access to bases and airspace in the region. This could encourage China to compete on terms favorable to the United States.[67]

China can be expected to continue to invest in the development of a world-class air force, one commensurate with its status as a major power and emerging global interests. That said, an increasingly tense rivalry with the United States and its regional allies and partners would likely deepen the intensity of the strategic competition in military aviation, and probably in other areas, by motivating China to focus even more sharply on countering or undermining US advantages. Defense S&T competition could spill over into other domains, potentially causing greater friction in the US-China economic relationship, as evidenced by tension over cyber espionage and theft of commercial secrets in recent years.

Finally, the United States may find cost-imposing strategies and attempts to inspire self-defeating behavior less effective than strategies of denial, which "seek to prevent a competitor from being able to translate its operational means into the political ends that it seeks."[68] It will be difficult if not impossible to get the Chinese to spend more than they can afford, as Chinese analysts have studied the collapse of the Soviet Union extensively and determined that one reason for its disintegration was that it fell into the trap of excessive defense spending. That China has slowed the rate of increase in defense spending in line with slowing economic growth suggests this remains an important consideration for Beijing. China will be wary of responses to US actions that seem designed to achieve similar results. Moreover, even if China's defense budget is considerably larger than the official figures, it still likely accounts for an affordable share of GDP. Slowing economic growth may compel China to reduce annual increases in defense spending to more moderate levels, and more technologically advanced and expensive programs like aircraft carriers and stealth fighters may lead to greater resource competition within China's defense establishment. Nonetheless, China does not seem to be close to the point of painful tradeoffs between defense and other categories of government spending, much less one at which it could no longer afford to compete with the United States militarily.

Additionally, US understanding of Chinese decision-making may not be deep enough to allow for prediction of Chinese responses to US actions with the high degree of confidence needed for competitive strategies. This could be challenging, because Chinese responses may be shaped not only by China's interpretation of US actions and assessments of the optimal responses in strategic or operational terms, but also by factors that might be difficult to understand with great precision, such as competition between the PLA's services, the interests and preferences of defense industry organizations, and other bureaucratic and domestic political dynamics. Therefore, Washington should concentrate on developing platforms and operational concepts focused on denying China the ability to achieve its objectives by force. Focusing on deterrence by denial should also offer the added benefit of doing more to assure US allies and partners.

NOTES

1. Jim Sciutto, "Exclusive: China Warns US Surveillance Plane," CNN, September 15, 2015, http://www.cnn.com/2015/05/20/politics/south-china-sea-navy-flight/.

2. Thomas Gibbons-Neff, "Chinese Jets Intercept US Recon Plane, Almost Colliding Over South China Sea," *Washington Post*, May 18, 2016.

3. Barbara Starr, "US: Chinese Jet Makes 'Unsafe' Intercept of US Air Force Plane," CNN, June 8, 2016, http://www.cnn.com/2016/06/07/politics/us-china-planes-unsafe-intercept/.

4. Ryan Brone, "Chinese and US Aircraft in 'Unsafe' Encounter," CNN, February 10, 2017, http://www.cnn.com/2017/02/09/politics/us-china-aircraft-unsafe-encounter/.

5. Ryan Brone and Brad Lendon, "Chinese Fighter Flew Inverted over US Air Force Jet," CNN, May 19, 2017, http://www.cnn.com/2017/05/18/politics/china-us-jets-intercept/.

6. Andrew Tilghman, "The US Military Is Moving into These Five Bases in the Philippines," *Military Times*, April 1, 2016.

7. "PACAF, PACFLT Coordinate Arrival of Electronic Attack Squadron Detachment in Philippines," US Pacific Command, June 20, 2016, http://www.pacom.mil/Media/News/NewsArticleView/tabid/11348/Article/805535/pacaf-pacflt-coordinate-arrival-of-electronic-attack-squadron-detachment-in-phi.aspx.

8. Franz-Stefan Gady, "US Air Force Rotates Supersonic Strategic Bombers in the Asia-Pacific," *The Diplomat*, February 11, 2017, http://thediplomat.com/2017/02/us-air-force-rotates-supersonic-strategic-bombers-in-the-asia-pacific/.

9. Shen Jinke and Li Hongbin, "Zhu jian buneng wang zhan chengwei kongjun guanbing gongshi gong wei" 来源: 中国军网作者: 申进科 李洪斌责任编辑: 陈婕 [Do not forget that warfighting is the consensus of air force officers and men], *PLA Daily*, May 24, 2016, http://www.81.cn/jmywyl/2016-05/24/content_7070722_2.htm; "Xi Jinping: jiakuai jianshe yi zhi kongtian yiti, gongfang jianbei de qiangda renmin kongjun" 习近平: 加快建设一支空天一体、攻防兼备的强大人民空军 [Xi Jinping: Accelerate the building of an integrated air-space power with simultaneous offensive-defensive capabilities], Xinhua, April 14, 2014, http://news.xinhuanet.com/politics/2014-04/14/c_1110234957.htm.

10. "Quanmian shishi gaige qiangjun zhanlue" 关于全面实施改革强军战略 [Regarding comprehensive implementation of military reform and modernization], *PLA Daily*, May 26, 2016, http://navy.81.cn/content/20 16-05/26/content_7073171_4.htm.

11. United States Air Force, "America's Air Force: A Call to the Future," July 2014, 6, http://www.af.mil/Portals/1/documents/SECAF/AF_30_Year_ Strategy.pdf.

12. Michael S. Chase and Cristina L. Garafola, "China's Search for a 'Strategic Air Force,'" *Journal of Strategic Studies* 39, no. 1 (2016), 4–28.

13. The new CMC unveiled following China's 19th Party Congress in October 2017 no longer includes any of the service commanders. However, PLAAF officer Xu Qiliang was promoted to senior vice chair of the CMC. Xu's promotion appears to reflect the PLAAF's growing status as well as China's determination to forge a more joint PLA.

14. Office of the Secretary of Defense, *Annual Report to Congress: Military and Security Developments Involving the People's Republic of China 2017* (Washington, DC: US Department of Defense, 2017), 28.

15. Ibid.

16. See Zhu Hui, ed., *Strategic Air Force* (Beijing: Blue Sky Press, 2009).

17. Office of the Secretary of Defense, *Annual Report to Congress: Military and Security Developments Involving the People's Republic of China 2016* (Washington, DC: US Department of Defense, 2016), 30–31.

18. "Air Force Planes Sent to Nepal for Quake Relief," Xinhua, April 27, 2015, http://news.xinhuanet.com/english/2015-04/27/c_134188680.htm.

19. "J-20, Y-20 Aircraft Shown in Pilot Recruitment Ads," Xinhua, February 27, 2015, http://english.chinamil.com.cn/news-channels/china-military-news/2015-02/27/content_6370521.htm.

20. US Department of Defense, *Developments Involving the People's Republic of China 2016*, 31.

21. Ibid., 67.

22. Ibid.

23. US Department of Defense, *Developments Involving the People's Republic of China 2017*, 28.

24. US Department of Defense, *Developments Involving the People's Republic of China 2016*, 38.

25. For a more complete discussion, see *The Science of Military Strategy 2013*, 98–100.

26. Yu Jixun, ed., *The Science of Second Artillery Campaigns* (Beijing: PLA Press, 2004).

27. A coercive or demonstrative use of conventional missile firepower, such as the series of launches China conducted during the 1995–1996 Taiwan Strait Crisis, could also be related to this type of campaign, and could escalate to a conventional missile attack campaign if intimidation fails to achieve the desired objectives.

28. Zhang Yuliang, ed., *The Science of Campaigns* (Beijing: National Defense University Press, 2006), 292.

29. Bi Xinglin, ed., *Campaign Theory Study Guide* (Beijing: National Defense University Press, 2002), 225–226.

30. Zhang Yuliang, *The Science of Campaigns*, 535.

31. This campaign could be conducted as a standalone campaign, but it is more likely to be conducted if the PLA's execution of another campaign results in conventional air attacks against Chinese territory. See Zhang Yuliang, *The Science of Campaigns*, 331.

32. Zhang Yuliang, *The Science of Campaigns*, 312.

33. The Army has 22 aviation brigades, the Navy 10 carrier air wings, and Special Operations 259 mobility and fire support aircraft and 83 ISR aircraft. US Department of Defense, *Quadrennial Defense Review 2014* (Washington, DC: US Department of Defense, 2014), 40–41. Hereafter QDR 2014.

34. Eric Heginbotham, *The US-China Military Scorecard: Forces, Geography, and the Evolving Balance of Power, 1996–2017* (Santa Monica, CA: RAND Corporation, 2015), 80.

35. US Air Force, "USAF Force Structure Changes: Sustaining Readiness and Modernizing the Total Force," February 2012.

36. QDR 2014, 36.

37. As a comparison, the general trend according to USAF Almanacs from 2011 to 2014 shows a steady decrease in total US Air Forces in Europe (USAFE) military and civilian personnel from approximately 32,000 to a shade under 30,000 by 2014; USAFE aircraft numbers mostly stayed the same, hovering around 220 between 2011 and 2014.

38. Amy McCullough, "Bombers on Guam," *Air Force Magazine*, August 2015.

39. David Axe, "Get Ready, China: Lethal A-10 Warthogs Are Patrolling the South China Sea," *The National Interest*, April 22, 2016, http://nationalinterest.org/blog/the-buzz/get-ready-china-lethal-10-warthogs-are-patrolling-the-south-15886.

40. Heginbotham, *The US-China Military Scorecard*, 37, 42.

41. Robert Work, "The Third US Offset Strategy and Its Implications."

42. QDR 2014.

43. Ibid., ix.

44. Ibid., 28.

45. Dan Katz, "Program Dossier: F-35 Lightning II," *Aerospace Daily and Defense Report*, September 16, 2014, 3.

46. "Program Profile: F-35 Lightning II," *Aviation Week and Space Technology*, Accessed June 3, 2016.

47. Kris Osborn, "F-35 Stealth Fighter Prepares for the Unthinkable: War with China or Russia," *The National Interest*, April 27, 2016, http://nationalinterest.org/blog/the-buzz/f-35-stealth-fighter-prepares-the-unthinkable-war-china-or-15956.

48. Thomas Donnelly and Phillip Lohaus, *Mass and Supremacy: A Comprehensive Case for the F-35* (Washington, DC: American Enterprise Institute, 2013), 18–20.

49. Thomas P. Ehrhard, *An Air Force Strategy for the Long Haul* (Washington, DC: Center for Strategic and Budgetary Assessments, 2009), 44.

50. Dan Katz, "Program Dossier: KC-46 Pegasus," *Aerospace Daily and Defense Report*, May 14, 2015, 7.

51. Arthur J. Lichte, "Why the US Needs a New Tanker," *National Defense Magazine*, October 2009, http://www.nationaldefensemagazine.org/archive/2009/October/Pages/WhytheUSNeedsaNewTanker.aspx.

52. Michael Isherwood, "The KC-X Opportunity," *Armed Forces Journal*, September 2007, 43.

53. Ehrhard, *An Air Force Strategy for the Long Haul*, 65.

54. Dan Katz, "Program Dossier: B-21," *Aerospace Daily and Defense Report*, March 3, 2016. 7.

55. David Axe, "Bombs Away: How the Air Force Sold Its Risky New $55 Billion Plane," *Wired*, March 26, 2012, https://www.wired.com/2012/03/airforce-bomber-gamble/.

56. International Institute for Strategic Studies, *The Military Balance 2016* (London: Routledge, 2016), 30.

57. David Axe, "Will the $55 Billion Bomber Program Fly?" The Center for Public Integrity, March 26, 2012, https://www.publicintegrity.org/2012/03/26/8498/will-55-billion-bomber-program-fly.

58. QDR 2014, 37; Hans M. Kristensen, "Forget LRSO; JASSM-ER Can Do the Job," *Strategic Security* (blog), Federation of American Scientists, December 16, 2015, https://fas.org/blogs/security/2015/12/lrso-jassm/.

59. Eleni Ekmektsioglou, "Hypersonic Weapons and Escalation Control in East Asia," *Strategic Studies Quarterly 9,* no. 2 (2015): 58; Kristensen, "Forget LRSO."

60. Roger Cliff, *Shaking the Heavens and Splitting the Earth* (Santa Monica, CA: RAND Corporation, 2011), 241–242.

61. Robert Martinage, *Toward a New Offset Strategy: Exploiting US Long-Term Advantages to Restore U.S. Global Power Projection Capability* (Washington, DC: Center for Strategic and Budgetary Assessments, 2014), 51.

62. Jeff Hagen, "Potential Effects of Chinese Aerospace Capabilities on US Air Force Operations," testimony presented at the US-China Economic and Security Review Commission Hearing on China's Emergent Military Aerospace and Commercial Aviation Capabilities, May 20, 2010, 4–5.

63. Bradford A. Lee, "Strategic Interaction: Theory and History for Practitioners, in Mahnken, *Competitive Strategies for the 21st Century.*

64. QDR 2014, 38.

65. For more on threats to air bases and resiliency efforts, see Oriana Skylar Mastro and Ian Easton, "Risk and Resiliency: China's Emerging Air Base Strike Threat," Project 2049 Institute Report, November 8, 2017.

66. David Ochmanek, "The Role of Maritime and Air Power in DoD's Third Offset Strategy," testimony presented before the House Armed Services Committee, Subcommittee on Seapower and Projection Forces, December 2, 2014, 8.

67. Stephen Peter Rosen, "Competitive Strategies: Theoretical Foundations, Limits and Extensions," in Mahnken, *Competitive Strategies for the 21st Century,* 12; Thomas Mahnken, "Thinking About Competitive Strategies," in Mahnken, *Competitive Strategies for the 21st Century,* 7.

68. Thomas G. Mahnken, *Cost-Imposing Strategies: A Brief Primer* (Washington, DC: Center for a New American Security, 2014), 6.

CHAPTER 6

STRATEGIC COMPETITION BETWEEN THE UNITED STATES AND CHINA IN THE MARITIME REALM

Bryan Clark and Jordan Wilson[1]

The great power competition between the United States and China will likely not be uniform across different elements of national power. Using the framework of Chapter 1, for example, opponents may pursue similar strategies, such as cost imposition, creating a symmetric competition in one element of power. In other dimensions, the participants may employ different strategies, resulting in an asymmetric competition. This chapter provides an overview of current US and Chinese maritime strategies, then examines the nature and extent of the maritime competition between the

United States and China. It concludes with considerations of the advantages and disadvantages each side possesses in a maritime competition, yielding important insights for US strategy going forward.

OVERVIEW OF CHINESE MARITIME STRATEGIES

Strategic Documents

While Chinese strategic documents indicate that a significant shift in its maritime strategy may be underway, the implementation of this shift has been slow. Since 1949, the focus of the People's Liberation Army Navy (PLAN) has evolved outward in several steps, described by a 2012 article in *China Military Science,* a journal published by China's Academy of Military Science, as "coastline and river defense," "littoral defense," "near seas defense," and "distant seas defense."[2] The early focus on coastal and littoral defense gave way to "near seas defense" in the 1980s,[3] and a 2000 directive from then-President Jiang Zemin began a gradual expansion from "near seas defense" to "distant seas defense."[4] In 2015, the evolution continued, with China's defense white paper officially stating for the first time that the PLAN will shift its focus from "offshore waters defense" (near seas) to the combination of "offshore waters defense" with "open seas protection" (distant seas).[5] Practically, "offshore waters" or "near seas" can be defined as the area between China's coast and the "second island chain" (figure 7).[6]

Figure 7. First and second island chains.

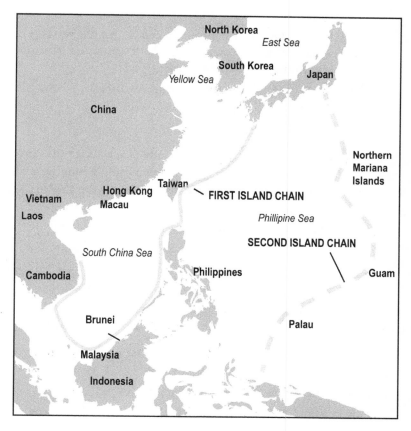

Source. Adapted from *Annual Report to Congress: Military and Security Developments Involving the People's Republic of China 2012* (p. 40) by US Department of Defense, 2012, Washington, DC: US Department of Defense.

The oft-referenced vision of General Liu Huaqing, the PLA Navy Commander from 1982 to 1987 often referred to as "the father of the modern Chinese Navy," can be placed in this context.[7] General Liu oversaw the shift to "offshore waters defense" (or "near seas active defense") during his tenure,[8] envisioning a three-phase strategy for the PLAN:

- Phase 1: by 2000, be able to control the Yellow Sea, the western East China Sea including Taiwan, and the South China Sea (essentially the area within the first island chain).
- Phase 2: by 2020, be able to control the area within the second island chain.
- Phase 3: by 2050, be a global navy.[9]

General Liu's vision likely does not exactly characterize the current strategy of China's leaders, but Beijing does envision a long-term shift that ends with a navy able to operate in distant seas. According to China maritime expert Bernard Cole, "Liu's most important achievement...was gaining civilian leadership support for the increased resources to develop a twenty-first century navy."[10]

With this support, the missions of the PLAN have evolved. The 2013 iteration of *The Science of Military Strategy*, one of China's most authoritative resources on military strategy, lists eight strategic missions for the Chinese navy, which touch on both near and far seas elements:

1. Participate in large-scale operations in the main strategic axis of operations.
2. Contain and resist sea-borne invasions.
3. Protect island sovereignty and maritime rights and interests.
4. Protect maritime transportation security.
5. Engage in protecting overseas interests and the rights/interests of Chinese nationals.
6. Engage in carrying out nuclear deterrence and counterattack.
7. Coordinate with the military struggle on land.
8. Protect the security of international sea space.[11]

Other changes are also taking place. Although China's current national-level Weapons and Equipment Development Strategy—a classified document that forecasts the international strategic environment and sets military armaments requirements—runs through 2023, the shorter-term naval weapons development plans subordinate to this strategy may be under revision. PLAN Commander Admiral Wu Shengli, speaking at the PLAN Party Committee's 8th plenary session in January 2015, described the PLAN as being in "a critical period of strategic transformation" due to expansions to its missions and ongoing military reforms. He specifically discussed the need to "revise and perfect" PLAN development strategies.[12] The Chinese government announced in July 2016 that it intends to formulate its first "national maritime strategy," which will likely set long-term guidelines for maritime development in conjunction with legal assertions of its maritime rights and interests, further shaping China's naval trajectory.[13]

Continued Near Seas Focus

Most US analysts have emphasized that the PLAN's primary mission will continue to be China's near seas—the area between China's coast and the second island chain—regardless of how its strategy shifts on paper.[14] This is evidenced by China's current political and military objectives as well as its force posture.

At the political level, Beijing's stated "core interests" include issues of sovereignty and territorial integrity.[15] China's 2015 defense white paper reaffirms that safeguarding "the sovereignty and security of China's territorial land, air, and sea" and "the unification of the motherland" (referring to Taiwan) are among the military's primary tasks, along with "overseas interests."[16] The goal of China's military strategy is listed as "winning local wars under informationized conditions,"[17] while its "primary strategic direction" is likely the "Taiwan Strait-Western Pacific" area.[18] Moreover, a "counterintervention" or "anti-access/area denial (A2/AD)" component exists within PLA missions,[19] in anticipation of potential outside interference in contingencies involving China's core interests; this is also likely to encourage continued focus on its near seas.[20]

China's shipbuilding priorities reflect an emphasis on the near seas. It has been building new ships at a tremendous pace, launching 67 large surface combatants and 16 submarines between 2005 and early 2015. This surpasses any other country's output in recent years, but did not grow the fleet, as the new ships replaced older, obsolete ones.[21] As a result, the composition of China's navy has not changed substantially since 1990 except for a slight decline in the share of nuclear-powered submarines (SSNs) and increase in the share of destroyers and frigates.[22]

Observers differ on whether this pace will be sustained, taper off as it nears predetermined objectives, or be increased due to China's pursuit of a far seas focus and global interests. Although assessing the trajectory is complicated by China's opaque military acquisition process, a 2013 report by the US Office of Naval Intelligence (ONI) projected that China's 2020 force structure would be very similar in composition to 2015 (table 8).[23]

Table 8. PLAN Force Structure and 2020 Projection.

	2015 force structure (% modern)	2020 force projection (% modern)
Aircraft carriers	1	1–2
Ballistic missile submarines	4	4–5
Nuclear attack submarines	5 (50)	6–9 (100)
Diesel attack submarines	57 (33)	59–64 (75)
Destroyers	26 (80)	30–34 (85)
Frigates	52 (70)	54–58 (85)
Corvettes	20	30–60 (100)
Amphibious ships	56	50–55
Missile-armed patrol craft	85	85

Source. Data from "China Naval Modernization: Implications for US Navy Capabilities—Background and Issues for Congress," (p. 47) by Ronald O'Rourke, 2016, Congressional Research Service report and *The PLA Navy: New Capabilities and Missions for the 21st Century* (p. 43) by the Office of Naval Intelligence, 2015, Washington, DC: Office of Naval Intelligence.

During the next 5 to 10 years, the PLAN will likely not grow substantially, but will improve its capabilities for near seas operations: more dedicated long-range intelligence, surveillance, and reconnaissance (ISR) assets (perhaps including more sky wave over-the-horizon radar and ISR satellites), and perhaps land- and ship-based unmanned aerial vehicles (UAVs); improved refueling aircraft (potentially extending the range of China's maritime strike aircraft); more advanced mines; and antisubmarine warfare (ASW) capabilities, which China had not prioritized in the past, including an "ambitious program to set up fixed sonar arrays on the sea bed in its proximate waters."[24] Additionally, China will likely continue investing in its maritime militia and Coast Guard, with implications for its ability to coerce other disputants in maritime territorial disputes in peacetime.

Beyond the next ten years, China's future shipbuilding rate and fleet size are uncertain. However, the PLAN is clearly modernizing and placing "a growing emphasis on ships that are both multi-mission capable and large enough to sustain far seas operations," according to ONI.[25] Aircraft carriers are a good example, potentially providing improved air defense as well as assistance to expeditionary forces. DoD projected in 2016 that China "could build multiple aircraft carriers over the next 15 years," and some sources suggest as many as five new carriers could be constructed, for a total of six.[26] The PLAN will likely continue to expand its presence in the Indian Ocean through longer and more frequent submarine patrols, which began in late 2013 and probably provide valuable training to its crews in conducting long-duration deployment and operating in less familiar waters.[27] This new emphasis could also mean that Beijing will seek access to foreign naval facilities or seek to establish its own bases in addition to its first military base in Djibouti, announced in February 2016.[28] China is also likely to emphasize the development of a sea-launched land-attack cruise missile capability.[29] The 2014 article in *China Military Science* mentioned earlier noted global naval trends towards long-range precision strikes, integrated forces, network-centric warfare, and shore-directed operations and recommended that China invest in these.[30]

Overall, these investments indicate that China aspires to a blue water navy in the long term, but is by no means shifting from its primary focus on the near seas, as will be discussed further later in this chapter.

OVERVIEW OF US MARITIME STRATEGIES

Strategic Documents

The current US maritime strategy, titled *A Cooperative Strategy for 21st Century Seapower (CS-21)* and published in 2015, updated its 2007 predecessor to acknowledge the return of great power competition and the need for the Navy to increase its emphasis on warfighting.[31] This shift in focus was reflected most explicitly in the new strategy's clear characterization of China and Russia as competitors and in its changes to the list of core naval functions—adding the function of All Domain Access, explicitly intended to address the anti-access strategies and capabilities being developed by China and Russia.

Despite these changes, the 2015 version of CS-21 remained rooted in the naval operations and security environment of the last decade—rather than emerging needs for naval forces over the next ten years. Its central discussion focuses on the ability of naval forces to maintain forward presence, facilitated by forward basing, greater reliance on partners, and tailored force packages. This discussion implies an emphasis on efficiency in deploying forces during fiscally challenging times, rather than warfighting effectiveness in the face of capable high-end opponents.

CS-21 does emphasize new concepts and capabilities to overcome anti-access networks, including some prioritized by the Third Offset Strategy such as networked distributed operations, electromagnetic spectrum warfare, and undersea warfare. Notably, its discussion of future power projection capabilities also focuses on how naval power projection will support gaining and maintaining access.

In his *Design for Maritime Superiority,* Chief of Naval Operations (CNO) John Richardson describes an emerging strategic environment dominated by greater interconnectedness, the rising importance of information systems, fiscal constraints, and an accelerating rate of technological change.[32] With the *Design,* the CNO is directing planners to start with new warfighting concepts when they plan the future fleet. New concepts in development that are likely to influence Navy plans include distributed lethality, electromagnetic maneuver warfare, littoral operations in a contested environment (LOCE), and operational logistics. These concepts all describe a much more distributed fleet with increased offensive firepower and greater maneuverability that is designed to deny enemy aggression and immediately punish adversaries for their actions.

Implementation

The long-term implementation of this design will be laid out in planning documents such as Navy force structure requirements, the Long-Range Plan for Construction of Naval Vessels, the Fleet Readiness and Training Plan, Congressional testimony of the CNO and other Navy leaders, and Navy budget materials. The Navy recently completed a Force Structure Assessment that determined the Navy needed 355 ships to meet its anticipated requirements, detailed in table 9.[33] The number of ships is driven predominantly by the Navy's robust overseas posture and its rotational model for naval force generation. The fleet needs at least three to five ships for each posture overseas; one is deployed, one is training in preparation for deployment, and one or more are undergoing maintenance.

Table 9. The US Navy's 2016 Force Structure Requirement.

Item	Number
Aircraft carriers	12
Large surface combatants	104
Small surface combatants	52
Amphibious warfare ships	38
Attack submarines	66
Guided missile submarines	0
Ballistic missile submarines	12
Combat logistics force	32
Expeditionary fast transport/High speed transport	10
Expeditionary support base	6
Command and support	23
Total	**355**

Source. "Executive Summary of Navy Force Structure Assessment" (p. 3) by Chief of Naval Operations, 2016, Washington, DC: US Department of the Navy.

The new force structure requirement grows the fleet relative to the former requirement of 308 ships established in 2012 to address the intensifying competition with China and Russia, and new operational concepts being pursued by the Navy.[34] For example, more submarines will be needed based on the emphasis in the *Design* on undersea warfare. For missions such as surveillance, bottom surveys, and intelligence gathering, the Navy is likely to increase its use of extra-large unmanned undersea vehicles (UUV) such as the *Orca*.[35] This 50–80 foot (depending on configuration) UUV could carry a 20 foot-long payload section and operate for six months at a time out of a friendly overseas port such as in Japan or Norway.

To implement new operational concepts such as distributed lethality and LOCE, the Navy will likely need to rely on a larger number of smaller platforms with adequate self-defense and greater offensive firepower. In littoral areas such as the South and East China Seas, small combatants such as guided missile frigates can be very costly to defeat in detail while being able to impose losses on an enemy. In comparison, larger ships such as guided missile destroyers and cruisers will be smaller in number and more expensive, increasing the value to an enemy of attacking them with an overwhelming number of anti-ship missiles. Small combatants will likely be complemented by the increasing use of unmanned vehicles for missions such as mining and mine clearing, counter-surveillance, anti-submarine warfare, search and targeting, and as weapons magazines. In particular, medium-displacement unmanned surface vehicles such as the *Sea Hunter* developed by DARPA can carry weapon and sensor payloads and operate for six months at a time independently or in concert with surface combatants.[36]

Distributed power projection operations will also be better enabled by a larger amphibious fleet with greater reach and lethality. This could lead the Navy to build more of its amphibious landing dock-size ships and focus its large amphibious assault ships (LHA/LHD) on longer-range fixed-wing strike-fighters such as the F-35B Lightning II instead of MV-22 Osprey troop transports and short-range attack helicopters. The Navy is studying how smaller, LHA/LHD-sized aircraft carriers could enable distributed strike and anti-surface operations and leverage the dramatic improvement in capability of the short take-off and landing F-35B compared to its predecessor, the AV-8B Harrier.[37] These carriers could be used in regions where the US today uses a large aircraft carrier (such as the Middle East), but without fully exploiting its capacity for sortie generation or high-end warfighting. This would enable large carriers to focus their efforts and preparation on large-scale, higher-end operations.

NATURE OF THE MARITIME STRATEGIC COMPETITION

In terms of the framework of Chapter 1, the Navy's approach to the competition with China could be characterized as a combination of cost imposition and denial. The Navy's sustained forward posture, combined with new operational concepts and Third Offset Strategy capabilities, are intended to gain and maintain access for US forces in areas contested by adversary anti-access networks. To sustain its counter-intervention strategy, China will need to invest in improved sensors and weapons and continue emphasizing near seas platforms such as diesel submarines and missile corvettes. Further, the ability of US naval forces to operate in the East and South China Seas near likely Chinese naval objectives such as Taiwan, the Senkaku Islands, or Scarborough Shoal increases the probability they could deny Chinese aggression against US allies.

The PLAN's approach to its maritime competition with the US Navy is also one of denial and cost imposition, focused on preventing US forces from intervening on behalf of allies such as Japan and the Philippines and increasing the defensive costs for the United States of honoring its alliance commitments. China's military strategy, weapons development priorities, and likely PLAN missions emphasize China's interests in the near seas, as described earlier, and are only slowly evolving to enable operations in support of China's stated objectives in the far seas.

This assessment is supported by the PLAN's projected force structure and capabilities. For example, the PLAN's balance of surface combatants is currently weighted toward small surface combatants, and the composition of its force is not likely to change fundamentally in the foreseeable future. In addition, only about one-third of PLAN surface combatants are large enough to carry a sufficient complement of defensive and offensive missiles in their vertical launch system magazines to both conduct independent offensive operations and protect the ship when deployed away from mainland-based defenses. Similarly, only about one-quarter of PLAN attack submarines are nuclear powered and able to sustain deployments overseas without having to snorkel frequently, which makes them more vulnerable to detection. These characteristics are consistent with near seas sea control rather than overseas power projection missions. Outside the PLAN, China's conventional ballistic missile buildup also is designed to address Chinese objectives in its near abroad, with only about 10 percent of its ballistic missiles able to range outside the "first island chain." The DF-21D anti-ship ballistic missile has been referenced as a *shashoujian* or "trump card"/"assassin's mace" weapon by China's leaders, referring to a unique capability used by a weaker power to defeat a stronger one.[38]

An emerging element of China's maritime strategy, however, is its use of "gray-zone" aggression in peacetime.[39] China has used proxy, civilian, and paramilitary forces in low-intensity operations to gain territory and influence in the South and East China Seas without creating a pretext for a US response. This approach includes activities such as building and equipping islands with precision missiles, harassing military vessels with fishing boats, and using coast guard ships to enforce unlawful maritime claims. Because it undermines the ability of the US Navy to protect allied resources and territory, the gray-zone approach could be considered as directly attacking the US maritime strategy. To implement it, China employs the world's largest coast guard and maritime militia, which can pursue sub-conventional aggression within range of mainland and naval defenses but are less effective at pursuing Chinese interests in the far seas.

Except for gray-zone aggression, the US Navy and PLAN strategies are symmetric in their approach, but asymmetric in their geographic focus. This could yield an advantage to the United States, if both sides effectively pursue their strategies. For example, the United States would likely impose costs on China's ASW efforts with more and larger submarine payloads, and the increased use of UUVs for undersea missions close to the Chinese coast. Moreover, US undersea warfare could deny PLAN offensives against targets such as Taiwan or the Scarborough Shoal. The PLAN could deny US undersea warfare with relatively inexpensive and easy ASW approaches combining sea-bed sonar arrays with standoff ASW missiles and "pouncer" aircraft to suppress—rather than destroy —US submarines inside the first island chain. The PLAN could attempt to counter larger UUVs using inexpensive area weapons such as depth bombs to damage them and sensor countermeasures to confuse them in coastal operating areas. The competition between US undersea capabilities and PLAN ASW could impose costs on both sides and deny both their objectives. However, because it is happening in China's near seas instead of in the open ocean or near the coast of the United States, the PLAN is prevented from projecting power overseas in support of its long-term strategy and is compelled to keep its emphasis on the near seas. The US Navy, on the other hand, continues an overseas posture in support of its maritime strategy and alliance commitments.

A similar dynamic emerges in air and missile defense (AMD). In response to US investments in new AMD capabilities such as electronic warfare and directed energy, China is likely to continue investments in regional precision-strike weapons and persistent targeting, combined with operating concepts and counter-sensor technologies to reduce the effectiveness of US AMD systems. Efforts by the US Navy to develop smaller, more lethal, and more distributed forces—if achieved—could mitigate these PLA efforts. Again, however, the competition is playing out in China's near seas rather than abroad, placing the PLA at a disadvantage relative to its desired strategy of projecting power and influence beyond the near seas.

In the longer term, China would like to expand the ability of the PLA, particularly the PLAN, to defend China's overseas interests. As this transpires, the nature of the competition could become more geographically symmetric, as China strives to produce a force of surface ships that eventually has the same capabilities and can undertake many of the same missions as the US Navy. This could provide opportunities for the US Navy to complement its approach of denial and cost imposition by also implementing a strategy of directly attacking the PLAN maritime strategy by holding PLAN forces at risk in the far seas.

The impact of gray-zone aggression remains to be seen. Because it essentially attacks the US maritime strategy, it creates a new, asymmetric, element of the US-China maritime strategic competition. However, although this element of China's peacetime strategy is increasingly yielding benefits in the near seas, it does not support their overall strategy of shifting focus to the far seas. Gray-zone aggression also does not necessarily contribute to the PLAN's competition with the US Navy, although the militarization of some islands in the South China Sea could improve the PLAN's denial and cost imposition strategies.

INTENSITY OF STRATEGIC COMPETITION

The symmetry of strategic approach and asymmetry of geography between the United States and China suggest an action-reaction dynamic between each side's maritime strategy and approach is occurring in the near term, but in the far term the coupling between US and Chinese maritime strategies and implementation is much less evident.

China

China's military strategy, likely PLAN missions, and the A2/AD component within such missions are designed to counter US intervention. The network of US military bases and alliances in the Asia-Pacific is seen as complicating China's freedom of action in potential contingencies,[40] and some Chinese academic and military writings declare the United States to be pursuing a long-term strategy to "strategically encircle" or "contain" China.[41] They argue that the United States relies primarily on bases and alliances throughout the "first island chain" and "second island chain" to carry this out.[42] This has, as already described, incentivized China's development of capabilities to blunt US force projection. James Holmes of the US Naval War College has pointed out that the 1995–1996 Taiwan Strait crisis in particular served to galvanize China's naval development and its efforts to exploit US vulnerabilities and forestall potential interventions.[43] China's near- to medium-term strategy and plans are expected to focus on improving the PLA's ability to rapidly defeat US naval forces in the "near seas," and to achieve territorial objectives with actions calculated to fall below the threshold that would constitute acts of war. This is consistent with its competitive strategy of denial and cost imposition, focused on the near seas, and is highly coupled with US efforts to gain and maintain maritime access. China's recent efforts at gray-zone aggression, although associated with an approach of attacking US strategy, are still a direct response to the continued US ability to operate in the near seas, albeit at increasing levels of risk.

On the other hand, China appears to be pursuing a host of capabilities to further its own interests not directly connected to the United States. Some analysts argue that China is attempting to emulate the US Navy, striving to produce a force of surface ships that has the same capabilities and eventually can undertake similar missions. China may construct carrier battle groups for far seas operations and seek access to additional foreign facilities for reasons other than competition with the United States, such as domestic and international prestige, non-war military missions, and protecting Chinese interests and citizens abroad.[44] The PLAN differs from the US Navy in the way it would employ its attack submarines, but this is likely due to current technical shortcomings in its submarines' abilities. Ultimately, China has sought to pursue a broad range of capabilities regardless of US choices, even while it invests in technologies to counter the US military in some cases.

The United States

On the US side, new maritime strategic documents and efforts are designed to specifically address the access challenges posed by China to a greater extent than before, as discussed above. The current direction of the US Navy's operating concepts and plans suggest it will be shifting to a greater focus on distributed operations, undersea and electromagnetic spectrum warfare, and capabilities for smaller, more lethal engagements. These operational approaches and capabilities will better position the Navy, compared to today's fleet, to counter current Chinese operations, which rely on persistent assertions of sovereignty and control over waters in China's "near abroad."[45]

Smaller, more distributed US Navy forces could specifically provide an improved ability to execute proportional responses to Chinese gray-zone aggression. The PLAN and China Coast Guard have shouldered, used water cannon, and in some cases fired upon neighboring countries' navies to assert China's territorial claims. The small-scale nature and low lethality of these engagements makes traditional US responses such as air strikes and shows of force disproportionate. The deployment of smaller, more distributed platforms in regions such as the South and East China Seas would enable small-scale, immediate responses or countermeasures to be applied against Chinese aggression. Further, the Navy's intent to ensure these distributed platforms have adequate self-defense will reduce the ability of China's anti-access weapons on shore or at sea to escalate in a way that could be catastrophic for US forces.

More broadly, new science and technology initiatives such as the Third Offset Strategy and Defense Innovation Initiative compete directly with China as a near-peer technological competitor. At the whole-of-government level, the United States has sought to strengthen its presence and leadership in the Asia-Pacific with the "Rebalance to Asia" strategy, initiated in 2011 but building upon initiatives begun under the Bush administration. The strategy incorporated security, economic, and diplomatic elements and sought to uphold the rules-based international order in the Asia-Pacific in an era of new challenges, including that posed by China in the maritime realm. On the security front, it includes stationing 60 percent of the US Navy in the Pacific by 2020, new basing and access agreements, new partner capacity-building initiatives, and the deployment or planned deployment of the most advanced US maritime asset types to the region. These would include the F-35 strike-fighter, E/A-18G Growler airborne electronic attack aircraft, *Virginia*-class attack submarines, *Zumwalt*-class stealth destroyers, Aegis missile defense-equipped vessels, littoral combat ships, and P–8 patrol aircraft, among others.[46]

These efforts are reflective of the highly coupled nature of the near-to medium-term maritime strategic competition between the United States and China. In the far term, US Navy plans are less reflective of China's blue-water aspirations and instead, like the PLAN, are designed to support US interests independent of China. This suggests, however, that a far seas focused strategy by the United States could give the US Navy an at least temporary advantage, because the PLAN is not focused on responding to it.

CONSIDERATIONS FOR US COMPETITIVE STRATEGY

In addition to assessing the nature and level of competition thus far, an evaluation of "medium-term" (defined here as approximately 10–20 years) and "enduring" competitive advantages is helpful in considering US strategy options in a long-term competition with China. A comparison of potential advantages held by each side, which draws on a review of analyses by experts inside and outside China, is presented in table 10, and discussed in detail below.

Advantages for China in the Medium Term

Relative Growth in Resources
China's defense spending hikes have roughly tracked its GDP growth, adjusting for inflation, and several external assessments have pointed out that China should be able to finance its high level of military moderniza-tion for the foreseeable future.[47] IHS Jane's Defense Budgets, as quoted by DoD in 2016, "expects China's defense budget to increase by an annual average of 7 percent, growing to $260 billion by 2020."[48] Other factors may play in as well, such as lower labor costs and China's dedication to maritime spending relative to other military branches. Robert Ross notes that the superiority China has enjoyed on its interior frontiers since the Cold War has enabled the PLA to redirect military spending toward

maritime assets; and China will thus have the resources to construct a large navy regardless of reductions in economic growth.[49]

Table 10. Summary of Chinese and US Advantages in Potential Maritime Competition.

Advantages for China	Advantages for the United States
Medium term	
Relative growth in resources: Based on economic growth, but may not persist	*Proficiency:* Temporary technical limitations to China's shipbuilding industrial base and relative proficiency of US naval personnel
Local capacity: PLA can focus attention on East and South China Seas	*Global capacity:* Able to counter China in multiple theaters and sustain operations in a protracted conflict
Other: Growing A2/AD "envelope"; non-accession to INF Treaty	*Other:* Undersea warfare capabilities
Enduring	
Geography for competition in near seas: China enjoys benefits of proximity, has yielding cost advantages in an offense-dominant missile competition	*Geography for competition outside the near seas:* China few exits through first island chain; is vulnerable to blockade
Initiative: China can choose when, where, and how to apply coercive pressure or begin hostilities	*Maritime norms:* Friction with international order may impose costs on China or facilitate US alliance-building
International politics: Potential for cooperation with states that share opposition to the international order, e.g. Russia	*International politics:* US regional and global partnerships and alliances

Although China will probably close the gap in defense spending with the United States in the foreseeable future based on its higher economic growth rate, it will likely face a rising cost curve and diminishing returns. Studies have observed that the cost of ships and weapons tends to rise faster than the inflation rate, eventually requiring continuous spending increases to avoid force reductions.[50] Andrew Erickson noted in 2014 that a buildup of aircraft carriers and other large vessels could have a particular impact in this regard.[51] IHS Jane's Defense Forecast suggested in 2012 that China's spending on shipbuilding would settle at around $3 billion annually from 2018, down from a peak of $5.2 billion in 2012 (due to the large number of ships being built at that time).[52] For context, however, the US Congressional Budget Office estimates that the US Navy will spend an average of $18.4 billion per year on new ships under its new 30-year shipbuilding plan, adjusted for inflation.[53] While China may gain ground, it thus faces a significant gap. Due to the uncertainty of China's future economic growth, relative growth in resources is best seen as a medium-term, rather than an enduring, advantage.

Local Capacity
Assessments generally characterize the regional US-China naval military balance as shifting or "eroding."[54] Based on the ONI projections in table 1, China will have 106 major conventional warships (aircraft carriers, cruisers, destroyers, amphibious ships, and attack and cruise missile submarines) in 2020, while the United States is projected to have about 109 homeported in the Pacific, based on the 60 percent target of the US maritime strategy. China would also have 72 attack submarines, of which approximately three-quarters will be modern, as opposed to 29 for the United States in the Pacific. Although the US submarines have greater endurance, sensor capability, and payload capacity, it is unclear that the United States will increase its Pacific submarine posture, while China likely will.[55]

In addition, observers have argued that China is currently better equipped to handle space denial than the United States,[56] that China's land-based H-6K bombers and Su-30 fighters outrange the US carrier-based air wing,[57] and that US refueling aircraft in the Western Pacific might be vulnerable to attack.[58] The United States has also not invested heavily in developing new air- and surface-launched ASCMs since the end of the Cold War, meaning China (likely temporarily) has a range advantage in this regard.[59] Because the PLA will continue to lack the basing and refueling capabilities to project power beyond the first and second island chains, however, this range advantage, like the capacity advantage described above, will be localized.

Enduring Chinese Advantages

Geography for Competition in Near Seas

A wide consensus of sources note the advantage of proximity to a potential conflict and the cost advantages this confers given the current offense-dominant missile competition.[60] The *China Military Science* article referenced above notes the importance of China's proximity to an area that "regulates the operations of the global maritime economic system, and affects and even controls the global strategic situation."[61] From another perspective, if China sought a "breakthrough" in a conflict, it need not contest the entire island chain but can choose when and where to make an attempt.[62] China's occupied features in the South China Sea could host ground-based radar that could assist China's efforts to detect and target carrier strike groups that area with ASBMs, pending a more robust space-based ISR architecture. One such installation is already in place on Cuarteron Reef in the Spratly Islands.[63]

This assessment, however, misses that China seeks to be a global power and to project its power and influence broadly. Being able to contest or deny the near seas is desirable for defense of the Chinese mainland, but does not further this larger goal. Moreover, seen from this perspective, the proximity of the first island chain becomes a vulnerability rather than a source of targets. To reach beyond the near seas, the PLAN must neutralize threats around this periphery. It must then also develop a fleet and support infrastructure able to sustain global operations.

Initiative

As a Center for Strategic and Budgetary Assessments' report noted in 2010, China "would have the strategic and operational initiative in choosing when, where and how war begins" should a contingency ever reach the level where it began hostilities.[64] This does not mean China would be the first to escalate to strikes against land targets; in fact, it implies that it could choose not to do this and force the costs of escalation on the United States.[65] At the tactical level, fixed bases and surface ships are vulnerable to the first use of force, presenting an unfortunate and destabilizing incentive.[66] Beijing could also continue to be selective in applying coercive pressure below the threshold of conflict.

International Politics

States in tension with the US-led international order, should their interests align with Beijing's in certain cases, may provide China with support. Scholars in China have debated the extent to which China has shared interests with Russia and whether this could be a strategic asset, for example.[67] Many observers have assessed that prospects for greater Sino-Russian cooperation will likely be limited by factors such as "strategic mistrust,"[68] geographic competition, and conflicts of interest over issues such as oil prices,[69] but advise the United States not unnecessarily make it convenient for China and Russia to band together.[70] Limited cooperation could also be useful for China. Russian defense exports played a significant role in China's maritime development in the past, and its assistance could benefit Chinese nuclear propulsion technology going forward, for example.[71]

Advantages for the United States in the Medium Term

Proficiency

The United States will likely enjoy technical advantages in shipbuilding and in a qualitative advantage in the proficiency of its naval personnel in the medium term. Analysts have pointed out that the United States is not likely to have an enduring advantage in this area, however. Experts at the 2015 China Maritime Studies Institute Conference, hosted by the Naval War College, agreed that "the PRC's shipbuilding industry appears to be on a trajectory to build a combat fleet quantitatively and qualitatively on a par with the US Navy by 2030."[72]

Experts note that China has often exceeded US estimates of its military capability and capacity, specifically making rapid strides in the areas of anti-air warfare, antisurface warfare, and ISR, while beginning to make progress in anti-submarine warfare.[73] At the technical level, they note improvements in design techniques and even naval propulsion; while production runs have lengthened and the role of foreign technology has clearly diminished.[74] Others note that China's naval shipbuilding enterprise is generally very well resourced, and that China's government has assigned the overall shipbuilding industry a key role in China's development as a great power.[75] While sources disagree, some state that civil-military diffusion has been beneficial to China's naval shipbuilding efforts; DoD noted in 2016 that collaboration between the two major naval SoEs lends efficiency and also referenced China's growing overall R&D and S&T base.[76] Finally, some experts have suggested that this is to be expected from a historical perspective, given the rapid speed at which rising navies have gained on established ones in the past, and because "naval technology flows more or less freely across borders among the world's most powerful nations" in the long run.[77]

Global Capacity

Despite changes in the military balance in the Asia-Pacific, the United States retains an overwhelming military advantage in the far seas, and could bring additional forces into the region in the event of a contingency. One Chinese source also noted that 14 of the 17 largest global fleets by tonnage (after the United States) in 2010 belonged to US allies.[78] The United Kingdom and France will likely deploy 2 carriers, 6–8 Aegis-like destroyers, and 7 SSNs and 1 carrier, 2 Aegis-like destroyers, and 6 SSNs by 2020, respectively.[79] Despite their distance, both participate in RIMPAC.[80] France refers to itself as a "Pacific power" and announced in July 2016 that it plans to coordinate fellow European Union nations to conduct freedom of navigation operations in the South China Sea.[81]

Enduring US Advantages

Geography for Competition Outside Near Seas

China does not control its decisive maritime geography, presenting an enduring disadvantage.[82] Numerous sources both inside and outside China view the "island chains" concept as posing real disadvantages based on the potential for sensors and missiles based there to complicate Chinese military planning and the presence of limited numbers of narrow "exits" through the first island chain, creating "chokepoints."[83] Although China and the United States are pursuing similar overarching strategies in the near seas, there is a great asymmetry of risks. The East and South China Seas are essentially China's home waters and China must have high confidence of success in a near seas operation. In contrast, the United States only needs to create enough of a risk of failure to deter China and reassure US allies.

China encounters other geographic challenges as well. Taiwan is hurt by its proximity to China, but would still enjoy the advantages of island defense.[84] Even potential sites for foreign naval facilities such as Bangladesh, Pakistan, and Sri Lanka happen to be close to India and could further affect that country's perceptions.[85] The United States, in contrast, sustains a globally-deployed fleet supported by numerous bases on allied territory outside the range of all or most of China's shore-launched cruise and ballistic missiles.

Chinese and US sources also frequently mention the "Malacca dilemma" posed by China's vulnerability to a blockade of the Malacca Strait.[86] Foreign bases and a blue water navy could in theory counter this threat in a conflict, but analyses of China's current carrier program indicate it is better prepared to bolster fleet air defense than to be a useful power projection tool.[87] The United States can surge global forces and call upon allies (addressed under "international politics" below); at best China could deploy submarines to slow their advance.[88]

Maritime Norms

Beijing's gray-zone aggression in the East and South China seas, in direct violation of international maritime norms, has caused other countries in the region to look to the United States for support.[89] China does not reject the current "rules-based international order" outright, but rather appears to pick and choose its involvement based on interest, while seeking to participate in writing the rules where possible.[90] This stance is itself in friction with countries that generally accept the order. To the extent that this raises the costs of China's coercive peacetime activities, or aids US alliance-building efforts, China will face an enduring disadvantage. Some sources in China have discussed the issue of US-supported maritime norms: for example, one scholar argues that "the exercise of American sea power in East Asia rests on the norm of freedom of navigation;" another that the US is undermining China's "soft environment."[91] Sources also advocate that China must "contribute more" to the international maritime legal system in order to shape it.[92]

International Politics

US allies and partners in the Asia-Pacific could provide numerous contributions going forward. Observers have noted their potential for facilitating the dispersion of US military assets—which would also present China with the risk of drawing in greater numbers of opponents should it target US regional bases in a conflict—or providing outposts for sensors that could detect Chinese submarines traversing the chokepoints in the first island chain.[93] They may also be able to augment the offensive strike capabilities of the US "side" by virtue of not being bound by the INF treaty.[94] In the longer-term, US assistance to the Philippines, Vietnam, Indonesia, Malaysia, and Thailand under the recently-introduced "Southeast Asia Maritime Security Initiative" will take time, according to experts, but so did its assistance to the now-modernized militaries of Japan, South Korea, and Taiwan begun decades ago.[95] In recent years the United States has established new basing or access agreements in Australia, the Philippines, and Singapore, while Japan has passed new security laws allowing it to defend allies if they are attacked.[96] Countries along China's periphery will likely continue to look to the United States for reassurance in the future, presenting opportunities if the United States can continue working to transition its alliances into a stronger regional security network.[97]

CONCLUSION

To summarize the chapter's assessments, enduring Chinese disadvantages are likely to be geopolitical rather than technical in nature. This implies that whole-of-government strategies, which emphasize all elements of statecraft and include coalition building and support for maritime norms, will be crucial to US maritime competition and efforts to deter conflict in the long term. On their own, policies that are strictly technical in nature may not fully exploit China's areas of weakness.

From a maritime perspective, China's focus is still largely on its near seas and on capabilities to blunt US force projection. China has lagged in shifting to the far seas-focused capabilities called for in its strategic documents. This will make US efforts to sustain naval access in the near seas more challenging, but also compels China and the PLAN to continue to emphasize coastal and littoral defense. Rather than abandoning or slowing implementation of concepts such as AirSea Battle (now the Joint Concept for Access and Maneuver in the Global Commons), or technological initiatives such as the Third Offset and DII, these efforts should continue to impose costs on the PLAN and increase the risk of Chinese aggression being denied in the East or South China Seas. As noted above, the geographic asymmetry of the US and China competition in the near seas means that China must have high confidence of success in a near-seas operation, whereas the United States only needs to create enough of a risk of failure to deter China and reassure US allies.

The United States should continue its strategy of denial and cost imposition by pursuing concepts and capabilities to operate in highly contested environments, given its key interests in the Asia-Pacific and the presence of numerous allies and partners that are vulnerable to potential aggression. As noted above, these efforts do not have to create certainty that a US response would succeed in denying Chinese aggression; they only need to create enough uncertainty that Chinese leaders will be dissuaded from pursuing aggression.

The United States could complement its cost imposition and denial strategy by directly attacking China's far-term strategy through an approach that puts Beijing's interests at risk in the far seas. This could broadly include the development of new operational concepts that signal the willingness of the United States to threaten China's sea lines of communication and strategic chokepoints in a conflict. It could build on previous US efforts such as the Rebalance to Asia that seek to preserve strength and leadership in the Asia-Pacific on all fronts, such as investment in regional bilateral and multilateral alliances, building partner capacity, expansion of regional maritime domain awareness, broader regional basing and access, and deployment of additional forces forward to the region. Additional research is needed to fully develop such a strategy, but a guiding principle could be to demonstrate that the United States would respond to aggression or a potential conflict in ways that could be countered only by substantial investment in foreign bases and a blue water navy on China's part.

Shifting toward a far seas-focused competition while retaining the ability to operate in the near seas is well suited to the current nature and level of maritime strategic competition between China and the United States, and would benefit US interests in many ways. First, it would allow the United States to build on its advantages, most notably global capacity, favorable maritime geography, and regional and global alliances and partnerships. Second, it could place the United States in a better position for a long-term competition at the technical level, based on the potential to employ unmanned and distributed systems and their utility for operational functions such as a blockade. Third, it could advance regional stability by demonstrating US resolve and readiness to involve its global capacity, making it evident that a short conflict in which China could move quickly and consolidate its gains is unlikely. Fourth, it would demonstrate commitment to US allies and partners in the region, and potentially further these countries' willingness to assist US efforts to defend the rules-based regional order. Fifth, it could preserve US internal lines of communication in a potential conflict, as these would likely be disrupted inside China's A2/AD envelope. Finally, and most important, it could attack China's desired far-term strategy by undermining its still-weak implementation. In theory, China would have to respond with investments in a blue water navy, a wider network of basing and access agreements, and international partnerships and alliances, precisely where the United States is well positioned to compete in the long term.

Notes

1. The views in this chapter are Jordan Wilson's own and do not imply endorsement by the U.S. Department of Defense.

2. Liu Yonghong, "Strategic Consideration on the Transformation of the PLA Navy under the New Situation," *China Military Science,* November 30, 2012.

3. Daniel Hartnett, "The Father of the Modern Chinese Navy: Liu Huaqing," Center for International Maritime Security, October 8, 2014, http://cimsec. org/father-modern-chinese-navy-liu-huaqing/13291.

4. Liu Yonghong, "Strategic Consideration on the Transformation of the PLA Navy."

5. Caitlin Campbell, "Highlights from China's New Defense White Paper, 'China's Military Strategy,'" US-China Economic and Security Review Commission Issue Brief, June 1, 2015, 1.

6. The first island chain refers to a line of islands running through the Kurile Islands, Japan and the Ryukyu Islands, Taiwan, the Philippines, Borneo, and Natuna Besar. The second island chain is farther east, running through the Kurile Islands, Japan, the Bonin Islands, the Mariana Islands, and the Caroline Islands. The precise boundaries of the island chains vary among Chinese sources and have never been officially defined by China's government. Andrew S. Erickson and Joel Wuthnow, "Barriers, Springboards and Benchmarks: China Conceptualizes the Pacific 'Island Chains,'" *China Quarterly* 225 (2016): 3, 7–9, 17. http://journals.cambridge. org/abstract_S0305741016000011; Bernard D. Cole, *The Great Wall at Sea: China's Navy in the Twenty-First Century* (Annapolis, MD: Naval Institute Press, 2010), 174–176; see also Michael McDeavitt, "China's Far Sea's Navy: The Implications of the 'Open Seas Protection' Mission," paper presented at the "China as a Maritime Power" conference, Center for Naval Analyses, Arlington, Virginia, April 2016, 2, https://www.cna.org/ cna_files/pdf/China-Far-Seas-Navy.pdf.

7. Hartnett, "The Father of the Modern Chinese Navy"; Edward Wong, "Liu Huaqing Dies at 94; Oversaw Modernization of China's Navy," *New York Times,* January 16, 2011, http://www.nytimes.com/2011/01/1 8/world/asia/18liu.html.

8. Christopher H. Sharman, *China Moves Out: Stepping Stones toward a New Maritime Strategy* (Washington, DC: National Defense University Press,

2015), 1; Toshi Yoshihara and James R. Holmes, *Red Star over the Pacific: China's Rise and the Challenge to US Maritime Strategy* (Annapolis, MD: Naval Institute Press, 2010), 24–25.

9. Hartnett, "The Father of the Modern Chinese Navy"; Cole, *The Great Wall at Sea*, 174–76.

10. Bernard D. Cole, *China's Quest for Great Power: Ships, Oil, and Foreign Policy* (Annapolis, MD: Naval Institute Press, 2016), 93.

11. Andrew S. Erickson, "China's Blueprint for Sea Power," *China Brief* 16, no. 11 (2016), http://www.jamestown.org/single/?tx_ttnews%5Btt_news %5D=45570&tx_ttnews%5BbackPid%5D=7&cHash=e717a7332ee80a4556 1860be75770b15#.V4_7ifmAOko.

12. Tai Ming Cheung (director, UC Institute on Global Conflict and Cooperation), e-mail communication with author, July 2016.

13. Zhang Yunbi, "Coordination Is Key to New Maritime Strategy," *China Daily*, July 22, 2016, http://www.chinadaily.com.cn/china/2016-07/22/ content_26190319.htm.

14. Craig Murray, Andrew Berglund, and Kimberly Hsu, "China's Naval Modernization and Implications for the United States," US-China Economic and Security Review Commission Staff Research Backgrounder, August 26, 2013, 3, http://www.uscc.gov/sites/default/ files/Research/Backgrounder_China's%20Naval%20Modernization%20 and%20Implications%20for%20the%20United%20States.pdf.

15. Alastair Iain Johnston, "The Evolution of Interstate Security Crisis Management Theory and Practice in China," *Naval War College Review* 69, no. 1 (2016): 40; Edward Wong, "Security Law Suggests a Broadening of China's 'Core Interests,'" *New York Times*, July 2, 2015. http://www.nytimes.com/2015/07/03/world/asia/security-law-suggests-a-broadening-of-chinas-core-interests.html; Ministry of National Defense of the People's Republic of China regular press conference, November 26, 2015; Caitlin Campbell et al., "China's 'Core Interests' and the East China Sea," US-China Economic and Security Review Commission Staff Research Backgrounder, May 10, 2013, 1–5, https://www.uscc.gov/sites/ default/files/Research/China's%20Core%20Interests%20and%20the%20 East%20China%20Sea.pdf.

16. State Council Information Office, "China's Military Strategy," May 2015; Wilson, "China's Expanding Ability," 4.

17. State Council Information Office, "China's Military Strategy," May 2015.

18. M. Taylor Fravel, "China's New Military Strategy: 'Winning Informationized Local Wars,'" *China Brief* 15, no. 13 (2015).

19. According to the US Department of Defense, "anti-access" actions are intended to slow the deployment of an adversary's forces into a theater or cause them to operate at distances farther from the conflict than they would prefer. "Area denial" actions affect maneuvers within a theater, and are intended to impede an adversary's operations within areas where friendly forces cannot or will not prevent access. China, however, uses the term "counter-intervention," reflecting its perception that such operations are reactive. Office of the Secretary of Defense, *Annual Report to Congress: Military and Security Developments Involving the People's Republic of China 2013* (Washington, DC: US Department of Defense), i, 32, 33; Air-Sea Battle Office, "Air-Sea Battle: Service Collaboration to Address Anti-Access and Area Denial Challenges," May 2013, 2.

20. Tai Ming Cheung et al., *Planning for Innovation: Understanding China's Plans for Technological, Energy, Industrial, and Defense Development.* Report for the US-China Economic and Security Review Commission by the University of California Institute on Global Conflict and Cooperation (La Jolla, CA: IGCC, 2016), 22; Harry J. Kazianis, "America's Air-Sea Battle Concept: An Attempt to Weaken China's A2/AD Strategy," China Policy Institute Policy Paper 2014: No. 4, 2, http://www.nottingham.ac.uk/iaps/documents/cpi/policy-papers/cpi-policy-paper-2014-no-4-kazianis.pdf; Cortez A. Cooper, "The PLA Navy's 'New Historic Missions,'" testimony at the US-China Economic and Security Review Commission hearing on the Implications of China's Naval Modernization for the United States, June 11, 2009. http://www.rand.org/content/dam/rand/pubs/testimonies/2009/RAND_CT332.pdf.

21. US Office of Naval Intelligence, *The PLA Navy: New Capabilities and Missions for the 21st Century* (Washington, DC: Office of Naval Intelligence, 2015), 4, 12; Murray, Berglund, and Hsu, "China's Naval Modernization," 2.

22. Ronald O'Rourke, "China Naval Modernization: Implications for US Navy Capabilities—Background and Issues for Congress," Congressional Research Service Report, May 31, 2016, 47–48.

23. US Office of Naval Intelligence, *The PLA Navy: New Capabilities and Missions for the 21st Century* (Washington, DC: Office of Naval Intelligence, 2015), 43.

24. Information on capabilities from Heginbotham, "The US-China Military Scorecard," 165; Ronald O'Rourke, "PLAN Force Structure: Submarines, Ships, and Aircraft," in *The Chinese Navy: Expanding Capabilities, Evolving Roles*, ed. Phillip C. Saunders et al. (Washington, DC:

National Defense University, 2011), 162; National Institute for Defense Studies (Japan), *NIDS China Security Report 2016: The Expanding Scope of PLA Activities and the PLA Strategy*, trans. Japan Times (Tokyo: National Institute for Defense Studies, 2016); Jesse Karotkin, "Trends in China's Naval Modernization," testimony for the US-China Economic and Security Review Commission hearing on PLA Modernization and its Implications for the United States, January 10, 2014; O'Rourke, "China Naval Modernization," 6; James R. Holmes, "The State of the US-China Competition," in Mahnken, *Competitive Strategies for the 21st Century*, 140–141. Quote from Lyle J. Goldstein, "A Frightening Thought: China Erodes America's Submarine Advantage," *The National Interest*, August 17, 2015.

25. Office of Naval Intelligence, *The PLA Navy*, 6.

26. Quote from Office of the US Secretary of Defense, *Developments Involving the People's Republic of China 2015*, 11. See Daniel J. Kostecka, "From the Sea: PLA Doctrine and the Employment of Sea-Based Airpower," *US Naval War College Review* 64, no. 3 (2011): 11; James Goldrick, "Why China's Next Aircraft Carrier Will Be Based on Soviet Blueprints," *The National Interest*, January 8, 2016; Kyle Mizokami, "China Wants Aircraft Carrier Battle Groups to Defend its Maritime Turf," *Popular Mechanics*, March 3, 2016.

27. *2015 Report to Congress*, 13, 250.

28. Oriana Skylar Mastro, testimony for the US-China Economic and Security Review Commission hearing on Developments in China's Military Force Projection and Expeditionary Capabilities, January 21, 2016; Chinese National Defense Ministry, "Official English Transcript of PRC National Defense Ministry's News Conference February 25, 2016"; Ankit Panda, "Construction Begins on China's First Overseas Military Base in Djibouti," *The Diplomat* (Japan), February 29, 2016; Jane Perlez and Chris Buckley, "China Retools its Military with a First Overseas Outpost in Djibouti," *New York Times*, November 26, 2015; US Department of Defense, *Developments Involving the People's Republic of China 2017*, ii.

29. US Department of Defense, *Developments Involving the People's Republic of China 2014*, 36; US-China Economic and Security Review Commission, testimony of Jesse Karotkin; Murray, Berglund, and Hsu, "China Naval Modernization."

30. Liu Yonghong, "Strategic Consideration on the Transformation of the PLA Navy."

31. Jonathan Greenert, James Amos, and Paul Zunkuft, *A Cooperative Strategy for 21st Century Seapower* (Washington, DC: US Department of the Navy, 2015).

32. John Richardson, *Design for Maritime Superiority* (Washington, DC: US Department of the Navy, 2016).

33. Christopher Cavas, "Shaping the Fleet of the Future," *Defense News*, May 16, 2016, http://www.defensenews.com/story/defense-news/2016/05/08/navy-fleet-future-architecture-aircraft-carrier-cno-richardson-csba-bryan-clark-force-structure-mccain/84002628/.

34. Deputy Chief of Naval Operations (Integration of Capabilities and Resources), "Report to Congress: Navy Combatant Vessel Force Structure Requirement," January 2013; Deputy Chief of Naval Operations (Integration of Capabilities and Resources), "Report to Congress on the Annual Long-Range Plan for Construction of Naval Vessels for FY2015," June 2014.

35. Alex Davies, "Boeing's Monstrous Underwater Robot Can Wander the Oceans for Six Months, *Wired*, March 21, 2016, https://www.wired.com/2016/03/boeings-monstrous-underwater-robot-can-wander-ocean-6-months/; Chief of Naval Operations, Undersea Warfare Directorate, "Report to Congress: Autonomous Undersea Vehicle Requirement for 2025," February 2016, 5.

36. Sydney Freedberg, "DSD Work Embraces DARPA's Robot Boat, Sea Hunter," *Breaking Defense,* April 7, 2016, http://breakingdefense.com/2016/04/dsd-work-to-christen-darpas-robot-boat-sea-hunter/.

37. The US Navy's Nimitz and Ford-class carriers displace about 100,000 tons. A LHA/LHD displaces about 40,000 tons. See also James Hasik, "Are Aircraft Carriers About to Become Obsolete?" *The National Interest,* April 3, 2015, http://nationalinterest.org/blog/the-buzz/are-us-aircraft-carriers-about-become-obsolete-12540.

38. Andrew S. Erickson, "Chinese Anti-Ship Ballistic Missile Development and Counter-intervention Efforts," testimony for the US-China Economic and Security Review Commission hearing on China's Advanced Weapons, February 23, 2017; People's Network, "Dong Feng 21D Troop Review Gives PLA Navy an Asymmetric 'Assassin's Mace,'" September 9, 2015; National Ground Intelligence Center, *China: Medical Research on Bio-Effect of Electromagnetic Pulse and High-Power Microwave Radiation,* August 17, 2005.

39. Michael J. Mazarr, *Mastering the Gray Zone: Understanding a Changing Era of Conflict* (Carlisle, PA: Strategic Studies Institute, 2015), 4, http:// www.

strategicstudiesinstitute.army.mil/pubs/display.cfm?pubID=1303; Hal
Brands, "Paradoxes of the Gray Zone," Foreign Policy Research Institute E-
Notes, February 5, 2016, http://www.fpri.org/article/2016/02/paradoxes-
gray-zone/.

40. Johnston, "Evolution of Interstate Security Crisis Management Theory,"
    34; Kazianis, "America's Air-Sea Battle Concept," 1–2; Lu Zhengtao,
    "PRC Article Urges PLA to Boost Air-Sea Force Building for Breaking US
    'Island Chain' Strategy," *China Youth Daily* (Chinese edition), Novem-
    ber 19, 2013; Yoshihara and Holmes, *Red Star over the Pacific*, 20; Bi Lei,
    "Sending an Additional Aircraft Carrier and Stationing Massive Forces:
    The US Military's Adjustment of Its Strategic Disposition in the Asia-
    Pacific Region," *People's Daily* (Chinese edition), August 13, 2004.

41. Wang Changqin and Fang Guangming, "PRC Military Sciences Academy
    Explains Need for Developing the DF-26 Anti-Ship Missile," *China Youth
    Daily* (Chinese edition), November 30, 2015; Toshi Yoshihara, "Japanese
    Bases and Chinese Missiles," in *Rebalancing US Forces: Basing and Forward
    Presence in the Asia-Pacific,* ed. Andrew S. Erickson and Carnes Lord
    (Annapolis MD: Naval Institute Press, 2014), 45; Lu Zhengtao, "PRC
    Article Urges PLA to Boost Air-Sea Force Building"; Gideon Rachman,
    "Obama and Xi Must Halt the Rise of a Risky Rivalry," *Financial Times,*
    June 3, 2013. http://www.ft.com/intl/cms/s/0/db366e3e-ca06-11e2-8f5
    5-00144feab7de.html#axzz3uKTMR2rn; Lin Limin, "A Review of the
    International Strategic Situation in 2012," *Contemporary International
    Relations* (Chinese), December 2012; Zhang Ming, "Security Governance
    of the 'Global Commons' and China's Choice," *Contemporary International
    Relations* (Chinese), July 26, 2012; Liu Bin, "The 'Roadmap' of the Asia-
    Pacific Military Bases of the US Military," *People's Daily* (Chinese
    edition) April 23, 2012; Aaron L. Friedberg, *A Contest for Supremacy:
    China, America, and the Struggle for Mastery in Asia,* (New York: W.W.
    Norton, 2011), 137; Liu Ming, "Obama Administration's Adjustment of
    East Asia Policy and Its Impact on China," *Contemporary International
    Relations* (Chinese), February 20, 2011; Chen Zhou, "Evolution of the US
    Strategy Toward China and China's Peaceful Development," *Peace and
    Development* (Chinese), November 1, 2008; Modern Navy (Chinese), *The
    Island Chains, China's Navy,* October 1, 2007; and Lu Baosheng and Guo
    Hongjun, "Guam: A Strategic Stronghold on the West Pacific," *China
    Military Online,* June 16, 2003.

42. Lu Zhengtao, "PRC Article Urges PLA to Boost Air-Sea Force Build-
    ing"; Liu Bin, "The 'Roadmap' of the Asia-Pacific Military Bases of the

US Military"; Hai Tao, "The Chinese Navy Has a Long Way to Go to Get to the Far Seas," *Guoji Xianqu Daobao*, January 6, 2012; Liu Ming, "Obama Administration's Adjustment of East Asia Policy"; CCTV-7, *Defense Review Week*, August 9, 2009; Chen Zhou, "Evolution of the US Strategy Toward China"; and Modern Navy (Chinese), *The Island Chains*.

43. Holmes, "The State of the US–China Competition," 135–36.
44. *2016 Report to Congress of the US-China Economic and Security Review Commission* (Washington, DC: US Government Printing Office, 2016), 256, 258–59, 261–63.
45. Catherine Wong, "PLA Navy Ready to Counter Aggression in South China Sea," *South China Morning Post*, July 19, 2016, http://www.scmp.com/news/china/diplomacy-defence/article/1991499/pla-navy-ready-counter-aggression-south-china-sea.
46. US-China Economic and Security Review Commission, *2016 Annual Report to Congress*, 478.
47. US Department of Defense, *Developments Involving the People's Republic of China 2016*, 77; International Monetary Fund, *World Economic Outlook Database*, April 2016; Chris Buckley and Jane Perlez, "China Military Budget to Rise Less Than 8%, Slower than Usual," *New York Times*, March 4, 2016. http://www.nytimes.com/2016/03/05/world/asia/china-military-spending.html; Andrew S. Erickson and Adam P. Liff, "Demystifying China's Defense Spending: Less Mysterious in the Aggregate," *China Quarterly* 216 (2013): 808; US Department of Defense, *Developments Involving the People's Republic of China 2016*, 77; Anthony H. Cordesman, Ashley Hess, and Nicholas S. Yarosh, *Chinese Military Modernization and Force Development: A Western Perspective* (Lanham, MD: Rowman and Littlefield, 2013), 32.
48. US Department of Defense, *Developments Involving the People's Republic of China 2016*, 77.
49. Robert S. Ross, "The Rise of the Chinese Navy: From Regional Power to Global Naval Power," *Journal of International Security Studies* (Chinese) (January/February 2016): 1.
50. Andrew Erickson, testimony for the US-China Economic and Security Review Commission hearing on China's Military Modernization and its Implications for the United States, January 30, 2014.
51. Ibid.
52. IHS Jane's Defense Forecast, 2012.

53. US Congressional Budget Office, *An Analysis of the Navy's Fiscal Year 2016 Shipbuilding Plan*, October 29, 2015, https://www.cbo.gov/publication/50926#section1.
54. J. Randy Forbes and Elbridge Colby, "We're Losing Our Military Edge over China: Here's How to Get It Back," *The National Interest*, Marcy 27, 2014; Robert Haddick, "This Week at War: An Arms Race America Can't Win," *Small Wars Journal* [blog], June 8, 2012, http://smallwarsjournal.com/blog/this-week-at-war-an-arms-race-america-cant-win.
55. Haddick, "This Week at War."
56. Jan Van Tol, *AirSea Battle: A Point-of-Departure Operational Concept* (Washington, DC: Center for Strategic and Budgetary Assessment, 2010), 50, 67.
57. Andrew F. Krepinevich, *Why AirSea Battle?* (Washington, DC: Center for Strategic and Budgetary Assessments, 2010), 21.
58. Jamie Seidel, "South China Sea Escalations Leave Analysts Wondering Who Would Win if War Broke Out," *New Zealand Herald*, July 13, 2016.
59. Heginbotham, "The US-China Military Scorecard," 30; Office of Naval Intelligence, *The PLA Navy*, 217–19.
60. Forbes and Colby, "Losing Our Military Edge over China"; Yang Zhen, Zhao Juan, and Bian Hongjin, "On the Development of [the] Chinese Navy in the Era of Sea Power and Aircraft Carriers," *World Regional Studies* (Chinese) 22 (2013):4; Harold Brown, Joseph W. Prueher, and Adam Segal, *Chinese Military Power* (New York: Council on Foreign Relations Press, 2003), 3; Anthony H. Cordesman, Steven Colley, and Michael Wang, *Chinese Strategy and Military Modernization in 2015: A Comparative Analysis* (Lanham, MD: Rowman and Littlefield, 2015), 319; Peter M. Swartz, "Rising Powers and Naval Power," in *The Chinese Navy: Expanding Capabilities, Evolving Roles*, ed. Phillip C. Saunders et al. (Washington, DC: National Defense University, 2011), 118.
61. Liu Yonghong, "Strategic Consideration on the Transformation of the PLA Navy."
62. Toshi Yoshihara, "Chinese Maritime Geography," in Mahnken and Blumenthal, *Strategy in Asia*, 54.
63. Andrew S. Erickson, "Raining Down: Assessing the Emerging ASBM Threat," Princeton-Harvard China and the World Program, March 30, 2016.
64. Lyle J. Goldstein, "A Frightening Thought: China Erodes America's Submarine Advantage," *The National Interest*, August 17, 2015; Van Tol, "AirSea Battle," 50, 67.

65. Haddick, "This Week at War."

66. Peter Dutton, "A Maritime or Continental Order for Southeast Asia and the South China Sea?" *Naval War College Review* 69, no. 3 (2016): 10.

67. David Lampton, "Rethinking How America Engages China," testimony for the US-China Economic and Security Review Commission hearing on China and the US Rebalance to Asia, March 31, 2016; Chu Shulong and Tao Shasha, "Responding to Our Peripheral Security Challenges," *Journal of Contemporary International Relations* (November/December 2013).

68. Michael Green et al., *Asia-Pacific Rebalance 2025: Capabilities, Presence, and Partnerships* (Lanham, MD: Rowman and Littlefield, 2016), 25; Franz-Stefan Gady, "Russia's Foreign Minister Slams US over Military Buildup in Asia," *The Diplomat*, August 6, 2015; Märta Carlsson, Susanne Oxenstierna, and Mikael Weissmann. "China and Russia-A Study on Cooperation, Competition and Distrust," FOI Research Report, June 2015, 79–84; Yoichi Kato, "Interview: Michael Green: Concerns About China's Rise Boost Support for US Rebalance to Asia," *Asahi Shimbun*, June 20, 2014; Stephen Kotkin, "The Unbalanced Triangle," *Foreign Affairs*, September/October 2009.

69. US-China Economic and Security Review Commission, testimony of David Lampton.

70. US-China Economic and Security Review Commission, testimony of Dan Blumenthal, March 31, 2016; US-China Economic and Security Review Commission, testimony of David Lampton.

71. Andrew S. Erickson, "Personal Summary of Discussion at China's Naval Shipbuilding: Progress and Challenges," conference held by China Maritime Studies Institute Conference, US Naval War College, May 19–20, 2015, 4, http://www.andrewerickson.com/2015/07/quick-look-report-on-cmsi-conference-chinas-naval-shipbuilding-progress-and-challenges/.

72. Ibid.

73. Holmes, "The State of the US-China Competition," 138; Heginbotham, "The US-China Military Scorecard," 30, 160–62, 208; Office of Naval Intelligence, *The PLA Navy*, 11, 43; Nan Li, "Evolution of Strategy: From 'Near Coast' to 'Far Seas,'" in Saunders et al., *The Chinese Navy: Expanding Capabilities, Evolving Roles*, 121; US-China Economic and Security Review Commission, testimony of Jesse Karotkin.

74. US Department of Defense, *Developments Involving the People's Republic of China 2016*, 80; Erickson, "China's Naval Shipbuilding: Progress and Challenges," 4; Office of Naval Intelligence, *The PLA Navy*, 10, 11; US-

China Economic and Security Review Commission, testimony of Jesse Karotkin.

75. National Institute for Defense Studies, *China Security Report 2016*; Kyunghee Park, "China Shipbuilding Sector Set to Contract," *Bloomberg*, April 30, 2015. http://www.bloomberg.com/news/articles/2015-04-30/china-shipbuilding-industry-is-set-to-contract-yangzijiang-says.

76. US Department of Defense, *Developments Involving the People's Republic of China 2016*, 77, 80.

77. Quote from Swartz, "Rising Powers and Naval Power," 14. See also Holmes, "The State of the US-China Competition," 137.

78. Zhao Qinghai, "US Maritime Threats to China and Thoughts on China's Countermeasures," *China International Studies* (English) (March/April 2015): 92.

79. Michael McDeavitt, *Becoming a Great 'Maritime Power:' A Chinese Dream* (Arlington, VA: Center for Naval Analyses, 2016), 46, https://www.cna.org/cna_files/pdf/IRM-2016-U-013646.pdf.

80. French Republic Ministry of Defense, "France and Security in the Asia-Pacific," April 2014, 12; "RIMPAC 2014: Participating Forces," Commander, US Pacific Fleet, June 30, 2014, http://www.cpf.navy.mil/rimpac/2014/participants/.

81. French Republic Ministry of Defense, "France and Security in the Asia-Pacific," 8; Yo-Jung Chen, "South China Sea: The French Are Coming," *The Diplomat*, July 14, 2016. http://thediplomat.com/2016/07/south-china-sea-the-french-are-coming/.

82. Roy Kamphausen, "Asia as a Warfighting Environment," in Mahnken and Blumenthal, *Strategy in Asia*, 19.

83. Wilson, "China's Expanding Ability," 5–6; Yoshihara, "Chinese Maritime Geography," 47; Chen Guangwen, "Distant Seas Training is the Chinese Navy's Best Option," *China Youth Daily* (Chinese), June 4, 2014. http://youth.chinamil.com.cn/qnht/2014-06/04/content_5937763.htm; *Global Times* (Chinese), "Large Adjustment to Break Maritime Channel Blockages," January 18, 2012; Van Tol, "AirSea Battle," 14; Cote, "Assessing the Undersea Balance," 190; Jacqueline Newmyer Deal, "Chinese Dominance Isn't Certain," *The National Interest*, June 23, 2014.

84. Cordesman, Colley, and Wang, *Chinese Strategy and Military Modernization in 2015*, 404.

85. Ibid., 535.

86. Zhao Qinghai, "US Maritime Threats to China"; Zhou Yunheng and Yu Jiahao, "Security of Maritime Energy Channels and the Development

of China's Sea Power," *Pacific Journal* (Chinese) 22 (2014): 3; "Commentary: Why Did Australia Call China's Naval Exercises Provocative?" *China Youth Daily*, February 17, 2014; *Global Times*, "Large Adjustment to Break Maritime Channel Blockages"; Van Tol, "AirSea Battle," 75.

87. Heginbotham, "The US-China Military Scorecard," 34; US Department of Defense, *Developments Involving the People's Republic of China 2015*, 11; Office of Naval Intelligence, *The PLA Navy*; Cordesman, Hess, and Yarosh, *Chinese Military Modernization*, 174.

88. Cordesman, Hess, and Yarosh, *Chinese Military Modernization*, 498; Michael Pilger, "China's New YJ-18 Antiship Cruise Missile: Capabilities and Implications for US Forces in the Western Pacific," US-China Economic and Security Review Commission Staff Research Report, October 28, 2015, 5.

89. US-China Economic and Security Review Commission, testimony of Dan Blumenthal; US-China Economic and Security Review Commission, testimony of David Lampton.

90. Richard Fontaine and Mira Rapp-Hooper, "How China Sees World Order," *The National Interest*, May-June 2016. http://nationalinterest.org/print/feature/how-china-sees-world-order-15846; Mira Rapp-Hooper, "The Rebalance in the South China Sea," testimony for the US-China Economic and Security Review Commission hearing on China and the US Rebalance to Asia, March 31, 2016.

91. Zhengyu Wu, "The Crowe Memorandum, the Rebalance to Asia, and Sino-US Relations," *Journal of Strategic Studies* 39, no. 3 (2016): 408, http://www.tandfonline.com/doi/pdf/10.1080/01402390.2016.1140648; Zhao Qinghai, "US Maritime Threats to China."

92. Zhao Qinghai, "US Maritime Threats to China," 93; Zhou Yunheng and Yu Jiahao, "Security of Maritime Energy Channels," 9.

93. Forbes and Colby, "Losing Our Military Edge over China"; Haddick, "This Week at War"; Cote, "Assessing the Undersea Balance," 190.

94. Toshi Yoshihara, testimony for the US-China Economic and Security Review Commission hearing on China's Offensive Missile Forces, April 1, 2015; Evan Montgomery, "Managing China's Missile Threat: Future Options to Preserve Forward Defense," testimony for the US-China Economic and Security Review Commission hearing on China's Offensive Missile Forces, April 1, 2015; Forbes and Colby, "Losing Our Military Edge over China."

95. Aaron Mehta, "Carter Announces $425M in Pacific Partnership Funding," *Defense News*, May 30, 2015. http://www.defensenews.com/story/defense/

2015/05/30/carter-announces-425m-in-pacific-partnership-funding/2820
6541/; US-China Economic and Security Review Commission, testimony
of Mira Rapp-Hooper; US-China Economic and Security Review
Commission, testimony of Dan Blumenthal.

96. Armando J. Heredia, "Analysis: New US-Philippine Basing Deal Heavy on
Air Power, Light on Naval Support," *USNI News*, March 22, 2016; Manuel
Mogato, "Philippines Offers Eight Bases to US Under New Military Deal,"
Reuters, January 13, 2016; Rob Taylor, "US Air Force Seeks to Enlarge
Australian Footprint," *Wall Street Journal*, March 8, 2016; Hayley Channer,
"Steadying the US Rebalance to Asia: The Role of Australia, Japan and
South Korea," *ASPI Strategic Insights*, November 2014, 3; BBC News, "US
P-8 Spy Plane Deployed to Singapore," December 8, 2015; Sam LaGrone,
"Two Littoral Combat Ships to Deploy to Singapore Next Year, Four
by 2017," *USNI News*, April 24, 2015; Erik Slavin, "Japan Law to Defend
US, Allied Troops Takes Effect Next Week," *Stars and Stripes*, March
22, 2016. http://www.stripes.com/news/pacific/japan-law-to-defend-us-
allied-troops-takes-effect-next-week-1.400421.

97. US-China Economic and Security Review Commission, testimony of
Mira Rapp-Hooper; Robert Burns, "Ash Carter Proposes Asia-Pacific
'Security Network,'" Associated Press, June 4, 2016, http://www.
militarytimes.com/story/military/2016/06/04/ash-carter-proposes-asia-
pacific-security-network/85398726/.

CHAPTER 7

ARTIFICIAL INTELLIGENCE, EMERGING TECHNOLOGIES, AND CHINA-US STRATEGIC COMPETITION

Daniel Alderman and Jonathan Ray

INTRODUCTION

The United States and China face a strategic paradox in their long-term competition to research, develop, and acquire new and emerging technologies. In the enormous commercial sphere, the two nations' research and development (R&D) of emerging technologies is now deeply integrated, potentially providing tremendous mutual benefit to each country's consumer markets. Not simply trading partners for finished goods, major commercial entities from each country increasingly seek cross-border talent and market access, and even perform research within the other country's borders. Chinese science and technology (S&T) planners are particularly enthusiastic about this intertwined relationship, and openly advocate for increased flows of talent and technology from the United States and other Western S&T leaders to China. However, despite this deep commercial fluidity, national security planners in each country continue to view each other as potential adversaries. This dynamic fosters national strategic competition and manifests itself in active planning by each country's defense establishments. Complementing previous chapters on competitive strategy frameworks for US-China interactions, this chapter examines both this strategic paradox of "friendship" in commercial and academic pursuits and "enemies" in military planning (hence "frenemies"). It then elucidates China's pursuit of emerging technologies in this context with analytical models and artificial intelligence (AI) as a case study.

The United States and China have fundamentally different approaches to fostering market-driven innovation. In the former, private investors seeking economic returns on future breakthroughs drive the commercial market for new and emerging technologies. Although government policies strive to incentivize innovation through legislation and executive action, no national targets are outlined by the president for the commercial sector. In an attempt to bridge this gap, the Third Offset Strategy is designed to maintain US defense technological advantages by leveraging AI and other technologies currently developed largely by commercial firms such as those in Silicon Valley. In contrast, China's S&T planning spans the commercial and defense realm, and a series of interlocking planning documents guide the entire nation's R&D activities. This dedication to a "whole of state" and goal-oriented planning process flows from a long history of central economic planning, which now aims to leverage the best parts of the market, while also firmly guiding commercial and defense S&T development.

As the United States and China continue their strategic competition for new and emerging technologies, research on AI and other machine learning concepts has emerged as a key enabling technology for both commercial and defense applications. This technology has the potential to provide exponential advances in a wide range of robotic, automation, and decision-making applications, all of which would be dramatically improved by AI processes that continually optimize outcomes to a higher quality than their inputs. Once such machine learning begins, the productivity of an AI-enabled process could dramatically outpace the abilities of its human developers. In the commercial sphere, Kevin Kelly of *Wired* has joked "the business plans of the next 10,000 start-ups are easy to forecast: Take X and add AI."[1] In the defense realm, Arati Prabhakar, the former director of DARPA, has said, "When we look at what's happening with artificial intelligence, we see something that is very, very powerful, very valuable for military applications, but we also see a technology that is still quite fundamentally limited."[2] These limitations are nearly certain to disappear in coming decades, but the relationship between their use in the commercial and defense market is largely uncharted.

This chapter presents AI R&D as a case study to build an analytical framework and unique models to show interactions between key players in China-US competition in emerging technologies. The goal is to contextualize key types of interaction within this competition for the next ten to twenty years. In reviewing this competition from the standpoint of competitive strategies, the rapid pace of innovation in the intertwined commercial markets is the dominant feature. Relentless technological disruption prevents leaders from disentangling the tradeoffs between essential economic growth through joint commercial advancements, and the possibility for threatening military advancements in parallel. The chapter's key goal is to provide a basic framework that helps organize these complex interactions and assists leaders as they formulate competitive strategies within this rapidly evolving environment. These dynamics are analyzed in four sections.

The first section provides a background on China-US technological competition, briefly surveying the historical legacies shaping the next ten to twenty years of competition.

The second section provides a simplified analytical framework for understanding the interplay between the commercial, scientific, and military actors driving research in emerging technologies. These relationships define the fluidity and barriers between key US and Chinese players and demonstrate how each country aims to pull emerging technologies from the commercial sphere into defense applications.

The third section builds upon the framework to introduce six models through which China pursues new and emerging technologies. Any strategy of US national security planners, such as a competitive strategies approach, must account for the following models:

1. Domestic Chinese R&D

2. Academic Exchange

3. Foreign R&D Investment

4. Mergers and Acquisitions

5. Talent Recruitment

6. Traditional Espionage

The chapter concludes with the fundamental problems and tests for both the US and Chinese competitors in emerging technologies such as AI. The economic gains, strategic risks, and fluid interactions of communities across borders make this competition unprecedented. Ultimately, the contest of "frenemies" will come down to the US ability to reform defense procurement and engage the private sector, versus the Chinese capability to truly indigenize innovation.

Background of the China-US Competition in Emerging Technologies

Although this chapter focuses on AI as the premier emerging technology because it will fundamentally alter and not merely advance existing technologies, the United States and China are no strangers to competition in emerging technologies. For example, unmanned systems have long been part of the US-China conversation, going back to the downing of a US D-21 unmanned aerial vehicle (UAV) in 1971. Similarly, the United States and China researched rail gun technologies in the 1980s, and the first US hypersonic systems such as the X-15 began flights in the late 1950s.

Other than design improvements, what will fundamentally change these technologies are increasingly autonomous controls and eventually AI that enables adaptation to more complex operations. Currently, advanced systems such as the X-47B are demonstrators that may operate autonomously but still in predetermined maneuvers and with a human operator in the loop. In future unmanned combat systems, integration of true AI and machine learning will allow the system to assess and execute decisions independently.[3]

What will differentiate the Third Offset Strategy from previous ones are shorter timelines, different challenges, and different roles for commercial, military, and academic entities. The First Offset in the 1950s envisioned nuclear forces as a counterbalance to larger Soviet conventional forces. For the Second Offset in the 1970s, the United States invested in precision-guided weapons, stealth technology, and space-based military communications and navigation to counter Soviet numerical advantages. The Third Offset Strategy, as first announced in November 2014, envisions the US military leveraging and incorporating breakthroughs in robotics, autonomous systems, miniaturization, big data, and advanced manufacturing to counter anti-access and area denial challenges.

These Third Offset advantages will not provide the decades-long advantages of their predecessors. Former DARPA Director Prabhakar has noted that technological competition today is measured month to month, not in large, long-term offsets.[4] Another differentiator from previous offset strategies is the central role of innovation in the private sector. Former US Secretary of Defense Ash Carter has repeatedly visited Silicon Valley, where an innovation office known as DIUx (Defense Innovation Unit Experimental) is now open, with an additional branch planned for Boston.[5] The Silicon Valley branch opened in August 2015, but as of mid-May 2016, it was reported that no contracts had been offered.[6] The office's ability to work through the longstanding bureaucracy of US defense acquisition remains to be seen.

Chinese media and scholars are closely following the rollout of the Third Offset Strategy and considering the implications for China's defense industry. Chinese analysts consider US advantages to include innovation, cutting-edge systems, contributions from independent think tanks, and a strong civilian-military integrated national defense industrial base. Challenges to this innovation include pressures on defense budgets, lessened economic strength compared to other countries, and the lack of "home field advantage" as the US military must project force farther. The United States also needs clear technological strategies, improved defense procurement and purchasing, deepened military-civilian fusion, increases in defense education and innovation, updated wargame and analytical tools, clear defense requirements, and active innovation.[7]

Zhang Xiaobin, an author affiliated with China's State Administration for Science, Technology and Industry for National Defense, presents one of the most detailed analyses of how China should respond to the Third Offset Strategy. In his view, the proper response is for China's national defense industry both to avoid overspending as the Soviets did in response to the Second Offset Strategy, and to leverage the political advantages of China's governance system to focus on key programs.[8] Most relevant to artificial intelligence, Zhang also writes that the global proliferation of new technologies and R&D is beneficial to China. China should recruit top-level talent in leading technologies so that China may grasp and understand them. Then China should support military-civilian fusion led by the government and military. Finally, China should create an environment and policies that support exploration and forgive failures in defense technology development.[9]

A Basic Analytical Framework for China-US Competition in Emerging Technologies

Long-term forecasts for any strategic competition are challenging for areas as dynamic as emerging technologies. Our framework distills this competition to its simplest institutional entities to enable analysts to conceptualize models of future China–US strategic competitions related to AI and other emerging technologies. The following are the three basic institutional pillars or variables that will determine the success of each country's research, development, and acquisition (RDA) strategies:

1. Commercial Industry: Emerging technologies will increasingly come from the private sector and not from government entities, making private companies a key player in this competition.

2. Academe: Universities and laboratories have traditionally made technological breakthroughs for both the US and Chinese militaries. Their role will continue to be important and evolve based on their relationships with each other domestically and across borders.

3. Defense Industry: Defense companies and contractors will continue to be the primary providers of combat and support systems to the US and Chinese militaries.

This distilled organizational framework is shown in figure 8.

Figure 8. An "iron triangle" for defense S&T analysis.

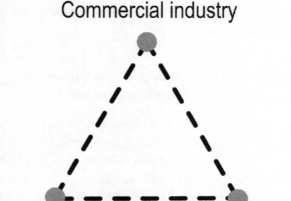

This framework of an 'iron triangle' is compatible with Chinese discussions of the same issues. Chinese S&T defense and civilian planning often refers to "industry, academe, and research institutes" (产学研).[10] Defense analysts see "three revolutions" that are disruptive to modern warfare, which are the scientific, industrial, and military revolutions.[11] Developments in each sector influence and rely upon the other two. This iron triangle of organizations provides a simplified visualization of the entities available to undertake R&D in any given country.

During the Cold War, this framework's RDA iron triangles were defined by barriers that largely prevented the transfer of technology, talent, and investment between the United States and the Soviet Union. Multilateral export control regimes and other regulations governed sales of strategic materials and technologies to Communist countries, and effectively blocked interactions between Western and Soviet bloc states. While both sides pursued open and clandestine activities to gather intelligence on the other's RDA accomplishments, the competition in the relationship significantly limited technology flows. Figure 9 provides a simplified visualization of this dynamic.

Figure 9. A simplified visualization of US-Soviet competition for emerging technologies.

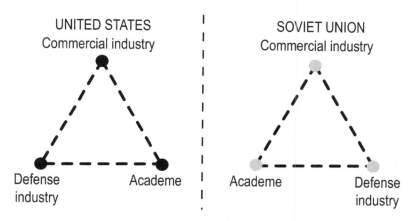

In complete contrast, today's China-US relationship sees deep fusion between the commercial industry and academe in both countries, and tremendous fluidity in transfers of technology, talent, and financing. Emerging technologies such as AI are being researched in facilities that are fully integrated between the two countries. While each country guards sensitive military projects, there is still significant fluidity between US entities and China's academic entities attached to the defense industry, such as the defense industrial universities associated with China's Ministry of Industry and Information Technology (MIIT). The deep integration of commercial and academic R&D between the US and China is visualized in figure 10. This simplified relationship is marked by extreme fluidity within Commercial Industry and Academe, which then selectively reaches back to the Defense Industrial base of each country.

Figure 10. A simplified visualization of China-US competition for emerging technologies.

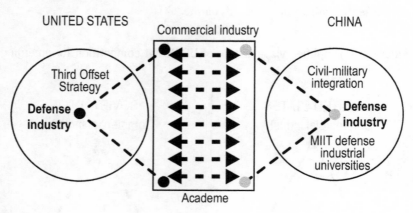

One underlying question within this framework is the extent to which commercial entities in each country are incentivized or compelled to cooperate with their respective defense establishments. There are clear economic incentives for both academic and commercial institutions to compete in each country's enormous civilian market. However, in the United States many primarily commercial entities have reportedly voiced concerns about the burdens of defense competition, in effect incentivizing them to compete in the global market rather than go through the painful bureaucratic exercises necessary for DoD vendors.[12] In contrast, China, as an authoritarian regime, is presumably able to compel commercial and academic entities to cooperate with their defense establishment. This asymmetric relationship between each country's defense and commercial entities permeates all six models in the next section.

China's Six Models for Achieving Strategic Objectives in AI and Other Emerging Technologies

Looking out over the next two decades, US and Chinese defense interests in the commercial space highlight the inherent fluidity of two systems that are at once friends and enemies. Based on the above framework, China pursues strategic objectives in AI and other emerging technologies through the six models below. Official Chinese writings do not explicitly detail this taxonomy, but official government planning and actions appear to sanction them. The end goal for each model is to transform China into the leading world power in emerging technologies. Each analysis below focuses on RDA efforts of AI technologies, and where necessary assesses emerging technologies more broadly or areas in which AI will be increasingly relevant.

A US Perspective on China's Models

China's prioritization of AI and other emerging technologies begins at the highest level with Xi Jinping's outlining of strategic objectives for S&T to 2030.[13] This announcement in November 2015, which now appears codified as "S&T Innovation 2030 Mega Projects" (科技创新2030重大项目), includes intelligent manufacturing and robotics as part of China's key S&T priorities.[14] Xi's personal announcement of key emerging technologies for strategic pursuit demonstrates the intense desire within China's leadership to provide top-level direction on the specific technological fields to be championed. Chinese media notes that China's 13th Five Year Plan (FYP) from 2016 to 2020 contains the first mention of artificial intelligence in a national-level FYP, and that the combination of AI as a subset of manufacturing and robotics marks a turning point in its importance within Chinese S&T planning.[15] In addition to these state plans, top-level initiatives such as "Made in China 2025" and "Internet Plus" explicitly state the importance for AI technologies in Chinese S&T development. In particular, the "Internet Plus" plan now has an entire sub-plan dedicated to AI, known as the "Internet + Artificial Intelligence

Three-Action Plan for Implementation" ("互联网+"人工智能三年行动
实施方案), discussed below.[16]

Model One: Domestic Chinese R&D Investment

Internal investment in domestic R&D is China's first model for achieving
its strategic objectives in AI and other emerging technologies, and is
the centerpiece on which all other models of technology acquisition and
transfer are built. This model directly allocates resources to national champions across commercial industry, academe, and the defense industry.
China's domestic R&D also drives other initiatives to acquire technology
and knowhow.

Chinese investment in S&T is guided by a series of planning documents
that begin at the highest levels of government and are implemented in
increasing detail down to individual laboratories. Key facets of these plans
include selecting national champion(s), increasing internal investment,
and training additional R&D personnel. This cult of self-reliance is a
hallmark of China's "Two Bombs One Satellite" ethos (despite having
benefited greatly from foreign tech transfer and knowhow).[17]

Despite the apparent displeasure of Chinese leaders with the S&T
funding programs, increased funding for R&D of AI and other machine
learning processes appears imminent. The massive restructuring of
domestic funding mechanisms currently underway, including the 863
and 973 programs, gives a glimpse into Chinese leadership's frustration
with the country's S&T progress in recent decades. Xinhua reports that
the restructure must "...address low efficiency resulting from redundant
programs."[18] Despite this apparent displeasure, the 13th FYP doubles down
on its selection of key technologies and institutions. The plan includes
massive investment and reorganization of state-owned enterprises in
combination with the first explicit mention of AI in an FYP.[19]

MIIT's planning document "Internet + Artificial Intelligence Three-
Action Plan for Implementation" demonstrates how Chinese S&T planning is domestically ramping up to pursue AI. It details development

goals for the integration of AI-enabling technologies through 2018. With sweeping calls for improved coordination between research and commercialization, the policies' overarching national goal is for China to "form myriad (one hundred billion) market applications for AI."[20]

The policy outlines the specific technological areas of interest and MIIT's broad goals for increased coordination between legacy and emerging research and commercialization. It calls for AI to span all areas of life including the home, automobiles, unmanned systems, and security. Another section of the plan outlines "Safeguards," or the six actions MIIT planners believe are necessary to achieve China's success in AI. In line with the historically domestic reliance of Chinese S&T, five of these six are focused on bolstering indigenous R&D and production, with only one mention of "international cooperation." These actions are the following:

1. Financial support (资金支持)
2. Standard system (标准体系)
3. Intellectual property rights (知识产权)
4. Talent cultivation (人才培养)
5. International cooperation (国际合作)
6. Organization and implementation (组织实施)

MIIT is directly responsible for managing China's state-owned commercial and defense conglomerates pursuing AI development. With this in mind, their first and most logical request is to increase financial support. What is interesting about this call for increased budgets is that it pivots from discussing central government's traditional role in coordinating national funding programs to highlighting the need to coordinate government funding with angel investors, venture capital, innovative capital funds, and capital market financing. The policy notes that these non-governmental streams of investment must be "guided and perfected" by the Chinese government. The policy therefore calls for both a doubling down of central government funding *and* an increased governmental role in directing investment types such as angel investors that would traditionally be thought of as private and fiercely independent.[21]

Model Two: Academic Exchange

China's global integration into the academic R&D of AI is a second key model for pursuing national objectives. Chinese researchers attached to academic institutions, whether universities or state-backed research institutes such as the Chinese Academy of Sciences (CAS), are fully integrated into the leading international communities for AI, machine learning, robotics, and other emerging technologies. Within our analytical framework, the entities driving this model reach beyond purely civilian academic organization to include defense-affiliated universities such as MIIT's seven universities and even research institutes affiliated with the People's Liberation Army (PLA).

Two case studies demonstrate how China leverages global academic exchanges to further its ambitions in AI. The first case study looks at the Beijing Institute of Technology (BIT) and its role as an organizational bridge between China's defense industry and global AI R&D. The second case study concerns the Chinese Association of Artificial Intelligence (CAAI), which both directly promotes China's interactions with the global AI community and is directly linked to the PLA.

One of China's leading engineering universities, BIT is directly affiliated with China's defense industry. It was overseen by the Commission for Science, Technology, and Industry for National Defense (COSTIND) through 2008, when COSTIND was merged into MIIT. BIT itself reports that the university also signed a "strategic cooperation agreement" with the PLA in June 2012.[22]

BIT is home to some of China's leading researchers of AI and robotics-related technologies, and plays host to leading defense entities. For example, the university hosts the Chinese Institute of Command and Control's Unmanned System Specialty Committee (中国指挥与控制学会无人系统专业委员会). This group brings together defense university-affiliated researchers, defense industry members, PLA research institutes, and PLA university researchers. The meeting's speaker list also includes the head of CAAI, profiled below.[23]

Despite its heavily PLA and defense-affiliated leanings, BIT is also deeply involved in global academic R&D of AI and robotics. BIT has at least three globally affiliated research centers attached to its School of Computer Science, each of which appears to research technologies applicable to AI and related advanced computing. These centers are:[24]

- BIT-DFKI Joint Lab of Language Information Processing, with German Research Center for Artificial Intelligence.
- The Joint Research Center for Neural Informatics, with Department of Linguistics State Key Laboratory of Brain and Cognitive Sciences, University of Hong Kong.
- Xilinx-BIT High Performance Networking Lab, with Xilinx, Inc., USA.

BIT also maintains significant ties to global commercial industry and academe. Relationships listed on its website include global leaders in AI and advanced computing such as Microsoft, IBM, Intel, and SAP.[25] Additional international exchanges have included undergraduates from the US Military Academy. Said to be working on robotics, these cadets visited BIT on a goodwill exchange.[26]

The CAAI is a second case that illustrates the fluidity that some members of China's academic community maintain between global AI R&D, the Chinese defense industry, and the PLA. Established in 1981, this national-level Chinese scientific society maintains 34 distinct subcommittees, covering the full spectrum of AI-related subfields.[27] CAAI's stated mission is to promote intelligent (智能化) S&T for China's economic development, civilized promotion, and security.[28]

CAAI is ostensibly a civilian academic organization, but many of its members, including its head, maintain direct connections to the PLA and China's defense-specific AI community. CAAI's chairman is Major General Li Deyi (李德毅), a researcher affiliated with the PLA General Staff Department's 61st Research Institute (总参第61研究所).[29] As a direct contributor to the PLA's highest S&T committees, Li's official biography reports that he is a member of the General Armament Department S&T Expert Committee (总装备部科技委委员), and the deputy director of the "All Army Informatization Office" (全军信息化工作办公室). His CAAI bio goes on to state that his research focuses on "command automation systems engineering and military informatization work" (指挥自动化系统工程和军队信息化工作).[30]

In addition to Li's direct affiliation to the PLA, he also maintains close ties to European and US academic communities. He received his PhD in the United Kingdom, and from 1994 to 1995 attended classes at Harvard before being named a major general in the PLA in 1996.[31] His contact with the global AI community has continued, and he regularly publishes in IEEE proceedings and is listed online as an academician in the International Academy of Sciences for Europe and Asia (国际欧亚科学院).

Furthermore, through his civilian affiliation with Tsinghua University, Li also routinely publishes internationally and in Western publications. An English-language biography for Li notes that he was a professor at Tsinghua University and that his "research interests include networked data mining, artificial intelligence with uncertainty, and cloud computing." [32] All of this information appears accurate, but neglects to mention Li's military affiliations.[33]

In 2014 Li was a coauthor with a leading US researcher and a Chinese colleague on a paper titled "Intelligent Carpool Routing for Urban Ridesharing by Mining GPS Trajectories." The paper provides a microcosm of the confluence of civilian, military, and international influences. The paper's lead author, Wen He, listed her affiliation as Tsinghua University, but the paper also notes her affiliation with the Institute of Chinese Electrical System Engineering (ICESE), which appears to be an alternative name for the 61st Research Institute.[34] The research is also a representative example of the tremendous fluidity between Chinese and US academic research and funding, as the US co-author was funded by a US multinational and a private investment fund, and the PLA participants were funded by a series of Chinese state funds.[35] The original international conference at which this research was presented in Beijing was jointly sponsored by the University of Illinois at Chicago, Microsoft, and MIT.[36]

Although only one micro-snapshot into joint China-US AI research, these papers provide a representative example of the fluidity possible in China-US research. From a funding standpoint, Chinese strategic national funds and private US funding can now easily be commingled in research. From the standpoint of China's civil-military integration, 61st Research Institute researchers are jointly undertaking research with Tsinghua University, China's premier S&T university, which is fully integrated into the global AI research infrastructure.

Model Three: Foreign R&D Investment
Direct foreign investment in R&D related to AI and other emerging technologies is a third model pursued by Chinese and US entities. This burgeoning model is bidirectional, with the creation of new R&D entities in the United States and Europe by Chinese entities and the establishment of R&D entities within China by US companies. The model is driven by commercial industry from the United States and China seeking improved economic returns and technological gains by directly placing their R&D investments abroad. Two cases demonstrating this model are Baidu's creation of an AI research center in Silicon Valley and Dell's establishment of a research center in China.

With Secretary of Defense Ash Carter stating that technologies from Silicon Valley are a key priority for DoD acquisition, it is interesting that a key investor of AI in the region is the Baidu Silicon Valley AI Lab (SVAIL/百度美国硅谷研发中心). SVAIL is the only US entity in a three-lab R&D cluster; its partner labs are based in Beijing. Its self-described mission includes "bring[ing] together top researchers, scientists, and engineers from around the world to work on fundamental AI research. Research areas include image recognition, speech recognition, natural language processing, robotics, and big data."[37]

Officially founded in 2013, SVAIL took off in 2014 when Baidu pledged to invest USD $300m in its Silicon Valley branch and hired Andrew Ng, a top AI researcher in the United States who previously served as the head of Google's successful Deep Learning project.[38] Baidu's US AI branch is now said to be home to more than 60 researchers, with an additional 100 Baidu employees working on non-AI issues nearby.[39] In looking forward, Baidu's recent financial success has led to it doubling down on Silicon Valley operations, stating that it plans to increase its AI work significantly, including in areas like driverless cars.[40]

In addition to Chinese-backed R&D investment in the United States, China also benefits from US investment in R&D within China. This dynamic is exemplified by Dell's recent US $125 million investment in China, which included the establishment of the "Artificial Intelligence and Advanced Computing Joint-Lab" (人工智能与先进计算联合实验室) as a joint venture with CAS.[41] Launched in 2015, details about the center's work are light, although it is reported to focus broadly on cognitive systems and deep learning.[42] Michael Dell has stated of his company's AI Lab, "Dell will embrace the principle of 'In China, for China' and closely integrate Dell China strategies with national policies in order to support Chinese technological innovation, economic development, and industrial transformation."[43]

According to some media reports, significant progress is already under way. Xu Bo, director of the CAS Institute of Automation, has stated, "CAS has built an artificial intelligence ecosystem, including theoretical innovation, core science and technology, and technology to application transfer, achieving a series of breakthroughs in recent years," and "... Dell has provided CAS R&D with an advanced computing platform."[44] With these transfers of technology and joint R&D underway, Dell's lab will be a key entity to watch as an example of the types of transfers that may continue developing within commercial industry in the China-US competition for emerging technologies.

It also appears that through their AI joint venture, Dell is expanding market access and interacting closely with defense-affiliated researchers. As a part of the initial launch of the lab and US $125 million investment, the partnership also included the launch of Dell-Kingsoft Cloud services, a partnership with China Electronics Corporation (CEC), and a relationship with Tsinghua Tongfang Co., Ltd.[45] In CEC and Tsinghua Tongfang, Dell has partnered with organizations that maintain close ties to the Chinese defense industry.[46]

Model Four: Mergers and Acquisitions

Under the Mergers and Acquisitions (M&A) model of competition, the Chinese government directs and supports Chinese companies acquiring foreign firms and, in turn, targeted technologies. Targeted acquisitions could provide Chinese firms with the intellectual property, quality controls, and brand recognition with which to reach international standards quickly. The risks and drawbacks include political backlash in the targeted countries and no guarantee that incorporating an innovative company will change the culture of the purchaser, that is, make it more innovative. This section uses China's recent moves in the semiconductor and integrated circuits (IC) industries as a case study to demonstrate the model, anticipating that as the commercial sphere for AI grows, so too will Chinese M&A activities in it.

China is investing heavily in its semiconductor industry after sporadic attempts since the 1970s. Consider that in the late 1990s China spent less than $1 billion in this field, whereas recently one bank assessed that the Chinese "government will muster $100 billion–$150 billion in public and private funds." This funding is backing widespread acquisitions to "buy as much foreign expertise as they can lay their hands on."[47]

In June 2014, China's State Council published its "National Guidelines for the Development and Promotion of the Integrated Circuit Industry" (国家集成电路产业发展推进纲要), which was drafted by China's MOF, MOST, MIIT, and NDRC.[48] The guideline calls for acceleration of China's IC design, manufacturing, and packaging industries and technology levels. To achieve these goals, the guideline calls for the establishment of a small group, a national industry investment fund, strengthened financial support, tax support policies, expanded application and use of secure and reliable software, strengthened industrial innovation, expansion of talent development and recruitment, and expanded opening toward the outside.[49] The guideline explicitly calls for recruiting foreign experts through the Thousand Talents program (explained in Model Five), indicating these models are not exclusive.

The IC funds warrant examination, as their financing, leadership, and roles in M&A deals all support and implement the State Council's guideline. The leading group is the China Integrated Circuit Industry Investment Fund (国家集成电路产业投资基金股份有限公司), established on September 24, 2014, by a large consortium including China National Tobacco, China Electronics Technology Corporation (CETC), and Tsinghua Unisplendour Co., Ltd. among others. Ding Wenwu, the fund's CEO, was the head of MIIT's Electronic Information Department, and may have served in that role at the same time as CEO as of November 2014.[50] By the end of 2014, the fund had already contributed to five offers to acquire foreign companies, including OmniVision Technologies Inc., maker of webcams for Apple.[51]

Questions remain as to how effective and politically viable this strategy will be for China's IC and semiconductor industries. As one skeptic notes, Chinese companies will have to shift from "a culture of cost to a culture of innovation," and one cannot simply buy cutting-edge research. Additionally, as seen in Tsinghua Unigroup's bid for US company Micron, the United States may deem such acquisitions as threats to critical infrastructure.[52] Tracking M&A activities by each of these funds warrants additional research, especially as computing demands for AI applications take form.

Model Five: Strategic Talent Recruitment

China's fifth model for pursuing advances in AI and other emerging technologies is the systematic recruitment of individuals possessing advanced knowhow in priority technologies. From the standpoint of the analytic framework, this recruitment incorporates nearly every entity within academe and commercial industry. China's talent recruitment takes place through dozens of national and local-level programs, each of which possesses its own process for advertising, vetting, and selecting recruits. Furthermore, each recruitment plan has its own guidelines regarding whether a person must be full or part-time in China, the length of their contract, and the amount of financial compensation and other benefits received.

Despite the variety of circumstances under which "talented persons" (人才) are recruited, there are a number of unifying forces behind these efforts. The case study below from CAS's Shenyang Institute of Automation (SIA) is an illustrative example of these commonalities.

First, across all of China's national and provincial-level recruitment programs, the Chinese government largely provides the financial incentives for recruited individuals, not the organization where the individual will work, such as a startup, state-owned enterprise, or university. Second, the Chinese government, through its national-level planning and global outreach, directly manages the specific technologies and types of individuals sought. Hence China's recruitment programs are focused on achieving breakthroughs and indigenous commercialization of targeted technologies, and are not driven by science for science's sake or economic motivations. Third, in the case of the Thousand Talents plan and its affiliated programs, the Chinese Communist Party's Organization Department directly manages the vetting and recruitment process. The Thousand Talents plan is China's largest and best-funded recruitment plan, and along with the CAS 100 plan, is the channel for recruitment in the SIA case study.

From the perspective of the proposed analytic framework, SIA straddles industry and academe, serving as an educational center, research institute, and production facility within CAS. Founded in November 1958, SIA describes itself as the national leader and "cradle of China's robotics technology" and has achieved "more than 20 'firsts' in robotics development."[53] SIA's R&D of emerging technologies is closely linked with the Chinese government and defense industry. Its mission is "making significant contributions to society, the economy, and national security."[54] In addition to its domestic role, SIA is active in global R&D networks, stating on its website that "[s]ince 1985, SIA has established exchange and collaboration programs with universities, research institutes and high-tech companies in the United States, Russia, Japan and various European countries. Nearly 100 SIA researchers travel abroad annually to participate in various exchange activities."[55]

SIA is also an active participant in the Chinese government's recruitment of individuals possessing specific technological knowhow. In May 2016, the Office of Educational Affairs of the PRC Embassy in the United States posted a recruitment notice for SIA, which provides specific guidance on the institute's goals and technological needs. The notice provides a list of scientific fields required for recruitment that includes "special robots, underwater vehicles, space automation, optical information technology, manufacturing technology and equipment, and industrial control networks and systems."[56]

Beyond specific technological knowhow sought, the announcement also details the recruitment mechanisms and significant financial incentives available to recruits. The three recruitment programs offered include the Thousand Talents Program, CAS 100 Talents Program, and the SIA 100 Talents Program. Each of these programs provides varying levels of funding from the Chinese government to individuals with a proven track record in the technologies sought. At the highest end, both the

Thousand Talents Program and CAS 100 Talents Program state in this recruitment ad that they can provide up to RMB 10 million (approx. USD $1.5 million) in funds.[57]

Model Six: Traditional Espionage

Under the traditional espionage model, government actors forgo their own domestic entities (academe, commercial, and potentially the military industry) to acquire foreign technologies illicitly from abroad, either physically or digitally. It is unclear whether China is or would directly spy on or penetrate the networks of US firms engaging in AI research. What is clear, however, is that Chinese espionage reportedly remains active in the form of cyber espionage and conspiracies to commit export control violations.

Cyber intrusions by Chinese actors have reportedly yielded massive amounts of data on sensitive technologies, including unmanned systems that could be future platforms for any AI breakthroughs. In 2013, an American cybersecurity firm covered Operation Beebus, a years-long operation by Chinese hackers to steal US designs and relevant technologies for UAVs.[58] In March 2016, Chinese national Su Bin pleaded guilty in a years-long conspiracy to hack into systems of major US defense contractor Boeing. Although unmanned systems were not mentioned specifically, Boeing's vast portfolio includes numerous unmanned systems.[59]

The US Department of Justice and Bureau of Industry Security have also released details of several instances of individuals conspiring to export components and technologies for unmanned systems. Six such cases involved UAV technologies such as autopilots, and one involved components for unmanned underwater vehicles.[60]

For AI research, the most relevant espionage risks likely involve insiders helping steal data or target systems for Chinese hackers. A consideration for US policymakers is the need to thoroughly vet researchers involved in emerging technologies to mitigate security risks. For private companies advancing AI, insider threats pose risks to both national security and their own intellectual property.

CONCLUSIONS

China-US competition in emerging technologies is unprecedented because the rapid disruption cycles in technologies and the deep fusion of cross-border research, talent exchanges, and investments. Instead of the Cold War's managed interactions between academic, defense, and commercial communities, US and Chinese companies are foundationally intertwined. The economic gains, strategic risks, and fluid interactions of communities across borders present a paradox for China-US competitive strategies, as both sides are at once friends and enemies. It is almost ironic that today both China's Baidu and the DoD's DIUx are aggressively pursuing AI in Silicon Valley.

To navigate this dynamic and for competitive strategies such as the Third Offset to succeed, it is important for US policymakers to take stock of this dynamic and the different strategies and advantages at play. This chapter's analytical framework and the six models that China adopts to pursue emerging technologies like AI can benefit these discussions. A key takeaway is that while China's defense procurement system may have many problems, there are few barriers against the government reaching into commercial industries for defense purposes. China's advantage of picking national champions can also prove crucial if it is able to predict key players and potential breakthroughs. With this advantage and other strategies ranging from M&A activity to talent recruitment, China has many tools to complement its pursuit of AI and other emerging technologies.

While a full comparison of US and Chinese strategies for pursuing technologies like AI is beyond the scope of this chapter, it is evident that with regard to competitive strategies, the United States and China have fundamentally different advantages and disadvantages. While the United

States has long-held advantages in its commercial and academic R&D, major structural problems exist in a DoD procurement system that often make it incompatible with startup costs. One analyst describes the system as "baroque" and comments that it forces US tech companies to choose between pursuing markets or making the Pentagon their sole customer.[61] In contrast, China has made tremendous investments but still lags in its commercial and academic R&D capabilities. It is easier for China, however, to target technologies, designate national champions, and gain access to technology breakthroughs in its academic and commercial sectors.

As a hypothetical for this point, consider Baidu and Google's pursuit of AI technologies and how any breakthroughs may benefit their host country. It is hard to imagine Baidu, with its political connections and oversight, refusing access by PRC government or military entities to algorithms, products, or other technologies. Google, on the other hand, has regularly contested US government access to data and supported Apple's refusal to decrypt an iPhone belonging to the San Bernardino shooter in 2015. Even if Baidu's AI technology lags that of Google (although this may no longer be the case), the PRC may leverage it much more easily and quickly.

Another initial observation from China's competition models is that the PRC holds a distinct advantage in informal and illicit technology acquisitions. PRC and political entities guide and oversee the recruitment of leading talent from abroad to support the country's technological development. This centralized approach enables the Chinese government to prioritize strategic concerns over market forces. Additionally, as China has benefited from illicit technology acquisitions through means such as cyberattacks, it is unlikely that the United States can benefit from such activities. Whereas the PLA could target US entities for Chinese commercial entities, the United States has formidable legal barriers and media oversight that prevent conducting similar activities for US commercial entities.

Ultimately, if one frames China-US competition for defense-use AI as a "race," the US Third Offset strategy is pitted against China's six models for technology acquisition defined in this chapter. Although the United States may be unable to compete in some of these models, it can and must get out of its own way by reforming its procurement practices and recalibrating incentives. Academic exchanges, commercial trade, and R&D in the United States are still the world's gold standard, and US competitive strategies must learn to leverage those advantages to ensure military technological advantages. For China, the key test will be whether it can develop a truly innovative and risk-taking culture in its domestic industries, as opposed to just pursuing technology transfer strategies. If China cannot do so, the technology transfer models in this chapter will continue to be a dependency and not an enabler for its pursuit of emerging technologies.

For the coming decades, the peacetime competition between China and the United States will likely continue to take place in a strategic paradox of "frenemies." As seen in this case study, the competition will largely come down to the US ability to reform defense procurement and engage the private sector, versus the Chinese capability to truly indigenize innovation. In the longer term, the United States must account for and respond to China's other models of technology acquisition. Moves in this competition may address talent recruitment, foreign investment and acquisitions, cyberattacks, and other means. Doing so will ensure that the United States maintains technological advantages in the China-US strategic competition.

Notes

1. Vivek Wadhwas, "The Amazing Artificial Intelligence We Were Promised Is Coming, Finally," *Washington Post*, June 17, 2016, https://www.washingtonpost.com/news/innovations/wp/2016/06/17/the-amazing-artificial-intelligence-we-were-promised-is-coming-finally/.

2. Mark Pomerleau, "DARPA Director Clear-Eyed and Cautious on AI," *GCN*, May 10, 2016, https://gcn.com/articles/2016/05/10/darpa-ai.aspx.

3. Clay Dillow, "What the X-47B Reveals about the Future of Autonomous Flight," *Popular Science*, July 5, 2013, http://www.popsci.com/technology/article/2013-05/five-things-you-need-know-about-x-47b-and-coming-era-autonomous-flight.

4. Christian Davenport, "Robots, Swarming Drones, and 'Iron Man': Welcome to the New Arms Race," *Washington Post*, June 17, 2016, https://www.washingtonpost.com/news/checkpoint/wp/2016/06/17/robots-swarming-drones-and-iron-man-welcome-to-the-new-arms-race/?hpid=hp_rhp-more-top-stories_no-name%3Ahomepage%2Fstory.

5. Aaron Mehta, "DIUX Expands to Boston, with New Leadership," *Defense News*, May 11, 2016, https://www.jsonline.com/story/defense-news/techwatch/2016/05/11/diux-expands-boston-new-leadership/84233338/.

6. Aaron Mehta, "Leadership, Structural Changes for DoD Silicon Valley Office," *Defense News*, May 11, 2016, http://www.defensenews.com/story/defense/innovation/2016/05/11/diux-silicon-valley-pentagon-ash-carter/84203664/.

7. Li Jian, "Xin dixiao zhanlüe: Meiguo yi jishu youshi mouqiu chixu jun-shi youshi de lao taolu he xin sikao" 新抵消战略#美国以技术优势谋求持续军事优势的老套路和新思考 [New offset strategy: An old means with new thinking for the us to maintain military dominance], 空天力量杂志 [Air and space power] 9, no. 2 (2015): 92–94.

8. Zhang Xiaobin, "Meiguo 'di san ci dixiao zhanlüe' dui guofang keji gongye de tiaozhan yu yingdui" 美国"第三次抵消战略"对国防科技工业的挑战与应对 [The challenge imposed by the third US offset strategy on the development of defense science and technology industry and contermeasures [*sic*]], 国防科技 [National defense science and technology] 36, no. 6 (2015): 74–76.

9. Ibid.

10. "Chan xue yan" 产学研 [Industry, academia, institutes], Baidu, http://baike.baidu.com/view/1319202.htm.

11. Wu Ji, Shen Xushi, Zhao Haiyang, and Xu Xiaoping, "Dianfu xing jishu de fazhan yu qiangzhan xin 'san da geming' zhanlüe zhigaodian" 颠覆性技术的发展与抢占新"三大革命"战略制高点" ["Grasping developping [sic] opportunities of disruptive technologies and surging to strategic highland of new 'tri-revolution'"], 国防科技 [*National Defense Science and Technology*] 36, no. 3 (2015): 23–26, 58.

12. Brian Fung, "The Huge Issue That's Keeping Silicon Valley and the Pentagon Apart," The Switch [blog], *Washington Post*, June 10, 2016, https://www.washingtonpost.com/news/the-switch/wp/2016/06/10/the-pentagon-wants-to-cozy-up-to-silicon-valley-heres-one-big-thing-keeping-them-apart/.

13. "Xi Jinping: guanyu 'Zhonggong Zhongyang guanyu zhiding guomin jingji he shehui fazhan di shisan ge wu nian guihua de jianyi' de shuoming" 习近平:关于《中共中央关于制定国民经济和社会发展第十三个五年规划的建议》的说明 [Xi Jinping: explanation of the 'Proposal of the CPC Central Committee on formulating the 13th five-year plan for national economic and social development] Xinhua, November 11, 2015, http://news.xinhuanet.com/politics/2015-11/03/c_1117029621_3.htm.

14. "Wan Gang: mianxiang 2030 linxian qidong hangkong fadongji deng yi pi keji chuangxin zhongda xiangmu" 万钢：面向2030遴选启动航空发动机等一批科技创新重大项目 [Wan Gang: target 2030 selection and launch of aero engines and other major projects for scientific and technological innovation], Xinhua, January 11, 2016, http://www.xinhuanet.com/fortune/2016-01/11/c_1117739527.htm. Other technological priorities are jet engines, quantum communications, cyberspace, deep sea and space exploration, key new materials, and neurosciences.

15. "'Shisanwu': Zhongguo kaiqi rengong zhineng shangyong xin jiyuan" "十三五"#中国开启人工智能商用新纪元 ['Thirteenth Five Year': China launches new era of artificial intelligence business], Phoenix News, March 8, 2016, http://finance.ifeng.com/a/20160308/14257713_0.shtml.

16. Ministry of Industry and Information Technology, "'Hulianwang+' rengong zhineng san nian xingdong shishi fang'an" "互联网+"人工智能三年行动实施方案 ['Internet Plus' artificial intelligence three-year action plan], May 18, 2016, http://www.miit.gov.cn/n1146290/n1146392/c4808445/part/4808453.pdf.

17. China's dedication to self-reliance has evolved into the concept of "indigenous innovation," which calls for adapting and re-innovating foreign technologies to suit Chinese needs.

18. "China Inaugurates National R&D Plan," Xinhua, February 16, 2016, http://news.xinhuanet.com/english/2016-02/16/c_135104108.htm.

19. "Xi Boosts Party Say in China's $18 Trillion State Company Sector," Bloomberg News, July 7, 2016, http://www.bloomberg.com/news/articles/2016-07-07/xi-boosts-party-say-in-china-s-18-trillion-state-company-sector; "'Shisanwu': Zhongguo kaiqi rengong zhineng shangyong xin jiyuan," March 8, 2016.

20. Ministry of Industry and Information Technology, "'Internet Plus' artificial intelligence three-year action plan." May 18, 2016.

21. Ibid.

22. Beijing Institute of Technology News, June 6, 2012, http://www.bit.edu.cn/xww/xys/blgxzdt/76907.htm.

23. "Beijing Ligong Daxue yu Jiefangjun Ligong Daxue qianshu zhanlüe hezuo xieyi" 北京理工大学与解放军理工大学签署战略合作协议 [Beijing Institute of Technology signs strategic cooperation agreement with PLA University of Science and Technology], http://www.bit.edu.cn/gbxxgk/gbxysz2/jdxy/jdxyxwdt/104138.htm.

24. "School of Computer Science and Technology," Bejing Institute of Technology, November 6, 2015, http://english.bit.edu.cn/academics/SchoolsDepartments/78025.htm.

25. Ibid.

26. "Summer Opportunities," Department of Electrical Engineering and Computer Science, US Military Academy West Point, http://www.westpoint.edu/eecs/sitepages/summer%20opportunities.aspx.

27. "Zhongguo rengong zhineng xuehui" 中国人工智能学会 [China association for artificial intelligence], December 18, 2015, http://www.caai.cn/index.php?s=/Home/Article/index/id/2.html.

28. Ibid.

29. "Li Deyi" 李德毅 [Li Deyi], Baidu, http://baike.baidu.com/view/1245508.htm.

30. "Zhongguo rengong zhineng xuehui," December 18, 2015.

31. "Li Deyi," Baidu.

32. Kai Hwang and Deyi Li, "Trusted Cloud Computing with Secure Resources and Data Coloring," IEEE Internet Computing (September/October 2010): 14–22, http://gridsec.usc.edu/hwang/papers/05562490.pdf.

33. "Li Deyi," Baidu.

34. "Wangluo shidai rengong zhineng yanjiu yu fazhan" 网络时代人工智能研究与发展 [AI research and development in the network age], 国家自然科学基金资助项目 (60496323, 60675032) [National Natural Science Foundation of China Fund subsidized project]; 国家973计划资助项目 (2004CB719401, 2007CB310800) [Nation 973 Plan subsidized project]. Li Deyi has previously listed his affiliation with ICESE when publishing in Chinese as a researcher from the GSD 61st.

35. Wen He, Kai Hwang, and Deyi Li, "Intelligent Carpool Routing for Urban Ridesharing by Mining GPS Trajectories," *IEEE Transactions on Intelligent Transportation Systems* 15, no. 5 (2014): 2286–2296.

36. "ACM SIGKDD International Workshop on Urban Computing (UrbComp 2012)," https://www.cs.uic.edu/~urbcomp2012/.

37. Baidu Research home page, http://research.baidu.com/.

38. Daniela Hernandez, "'Chinese Google' Opens Artificial Intelligence Lab in Silicon Valley," *Wired*, April 12, 2013, http://www.wired.com/2013/04/baidu-research-lab/; Paul Mozur and Rolfe Winkler, "Baidu to Open Artificial-Intelligence Center in Silicon Valley," *Wall Street Journal*, May 16, 2014, http://www.wsj.com/articles/SB10001424052702304908304579565950123054242; Pete Carey, "Andrew Ng, Chief Scientist, Chinese Search Giant Baidu," *San Jose Mercury News*, March 16, 2016, http://phys.org/news/2016-03-andrew-ng-chief-scientist-chinese.html.

39. Tekla S. Perry, "Checking in with Andrew Ng at Baidu's Blooming Silicon Valley Research Lab," *IEEE Spectrum*, February 12, 2016, http://spectrum.ieee.org/view-from-the-valley/robotics/artificial-intelligence/checking-in-with-andrew-ng-at-baidus-blooming-silicon-valley-research-lab.

40. David Ramli, "Baidu Flags More Spending on Cars after Profit Beats Estimates," Bloomberg, April 28, 2016, http://www.bloomberg.com/news/articles/2016-04-28/baidu-first-quarter-profit-revenue-outlook-beat-estimates.

41. "Dell Announces Its New "in China, for China" Strategy to Support Job Creation; Propel Entrepreneurship and Innovation," press release, September 10, 2015, https://www.dell.com/learn/us/en/vn/press-releases/2015-09-14-dell-announces-its-new-in-china.

42. March 3, 2012, http://china.huanqiu.com/article/2016-03/8694357.html.

43. Jack Clark, "Dell Expands in China with Venture Group, Creates AI Lab," Bloomberg, September 9, 2015, http://www.bloomberg.com/news/articles/2015-09-10/dell-expands-in-china-with-venture-group-creation-of-ai-lab.

44. "Zhongguo kexueyuan yu dai'er kaita zhineng keji yanfa xin lingyu" 中国科学院与戴尔开拓智能科技研发新领域 [Chinese Academy of Sciences and Dell open new areas for research and development of smart technologies], *China News*, May 26, 2015, http://www.chinanews.com/it/2016/05-26/7884607.shtml.

45. Dell press release.

46. James Mulvenon and Rebecca Samm Tyroler-Cooper, "China's Defense Industry on the Path of Reform," report prepared for the US-China Economic and Security Review Commission, October 2009, http://dtic.mil/dtic/tr/fulltext/u2/a523026.pdf.

47. "Chips on Their Shoulders," *Economist*, January 23, 2016, http://www.economist.com/news/business/21688871-china-wants-become-superpower-semiconductors-and-plans-spend-colossal-sums.

48. "Guojia jicheng dianlu chanye fazhan tuijin gangyao" 国家集成电路产业发展推进纲要 [National integrated circuit industry development outline], Electronic Information Industry Net, July 1, 2014, http://cyyw.cena.com.cn/2014-07/01/content_231406.htm; "Yang Xueshan jiedu 'Guojia jicheng dianlu chanye fazhan tuijin gangyao'" 杨学山解读《国家集成电路产业发展推进纲要》 [Yang Xueshan explains 'National integrated circuit industry development outline'], Netease, June 24, 2016, http://money.163.com/14/0624/17/9VH6FVI800254TI5.html.

49. "Guojia jicheng dianlu chanye fazhan tuijin gangyao," July 1, 2014.

50. "Shanghai chengli bai yi guimo jicheng dianlu jijin lianfake deng canyu" 上海成立百亿规模集成电路基金 联发科等参与 [Shanghai establishes 10 billion-scale integrated circuit fund; MediaTek and others participate], Sina, November 24, 2014, http://tech.sina.com.cn/it/2014-11-24/doc-icczmvun0274029.shtml; Ministry of Industry and Information Technology General Office, "Gongye he xinxihua bu bangongting guanyu juban di yi jie Zhongguo dianzi xinxi bolanhui de tongzhi" 工业和信息化部办公厅关于举办第一届中国电子信息博览会的通知 [Ministry of Industry and Information Technology General Office notice to hold first China electronic information expo], November 5, 2012, http://www.hfgj.gov.cn/10639/10641/201301/P020150905324843814031.pdf.

51. "Jicheng dianlu chanye touzi jijin lai xi quxiang hefang?" 集成电路产业投资基金来袭 去向何方? [Where did IC industry investment go?], Hexun, December 23, 2014, http://tech.hexun.com/2014-12-23/171694566.html; George Stahl, "OmniVision Agrees to $1.9 Billion Buyout," *Wall Street Journal*, April 30, 2015, http://www.wsj.com/articles/omnivision-agrees-to-1-9-billion-buyout-1430396689.

52. "Chips on Their Shoulders," *Economist*, January 23, 2016.
53. "Brief Introduction of SIA," Shenyang Institute of Automation, Chinese Academy of Sciences, updated December 30, 2013, http://english.sia.cas. cn/au/bi/201312/t20131230_115083.html.
54. Ibid.
55. Ibid.
56. "Zhongguo kexueyuan Shenyang zidonghua yanjiusuo chengji hai nei wai yingcai jiaru" 中国科学院沈阳自动化研究所诚邀海内外英才加入 [Chinese academy of sciences Shenyang institute of automation invites talents from home and abroad to join], Office of Educational Affairs of the Embassy of PR China in USA, May 23, 2016, http://www.sino-education.org/publish/portal131/tab6578/info126647.htm.
57. Ibid.
58. Edward Wong, "Hacking US Secrets, China Pushes for Drones," *New York Times*, September 20, 2013, http://www.nytimes.com/2013/09/21/world/asia/hacking-us-secrets-china-pushes-for-drones.html?_r=0; Alex Pasternak, "Hackers Are Helping China Build Cheap Clones of America's Drones," *Motherboard*, September 23, 2013, https://motherboard.vice.com/en_us/article/mgbqk8/hackers-are-helping-china-build-cheap-clones-of-americas-drones; John E. Dunn, "Chinese Malware Targeted US Drone Secrets, Security Firm Alleges," *TechWorld*, February 4, 2013, http://www.techworld.com/news/security/chinese-malware-targeted-us-drone-secrets-security-firm-alleges-3424289/.
59. Matt Apuzzo, "Chinese Businessman Is Charged in Plot to Steal US Military Data," *New York Times*, July 11, 2014, http://www.nytimes.com/2014/07/12/business/chinese-businessman-is-charged-in-plot-to-steal-us-military-data.html.
60. US Department of Justice, "Summary of Major US Export Enforcement, Economic Espionage, Trade Secret and Embargo-Related Criminal Cases (January 2010 to the Present: Updated June 27, 2016)," June 2016, https://www.justice.gov/nsd/files/export_case_list_june_2016_2.pdf/download.
61. Fung, "The Huge Issue That's Keeping Silicon Valley and the Pentagon Apart."

CHAPTER 8

RUSSIAN PERSPECTIVES ON THE THIRD OFFSET STRATEGY AND ITS IMPLICATIONS FOR RUSSIAN–CHINESE DEFENSE TECHNOLOGICAL COOPERATION

Vasily Kashin

The development of the US Third Offset Strategy has been closely watched by the Russian Ministry of Defense, the Russian defense industry, and Russian academics and government agencies. Although Russia has active technology development programs comparable to those associated with the Third Offset Strategy, the Russian authorities are paying close attention to what effects US technological breakthroughs might have on strategic, especially nuclear, stability. In light of worsening relations with the West, Russia seems to be reconsidering its previous model of defense industry cooperation with China. Joining efforts at this stage may be seen by Moscow and Beijing as the only way to prevent the United States from gaining a decisive military and technological advantage.

RUSSIAN VIEWS OF THE THIRD OFFSET STRATEGY

The Third Offset Strategy is rarely, if ever, directly mentioned in public statements by Russian officials. Russia's military leadership is dealing instead with separate US technological initiatives and projects associated with the strategy. Some of these are being emulated, others considered for the possibility of an asymmetrical response. At the same time, Russian government agencies and the academic community are closely monitoring the strategy as it develops.

The Third Offset Strategy is viewed by Russian researchers as a response primarily to China's expansion of its anti-access/area denial capabilities and secondarily to the growth of Russian defense capabilities. In examining the possible technological outcomes of the strategy, Russia has been paying close attention to its influence on strategic stability, since nuclear planning traditionally has been the basis of Russian security planning. The impact of the Third Offset Strategy on Russian conventional force capabilities is given lesser, but still significant, attention. As well, Russia has active counterparts of most of the US development programs associated with the Third Offset Strategy, such as robotics, artificial intelligence (AI), cognitive technologies, unmanned underwater platforms, additive technologies, and hypersonic weapons.

The introduction of the Third Offset Strategy happened at around the same time as major changes in relations between Russia and the West brought on by the 2014–2015 Ukrainian crisis. In the current climate of renewed confrontation between Russia and NATO, coupled with Western technology sanctions and an economic downturn, Russia is reconsidering its previous model of defense industry cooperation with

China. This cooperation is no longer the one-way street of the past, when Russia provided China with defense equipment and technology in exchange for cash.

The role of Russian companies as subcontractors in Chinese defense industry research and development (R&D) and production projects has grown in recent years. A good example of such cooperation is the agreement on an advanced heavy helicopter project signed during Russian President Vladimir Putin's visit to China in June 2016.

Russia and China may be moving to a mutually dependent industrial alliance, as opposed to the one-sided dependence of the past. This trend will be supported by increased Chinese participation in Russian civilian industries such as automobiles and electronics.

Sharing resources may be the best way for the two countries to counter overall US technological superiority. Two factors are making such cooperation increasingly effective now. Politically, both countries are experiencing a long-term deterioration of their respective relations with the United States. Additionally, after more than a decade of regular large-scale military exercises, the two countries' militaries have made significant progress in improving interoperability. Russia's military reform program in 2008–2009 can be seen as one of the key sources of inspiration for China's far-reaching military reform started by Xi Jinping at the end of 2015.

Russian writings on the Third Offset Strategy consider it a major US initiative aimed at maintaining general military and defense technology advantages over potential adversaries, primarily China and Russia, at a time when the US share of global GDP is gradually decreasing and the US armed forces are facing increasingly tight budgets. US policy is also increasingly influenced by technological factors. Previously, the US defense industry was a major technological driver of the civilian economy (for example, nuclear energy, aerospace, and the Internet). Now many important defense innovations are emerging from the civilian sector. The view of some Russian researchers is that the Defense Innovation

Initiative, the basis of the Third Offset Strategy, is aimed at maintaining US military technological superiority in the twenty-first century despite ongoing budgetary constraints.[1]

The US Second Offset Strategy had two main components: 1) aggressive investments into advanced technology development in the most promising areas; and 2) denial of technological achievements to adversaries through an extensive export control system. As the Third Offset Strategy develops, there is a general expectation that the US export control system will expand even more, seriously affecting civilian industries that are expected to contribute technology to the defense industry.

Russian researchers emphasize that the Pentagon is paying special attention to both mature and future civilian technologies.[2] This includes technologies that are already widely used in the civilian sector of the economy that could be transferred to the defense industry.

Russian specialists are also closely monitoring the ongoing discussion in the US defense community concerning the Third Offset Strategy and note that the response from the US defense community is increasingly skeptical. Although the majority of US defense technology experts are not against the strategy as such, many argue that trying to reproduce the experience of the 1970s likely will not work. In fact, while the previous offset strategy was widely considered a success, it was never tested in combat against a major military power.

Based on these factors, some Russian analysts conclude that

> there is every reason to believe that while implementing the Third Offset Strategy, the United States will be primarily focused on ensuring their technological superiority over the PRC as the main competitor to the United States in the Asia-Pacific.[3]

Secondary objectives are seen to be achieving and maintaining a decisive superiority over rivals such as Russia, Iran, and North Korea. This view of the Third Offset Strategy as primarily an "anti-Chinese" initiative, although having serious strategic implications for Russia, appears to be widespread. It can be found not just in scholarly publications, but also in the general circulation media outlets of the Russian Ministry of Defense.[4]

STRATEGIC STABILITY

Russia is most concerned with the potential effects of the Third Offset Strategy on strategic stability, with special attention paid to non-nuclear systems. For example, programs associated with long-range strike capability, such as the Long-range Strategic Bomber, possible upgrades to the B-2A Spirit stealth bomber, or future naval cruise missiles, could become elements of a US global surveillance and strike system. Other examples of such non-nuclear technologies affecting strategic stability are anti-satellite weapons, ballistic missile defense systems, and cyber weapons.[5] While many of these priorities existed before the Third Offset Strategy was initiated, they are viewed with increasing suspicion by the Russian government.

The key areas of Russian concern, such as development of ballistic missile defense technology and non-nuclear strategic weapon systems (such as the Prompt Global Strike program) were addressed in the national security strategy signed by President Dimitry Medvedev in 2009.[6] Per this strategy, Russia would undertake an asymmetric response to the deployment of US ballistic missile defense and PGS systems, while avoiding engagement in an arms race.[7] In 2012, then Prime Minister Vladimir Putin wrote that these new weapons systems can be comparable to nuclear weapons in their strategic effects while being more 'acceptable' to politicians and military leaders.[8]

The most important breakthroughs affecting strategic stability are expected to take place in cyber and hypersonic vehicles development. Another area of concern is robotic systems development. The impact of nanotechnology and cognition technologies is less clear. The industry that is expected to undergo the deepest transformation, according to Russian views, will be the aerospace industry. The development of new anti-ballistic missile defense and anti-satellite weapons, the emergence of new types of hypersonic vehicles, new generations of space carrier rockets, and other new systems create the potential for a turning point in this industry sometime after 2020.

THE RUSSIAN RESPONSE TO THE THIRD OFFSET STRATEGY

Russia so far has not undertaken any measures that can be seen primarily as responses to the Third Offset Strategy. However, the Third Offset Strategy is based on a number of US initiatives, ideas, and priorities that had been in existence long before the strategy was finalized or even announced, and these components have triggered Russian responses that affect its nuclear planning, institutional reforms, and technology policies.

For many years, Russia's military policy has been built on the assumption that a military conflict with a major foreign power is the main threat to Russian security. The adversary is expected to have a powerful defense industrial base and to do everything possible to achieve complete domination over Russia in defense technology. The greatest danger to the security of Russia, according to official Russian documents, is posed by the expected attempts by "major foreign powers" to develop new technologies that will reduce the effectiveness of Russian strategic nuclear forces. The emergence of the Third Offset Strategy seems to some Russian analysts to substantiate this view, thus warranting even closer attention by Russia to defense technology developments in the United States.

This shift in Russian views of future warfare is not new, however. It started after the NATO operation in Kosovo in 1999, when Moscow started to look seriously for the first time at the possibility of military confrontation with the West. After the 2008 military conflict with Georgia, the shift in the Russian viewpoint became irreversible. Russia now officially accepts the idea that the main source of external military threats would not be international terrorists but a major foreign power.

The "National Security Strategy of the Russian Federation to 2020," signed by President Medvedev in May 2009, stated that the main threats to Russian security in the military domain were the attempts of some "leading foreign countries" to achieve an "overwhelming advantage in the military field, especially in strategic nuclear forces" by developing new types of weapons, including non-nuclear strategic systems, space systems, information technology, and other high-technology methods and tools for warfighting.[9] This underscores the notion that Russian security planning has been based for a long time on the assumption that the United States was aggressively pursuing technological initiatives to achieve some kind of military dominance.

Russia is engaged in a number of high-profile nuclear programs while maintaining or even strengthening the role of tactical nuclear weapons, which are seen primarily as a way to offset Russian weaknesses in the conventional field. This brings to mind parallels to responses to the first US offset strategy, President Eisenhower's "New Look." For example, an article in the scientific journal of the Russian Ministry of Defense's 46th Research Institute, the main center responsible for long-term planning of Russian military R&D and procurement policies, argues that:

> for implementing the tasks of deterrence and repelling an aggression on the regional level, currently and for the mid-term perspective, the tactical nuclear weapons are and will be the balancer of forces, stripping NATO (and China) of their superiority in conventional weapons ... maintaining and development of the ground, air and sea-based tactical nuclear weapon systems should be one of the main dimensions of the Russian military technical policy.[10]

Since the late 1990s, Russia has invested resources into new types of tactical nuclear weapons, including nuclear warheads for naval and air-launched cruise missiles as well as ground-based short-range ballistic and cruise missiles and nuclear warheads for air defense systems and torpedo weapons. Rearmament of ground forces with the nuclear-capable Iskander (SS-26 Stone) family of short-range missile systems capable of using both ballistic and cruise missiles is one of the priorities of the State Program of Rearmament (GPV-2020). As of June 2016, seven Russian Army missile brigades were rearmed with SS-26s, and the Russian military expects to have 10 such brigades by 2020. Russian leaders publicly emphasize the nuclear capabilities of the new Russian tactical missile systems.

In December 2015, after Russian naval and air-launched cruise missiles were used for the first time in the Syrian war, President Vladimir Putin appeared on TV to emphasize that "these are new, modern, highly-effective weapons which can be equipped with a conventional or special warhead, which means nuclear warhead."[11] In March 2015, Putin had stated that during the Crimean crisis he was ready to use nuclear forces to protect this territory.[12] Russia is the only country that is deploying intermediate-range land attack cruise missiles on conventional submarines and small missile corvettes. The corvettes have a displacement of under 1,000 tons, which allows for their deployment in coastal areas and internal waterways.

In strategic weapons development, Russia seeks to maintain a high level of survivability and lethality of its nuclear arsenal in the face of US progress in ballistic missile defense, reconnaissance, and long-range precision-strike capabilities. Russian programs have included several new types of intercontinental ballistic missiles (ICBMs), including lightweight road-mobile ICBMs such as RS-26 Rubezh, new railroad-based ICBMs (Barguzin), a new heavy liquid-fuel ICBM (Sarmat), and the hypersonic reentry vehicle program (Avangard), in addition to the continued production of the RS-24 Yars (SS-27 Mod 2) system. In March 2018, Russia unveiled the beginning of deployment of a new hypersonic intermediate range cruise missile called the Kinzhal. Russia continues to develop its maritime nuclear forces with eight Borei-class ballistic-missile submarines (3 active, 4 under construction, 1 planned) each equipped with up to 16 Bulava ballistic missiles.

Russian leaders have officially confirmed plans to develop and procure new strategic bombers. Most likely, there will be 50 aircraft of a radically upgraded Tu-160 design. Russia expects to start test flights of these new Tu-160M bombers by 2021 and start serial production in 2023.[13]

Russia is also considering development of entirely new classes of strategic nuclear weapons. In November 2015, Russian TV leaked information (possibly intentionally) about the "Status-6" project—a long-range (more than 10,000 km) unmanned underwater vehicle that could be equipped with nuclear warheads for destroying coastal targets.[14] Another non-ballistic missile system unveiled in March 2018 was a nuclear powered cruise missile with "unlimited range."

The ultimate goal of Russian efforts in strategic weapons development is best described in a 2004 statement by Putin, when many of the programs were still at a very early stage: "to make any types of anti-ballistic missile defense, existing or future, useless."[15]

Major progress in the general modernization of the Russian conventional forces, which also started after 2008, is expected to be achieved by 2020. This is happening within the framework of the GPV-2020 program, which is intended to increase the share of modern equipment from around 10 percent in 2009 to 70 percent by 2020. The program has proved to be a major challenge for Russian producers of conventional weapon systems. Nuclear weapons complex and strategic systems producers received significant government funding throughout the post-Soviet period and, after 2008, needed to increase production. In contrast, from 1992 to 2008 conventional systems producers survived mainly by exporting their weapons. Since then, they have had to boost production rapidly for Russian domestic use.

The Russian Ministry of Defense has been of little help in attempts to boost production for the internal market. Its nearly obsolete procurement system lacks capable personnel and suffers from corruption. Development of something as basic but necessary as a working pricing mechanism has proved to be a major challenge. Lack of such mechanisms has caused constant struggles between the Ministry of Defense and the defense industry. However, most of these difficulties were overcome in 2012 through the decisiveness of then Minister of Defense Anatoly Serdyukov and constant attention from top leadership, including the president. By 2014, the defense industry was able to implement most of the GPV-2020 program requirements. In that year, the Russian Air Force alone received 101 new combat aircraft, compared with a single aircraft in 2008, and major R&D programs such as the T-50 fifth-generation fighter have been progressing more or less smoothly. The pace of procurement was to some extent reduced after 2014 because of sanctions and the economic crisis, but has still remained high. In 2016, the Russian armed forces received 69 new combat aircraft (and 139 new aircraft in total); 23 new ICBMs; 2 submarines; 24 surface combatants and auxiliary ships; 88 artillery systems; and 764 armored vehicles of various types.[16]

RUSSIA'S ADVANCED RESEARCH FOUNDATION

The main Russian initiative to boost innovation activity in the defense sector in the last several years was the establishment of the Advanced Research Foundation (ARF) in October 2012. Modelled initially on the US Defense Advanced Research Projects Agency (DARPA), the foundation is supposed to "encourage the implementation of high-risk breakthrough research in the interests of State defense and security." ARF can conduct economic activities only in areas designated by relevant Russian law and is to use its profits to support advanced research. Other state agencies cannot intervene in foundation activities and cannot influence decisions on what research should be supported.

The experts working for ARF are charged with identifying critical technological threats to national security and finding ways to neutralize such threats. ARF leadership then identifies companies and research institutions to conduct the relevant research. The intellectual property rights of the research results belong to ARF, and it can transfer these rights to defense industry companies, which are supposed to apply the results of the research.

ARF is supposed to prepare three-year research programs that are subject to yearly reviews. Projects to be included into the programs are to be chosen by the ARF Council on Science and Technology and then confirmed by the ARF board. This consists of the ARF director general and his deputies in charge of various research areas. Another important organ within ARF is its 15-member board of trustees, which includes the ARF director general. Seven members are appointed by the president and seven by the prime minister. ARF reportedly has some 100 employees who are supposed to oversee up to 150 projects simultaneously.

Andrei Grigoriev, the first director general of ARF, was appointed by Putin in January 2013. He had worked previously in the Federal Service of Technical and Export Control, a highly secretive organization responsible for the technological aspects of state security, including work on regulations for the defense industry and for the military.

In an August 2013 interview, Grigoriev talked about the differences between ARF and DARPA, commenting that the only thing they had in common was that both organizations were in charge of very long term R&D projects with very long timelines.[17] He also noted that DARPA exists in a different ecosystem, where it sometimes can choose the most promising projects underway at US universities and other research centers that already enjoy significant financial support via different channels. In contrast, ARF is set up to finance its projects from beginning to end. Grigoriev reiterated that ARF is not duplicating the functions of the Main Directorate for the Research Activities and Technological Support of Advanced Technologies, the Ministry of Defense department responsible for innovations. This directorate conducts analysis and research on current technological trends on behalf of the Ministry of Defense and coordinates the ministry's activities in this area.[18] ARF projects are aimed at a longer time horizon and are administered differently.

The foundation seems to finance a wide set of technologies, many of which are similar to known US priorities. These include robotics, including fully robotic combat platforms; hypersonic systems; additive technologies; advanced underwater technologies; cybersecurity; and cognitive technologies.[19] As one example, the projects on "advanced underwater systems" are supposed to help develop advanced unmanned underwater vehicles for both warfighting and natural resources exploration, create new technologies for tracking underwater objects, and find ways to reduce the acoustic detectability of underwater objects.[20] Russia also has active rail gun and directed energy weapons programs.[21]

The ARF and the Ministry of Defense appear to be choosing future programs primarily by monitoring global trends in technological development and listening to guidance from the Russian military, intelligence, and law enforcement agencies represented on the ARF board. Since the Third Offset Strategy is in an early stage of development, it is most likely not affecting ARF activities in a major way, but its influence is likely to grow.

RUSSIAN DEFENSE TECHNOLOGY COOPERATION WITH CHINA

Before the beginning of the Ukrainian crisis, Russian–Chinese defense industry cooperation was already on an upward trend after a period of decline from 2003 to 2010. After the biggest defense contracts of the 1990s, such as the Su-27SK fighter license production deal and the Su-30MK/Su-30MK2 contract, were fulfilled, the arms trade volume between the two countries dropped significantly below $1 billion per year. At some point, it seemed that Russian arms exports to China would drop to insignificant levels, and China would become self-sufficient. However, the Chinese tended to be too optimistic about their defense industrial capacity to fulfill domestic demand for some types of high-tech items, such as aircraft engines. The growing ambitions of the Chinese military and failure of the domestic industry to develop the necessary systems in time led to a resumption of bilateral defense trade growth in around 2010.

After major deals to supply China with aircraft engines and transport helicopters were signed, the defense trade volume came close to the $2 billion level in 2011 and 2012. In November 2012, Konstantin Bryulin, the deputy chief of the Federal Service for Military and Technical Cooperation, reported that China accounted for more than 15 percent of Russia's total arms trade. Based on the overall value of Russian arms deliveries to foreign customers that year, a 15 percent share translates to over $1.9 billion worth of deliveries. The value of new contracts signed that year with China was more than $1 billion in the aerospace segment alone. These contracts included a very important order for 184 D-30KP2 turbofan engines, which the Chinese need for their new H-6K bomber and new Y-20 transport aircraft. They are also likely to be used to retrofit the PLA Air Force's existing Il-76 transport aircraft.

In 2012, Russia made deliveries under a series of large aircraft engine contracts signed in previous years for the AL-31FN, D-30KP-2, and RD-93. In mid-2012, China placed several large new orders, including for 140 AL-31F engines and 52 Mi-171 helicopters that was worth a total of $1.3 billion. Deliveries on these contracts have already commenced.

Russia and China had signed contracts in 2005 to provide China with 34 Il-76 transports and 4 Il-78 air tankers, which Russia failed to fulfill because of a loss of production capacity in the aircraft's final assembly plant in Tashkent, Uzbekistan. However, after 2011 Russia started sales of secondhand Il-76s obtained from Russian Air Force reserves. In the initial contract, Russia was supposed to sell three of these to China; later the number was increased to ten. According to the chief executive of Rosoboronexport, China accounted for 12 percent, or roughly $2.1 billion, of the $17.6 billion in export contracts signed in 2012.[22] China was the third-largest spender on Russian weapons that year, after India and Iraq.

At around the same time, the two countries started negotiations on three other major programs: the S-400 SAM systems, the Su-35 fighter, and the Amur-1650 submarine. The long and difficult negotiations came to a conclusion in 2014 and 2015. The deal to supply four battalions of S-400 systems to China worth more than $1.9 billion was signed in the autumn of 2014, and a contract for 24 Su-35 fighters worth at least $2 billion was signed in November 2015. The first batch of four Su-35s was delivered to China in December 2016. The remaining aircraft and the S-400 systems are expected to be delivered from 2017 to early 2018. The current status of the Amur-1650 submarine program is unknown.

The growth trend in Russian–Chinese defense trade has continued since 2014. In early November 2016, Vladimir Drozzhov, the deputy director for the Federal Service for Military Technical Cooperation, stated that "Chinese interest in Russian armaments has been increasing" and that the total volume of outstanding contracts with China had reached $8 billion.[23] Later in November, Russian Defense Minister Sergey Shoigu stated that deliveries during 2016 exceeded $3 billion.[24]

We can expect an additional increase in the volume of deliveries in 2017–2018 when the majority of Su-35 planes and S-400 SAMs will be shipped to China. That will bring trade very close to the levels of the "Golden Age" of Russian–Chinese defense trade from the 1990s to the early 2000s. In a 2009 interview, Rosoboronexport CEO Anatoliy Isaykin said that at the peak of Russian arms exports to China, which lasted "a decade and a half," China was the destination of "up to 50 percent of Russian arms exports, with annual sales of up to $2.7 billion." The maximum volume of deliveries was reached in 2002, so the peak volume can be estimated at around $3.6 billion in 2016 dollars. Isaykin also reported that the total volume of sales to China in 2001–2009 was $16 billion.[25] The export deals that have not been identified in the Russian media most likely consist of contracts for military R&D, as well as deliveries of relatively small and inexpensive parts and components. These unidentified contracts (worth $800 million, or some 40 percent of trade in 2012 alone) include the repair and upgrade of previously supplied weaponry, which can generate significant revenue.

The resumption of large-scale Russian weapons sales to China can be explained by a mix of political and technological factors. Chinese military leaders want to increase the PLA's fighting ability rapidly as the military-political situation in the Asia-Pacific becomes more worrying for Beijing. Also, while the Chinese makers of finished weapons systems have made great progress in recent years, production of some key parts and components is still lagging behind.

An important trend in Russian–Chinese cooperation has been a gradual increase in joint R&D cooperation. As Russia's importance as a weapons provider gradually decreases, it has still played an important role as a technological partner and is often subcontracted work on various important elements of the overall design. Such a role is not new. The best-known examples of Chinese systems designed by Russia or with a major Russian contribution include the FC-1 fighter, the L-15 combat trainer, the WZ-10 attack helicopter, the PL-12 air-to-air missile, the HQ-9 and HQ-16 surface-to-air missiles, the ZBD-04 infantry fighting vehicle, and Type 054 frigates. Russia is now beginning to develop key elements of such platforms rather than whole platforms. Examples include suspension system elements for tracked vehicles, certain elements of aerial vehicle airframes, and specialized software. Such contracts are difficult to track, but their increased share in general cooperation was observed by the Russian arms export monopoly Rosoboronexport as early as 2011.[26]

Russia is ready to expand bilateral cooperation with the Chinese to new areas, notably in aircraft engines. The two sides are discussing possible cooperation on joint production of a fighter turbofan engine based on Russian 117S (AL-41F1) engine technology.[27] The 117S engine is used in Russian Su-35 fighters and early production fifth-generation T-50 fighters.

Russian concerns about theft of their technology by the Chinese are not nearly as great as they were in the 1990s. Current Russian arms exports to China fall into two broad categories: 1) partially modified Soviet systems that the Chinese cannot quickly copy for a variety of technological and/ or economic reasons; and 2) mass-produced post-Soviet designs.

Products in the first category include the Mi-17 and Ka-28 helicopters, the AL-31F, RD-93 and D-30KP2 aircraft engines. In addition, radically modernized Soviet systems and new technology were developed after the breakup of the Soviet Union. These include the S-300PMU2 Favorit SAM systems (deliveries began in the 2000s) Su-35 fighters, Amur-1650 submarines, and the S-400 SAM systems. In some cases, copying Russian technology is either impossible or does not make practical sense; helicopters are a good example. For some other products in this group, copying efforts have been long-standing, but still face great technical challenges.

As for the second category, the threat of Chinese copying still remains but is not nearly as great a threat as it was in the 1990s. After the breakup of the Soviet Union, many of the manufacturers or refurbishers of the mass-produced systems were left in the former Soviet republics. The Chinese found it easy to circumvent Russian restrictions and acquire the technologies from those republics to fully localize certain weapons systems. For example, Ukrainian companies were instrumental in China's efforts to launch production of local copies of the Su-27SK and Su-33 fighters, as well as the RD-93 engine.

Finally, Russia had a relatively weak counterintelligence system in the 1990s, making it easy for the Chinese to steal advanced military technologies. In recent years, however, Russia has pursued (with varying degrees of success) a program of excluding Ukrainian and Belarusian companies from the design and production cycle of Russian weaponry. The access of Commonwealth of Independent States members to the latest Russian defense technologies has been severely restricted or completely eliminated. As a result, China's ability to gain illicit access to Russian know-how and to copy Russian weapons systems is diminishing, even as the Chinese defense industry itself is becoming more capable.

New Trends in Cooperation and the Possible Impact of the Third Offset Strategy

The Ukrainian crisis and Western technology and financial sanctions imposed on Russia have had deep consequences for Russian defense industry behavior in the international arena and on Russian military and technological planning. The Russian defense industry has encountered difficulties in procuring spare parts, materials, technology, and industrial equipment in the West and in Ukraine. From the early stages of the crisis, the industry has encountered delays and breakups of contracts on delivery of industrial equipment. The import of defense products to Russia before the crisis used to be quite limited, amounting to $150–200 million (mostly from the European Union) before the crisis and dropping further to $70–80 million afterwards.[28] However, the industry has become dependent on some Western dual-use products such as electronic components (including for space vehicles) and naval diesels for surface ships.

The crisis served as a trigger for the Russian defense industry to search for alternative partners and suppliers in China. In some cases, the industry managed to find them. For example, Russia has started to procure naval diesel engines produced by Henan Diesel Engine Industrial Company instead of German MTU engines for its coast guard patrol ships and for 21631 missile corvettes.[29] In 2014, Russia and China began to examine the possibility of Russian sourcing of space-grade radiation-resistant electronic components and the relevant production technology from the state-owned China Aerospace Science and Industry Corp. in exchange for Russian RD-180 liquid-fueled space carrier rocket engines and production technology.[30] An agreement on intellectual property protection, which will enable the two sides to go forward with contracts, was signed during Putin's visit to China in June 2016.

Russian and Chinese defense industries are gradually moving toward creating new industrial alliances. During Putin's 2016 visit to China, the two sides concluded long and painful negotiations and signed agreements on the joint development of a wide-body passenger aircraft and an advanced heavy lift helicopter.

Russia and China have also signed an agreement on the integration of their respective satellite navigation systems (GLONASS and Beidou).

The two sides will jointly develop ground electronic equipment that will use signals from both systems for greater precision in navigation. The Norinco Group will co-develop the necessary electronic microchips with the Russians. The two sides will also cooperate in developing various applications for the systems.[31]

The Russian space industry has expressed a growing interest in developing a technological alliance with China, since joining efforts with China and other BRICS countries is seen as crucial to maintaining competitiveness. Andrei Ionin, chief analyst of the GLONASS Union, the official provider of GLONASS services in Russia, argues that the GLONASS-Beidou partnership is a first step that should be followed by others, such as creation of a BRICS satellite communications system competitive with the Iridium network.[32] It should be kept in mind that joint complex technology cooperation projects take years to negotiate and even more time to develop, so many of these initiatives are at an early stage.

Even before the Ukrainian crisis, the state-owned defense industrial corporations of the two countries had started to develop partnerships in civilian production. Rostec, for example, has cooperated with China Electronics Technology Corporation to build an LED factory in Tomsk.[33] Other reported areas of cooperation between Rostec and Chinese entities include civilian truck production, electronics, chemicals, rare earth metals processing, and medical equipment, among others.

RUSSIAN–CHINESE COOPERATION AND STRATEGIC COMPETITION WITH THE UNITED STATES

Chinese cooperation with Russia is expected to be an important factor in the China–US great power competition, under the influence of two emerging factors well understood by the leadership of the two countries.

First, both Russia and China understand that the United States will increasingly rely on its biggest remaining advantage, the strength of its R&D base, in order to achieve victory in strategic competition.

Second, since US resources and capabilities are seen to be declining, the coordinated policies and actions of Moscow and Beijing in the Atlantic and Pacific theaters respectively may have a decisive impact on the US ability to react to changing situations in these theaters—without requiring China and Russia to enter a formal military alliance treaty.

Since both governments see significant security challenges associated with US technological initiatives such as the Third Offset Strategy, they almost simultaneously began to reform and centralize their defense industry and defense innovation systems, allowing for greater concentration of resources. For example, the Defense Industrial Commission, the key Russian government body supervising the industry and traditionally chaired by the country prime minister has been headed by President Vladimir Putin since September 2014. The status of that body was raised from one of several cabinet-level commissions to a presidential commission. As a result, the president takes part in the commission meetings on a regular (more or less monthly) basis, contributes to key decisions, and has personal contact with the senior management of the defense industrial enterprises.

Chinese leadership has in the recent years undertaken significant efforts to upgrade existing regulations and organizational frameworks pertaining to integrated defense and civilian innovation management. The reform of the Central Military Commission led to centralization of many of its functions, including major R&D related policies supervision under the top leader. In January 2017, China established a new body, the Central Commission on Integrated Civil-Military Development, which is chaired by President Xi Jinping. Four of the seven Politburo Standing Committee members are also commission members. In December 2017, General Zhang Youxia, the Central Military Commission deputy chairman responsible for science and technology issues, took part in a yearly meeting of the Russian–Chinese commission on military technical cooperation in Moscow and was received personally by President Putin, an important sign of growing attention paid to the bilateral defense technology cooperation by the political leadership in the two countries.

China is the world's largest economy in terms of PPP-based GDP volume and industrial manufacturing capabilities and is a quickly growing defense industrial and technological power at the same time. Russia has a stagnant economy and lacks financial resources. But from 1990 into the 2000s Russia managed to preserve and, since 2011, rebuild, key elements of the Soviet defense innovation and industrial capacity. These established defense industrial capabilities are coupled with another crucial advantage that China lacks—rich combat experience gained in decades of military conflicts, including wars against foreign regular armies and expeditionary operations. That experience provides important contributions not only to Russian military capabilities, but also to defense industry development. Combining Chinese financial resources and manufacturing capacity with Russian expertise in the areas where Russia retains its competitive advantage seems a likely course of action in the coming years.

Facing Russia and China simultaneously as long-term strategic adversaries, Washington can no longer concentrate military resources in a single theater or shape its defense innovation policies to deal with the strengths and weaknesses of one specific country. Countering the Russian military in the European continental theater and China in the Pacific theater may dictate different military priorities and different technological choices. In contrast, Russia and China can jointly work to deal with the same threats or issues (for example, dealing with US carrier battle groups is relevant for both). They can develop a division of labor, for example, with the Russians investing more in submarines, littoral forces, and coastal defenses while the Chinese increasingly prioritize blue water capabilities.

More importantly, with US forces split between Europe, the Middle East, and the Asia-Pacific, Russia and China can work to prevent the United States from reaching and maintaining a decisive advantage on any of the three continents. This requires a deep understanding of each other's capabilities but does not require the establishment of a formal alliance. For example, large-scale Russian military exercises (similar to Zapad-2017 or larger) held in the Western part of the country at a moment of growing tension in the Taiwan Straits or South China Sea would likely draw a significant part of the overall expeditionary capabilities of the US Air Force and Navy to the Northern Atlantic even if on the political level there is a clear understanding that a Russian attack against NATO is not likely. Russia can dramatically reduce the US ability to react to Chinese actions in the Pacific even now, without any formal alliance with China.

At the same time, China and Russia can operate jointly to support allies and partners in the Middle East, combining Russian advantages in the fields of special operations, close air support, and air defense with the capabilities of the newly built Chinese blue water Navy.

Joint Russian–Chinese exercises in recent years, which have included joint deployments in the Eastern Mediterranean in 2015 and in Baltic in 2017, landing operations, and air defense and strike missions, suggest that such actions are being considered and prepared for.

Conclusion

Given the general trend toward closer industrial cooperation and the strengthening of political and military ties between Russia and China, it seems likely that the implementation of the US Third Offset Strategy will result in even closer cooperation between the two in the technology sectors prioritized by the Third Offset Strategy. Joining efforts at this stage may be seen as the only way to prevent the United States from gaining a decisive military and technological advantage.

The level of mutual trust, transparency, and cooperation in the military field between Russia and China is already very high, as evidenced by regular large-scale joint military exercises and other activities. Since 2005, Russia and China have held one large-scale ground and air forces exercise each year (the Peace Mission exercise). Annual naval exercises

(Naval Cooperation) have taken place since 2012. Anti-terrorism and security units (China's People's Armed Police and the Russian National Guard and Federal Security Service) hold joint exercises even more frequently. In some cases, exercises involve the creation of joint Russian–Chinese tactical groups under a single command or air groups implementing attacks jointly according to a joint plan. The two navies practice anti-submarine warfare, anti-air and anti-surface warfare, and landing operations.

Russian concerns about Chinese violations of intellectual property rights are not as strong as they were 10 to 15 years ago, and the two countries already have significant cooperation in some areas prioritized by the Third Offset Strategy. For example, in the 1990s Russia played an important role in development of the Chinese UUV industry. The first cooperation agreement between the Institute of Marine Technology Problems of the Russian Academy of Sciences (IMTP) in Vladivostok and Shenyang Institute of Automatics (SIA) of the Chinese Academy of Sciences was signed in 1991. IMTP and SIA jointly developed the UUV CR-1 with a maximum working depth of 6,000 meters. The CR-1 was equipped with an active sonar, video camera, acoustic profiler, and other systems. Initial tests took place in 1995 near Dalian. The next system, the CR-2, used Chinese electronic components and had improved onboard computer systems. There was also a third system, the MAKS-2, a remotely operated underwater vehicle for marine biological research.[34] None of the IMTP–SIA joint projects appear to have a military purpose. However, it is clear that in the 1990s there was a major Russian UUV technology transfer that opened the way for further Chinese progress. Similar cooperation is likely taking place today.

However, the framework of such cooperation will be different from the previous joint projects implemented in the 1990s–2000s, since the Chinese negotiating position has become stronger and the Russian one weaker. It is possible that China will come to dominate some projects where Chinese financing and technology are vital for success. In other cases, the projects will be implemented on a 50/50 basis, with Russia not able to withhold its state-of-the-art technology from its Chinese partners as it preferred to do in previous agreements.

Taking into account the deterioration of both countries' relations with the West and the rise of military tensions in both Eastern Europe and the Western Pacific, Russia and China have little choice but to expand cooperation. This reality was recognized by the Russian side in the early stages of the Ukrainian crisis. During his visit to Beijing in November 2014, Russian Defense Minister Sergei Shoigu noted that the two countries' cooperation in defense technology was becoming "especially important" because of the "complicated situation" in the world.[35] In May 2015 he stated that cooperation with China was receiving special attention from the top leadership and would be expanded.[36] Due to the long-term nature of modern high-tech defense and dual-use-related projects, many years may pass before this new drive towards cooperation produces concrete results.

It is likely that Russia and China will rely increasingly on combined defense and defense technology resources to counter current and future US technological initiatives. This will include both defense industrial and military cooperation, and the organizational and legal framework for such increased cooperation is already in place. The two countries' defense industries and militaries have already reached a significant level of interoperability and have pools of trained professionals with deep knowledge of the other side's strengths, weaknesses, and capabilities (something Russia and China lack in civilian economic cooperation). No additional high-level political action (such as a treaty) is needed for Russian–Chinese defense cooperation to become an important factor in the current global great power competition. Efforts to reach a high level of economic integration between Russia and China are still at a relatively early stage and face significant technical hurdles. However, in the military, defense industry, and security fields, most, if not all, necessary preparatory work has already taken place, and cooperation is moving ahead.

Notes

1. A. A. Kokoshin, V. I. Bartenev, and V. A. Veselov, Подготовка революции в военном деле в условиях бюджетных ограничений. Новые инициативы министерства обороны США [The preparation of a revolution in military affairs at a time of budgetary limitations: New initiatives of the US Ministry of Defense], США и Канада: экономика, политика и культура [US and Canada: Politics, economy, and culture] 11 (2015).

2. L. V. Pankova, Стратегическая стабильность и новая американская стратегия компенсации [Statement on strategic stability and the new american offset strategy], Международные отношения и мировая политика [Bulletin of the Moscow University] 3 (2015).

3. Kokoshin, Bartenev, and Veselov, "Preparation of a Revolution in Military Affairs."

4. I. Udaltsov, Третья стратегия [The third strategy], *Krasnaya Zvezda*, November 25, 2015, http://www.redstar.ru/index.php/syria/item/26749 -tretya-strategiya.

5. Pankova, "Strategic Stability."

6. "The National Security Strategy of the Russian Federation to 2020," May 12, 2009, https://rg.ru/2009/05/19/strategia-dok.html. English translation available at http://rustrans.wikidot.com/russia-s-national-security-strategy-to-2020.

7. A. Anin, Влияние стратегических наступательных вооружений в неядерном оснащении на стратегическую стабильность [The influence of non-nuclear strategic offensive weapons on strategic stability], Мировая экономика и международные отношения [International economy and international relations] 6 (2011), http://www.ebiblioteka.ru/browse/doc/25256650.

8. V. V. Putin, Быть сильными: гарантия национальной безопасности для России [To be strong: The guarantee of national security], *Rossiyskaya Gazeta*, February 20, 2012, https://rg.ru/2012/02/20/putin-armiya.html.

9. "The National Security Strategy of the Russian Federation to 2020."

10. O. B. Achasov and G. N. Vylegzhanin, Проблемы обеспечения эффективного решения задач силами общего назначения в современных условиях [The problems of ensuring the effective imple-

mentation of combat missions by conventional forces under current conditions], Вооружения и Экономика [Arms and economics] 1 (2014): 11.

11. Russian State TV report on Putin's speech, December 9, 2015, http://www.vestifinance.ru/articles/65255.

12. Russian State TV report on Putin's speech, http://www.vesti.ru/doc.html?id=2427105&tid=108263.

13. Шойгу назвал возобновление производства Ту-160 приоритетной задачей [Shoigu called the renewal of Tu-160 production a priority task], *Rossiyskaya Gazeta*, February 2, 2016, https://rg.ru/2016/02/02/shojgu-nazval-vozobnovlenie-proizvodstva-tu-160-prioritetnoj-zadachej.html.

14. Сверхсекретный Статус-6 напоминает идеи академика Сахарова [Top secret status-6 resembles academician Sakharov's ideas], *Vzglyad*, November 12, 2015, http://vz.ru/society/2015/11/12/777703.html.

15. The Russian Ministry of Defense TV Channel Zvezda report, January 23, 2015, http://tvzvezda.ru/news/krasnaya_zvezda/content/201501230547-labj.htm.

16. Ministry of Defense press releases; Moscow Center for Analysis of Strategies and Technologies data.

17. Мы готовы работать с любой компанией. Интервью с Андреем Григорьевым, генеральным директором Фонда перспективных исследований [We are ready to work with any company: Interview with Andrei Grigoriev, director general of the ARF"], *Eksport Vooruzheniy* 105, August 2013.

18. "Excerpts from the Regulation of the Main Directorate for Research Activities and Technological Support of the Advanced Technologies of the Ministry of Defense," http://doc.mil.ru/documents/quick_search/more.htm?id=11919505@egNPA.

19. Data from the ARF website, http://fpi.gov.ru/about/areas/physics/bisokoskorostnie_sredstva.

20. Data from the ARF website, http://fpi.gov.ru/about/areas/physics/perspektivnie_podvodnie_tehnologii.

21. On rail guns, see Россия создаст свой рельсотроню Российская Газета [Russia to build its own railgun], *Rossiyskaya Gazeta*, May 31, 2016, https://rg.ru/2016/05/31/rossiia-sozdast-svoj-relsotron.html. On directed energy weapons, see, for example, the well-known Sokol-Echelon airborne laser program. Ilya Schegolev, Как устроен А-60 и другие боевые лазеры России [What A-60 and other Russian lasers are like], October 31, 2014, https://rg.ru/2014/10/31/boevoilazer-site.html.

22. Китаю нужны русские крылья [China needs Russian wings], Rostec press release, February 14, 2013, http://rostec.ru/news/1118.
23. Китай вернулся в пятерку крупнейших импортеров российского оружия [China returned to the top 5 of the Russian weapons importers], *Vedomosti*, November 2, 2016, http://www.vedomosti.ru/politics/articles/2016/11/02/663309-kitai-krupneishih-importerov
24. Шойгу: Россия и Китай реализовали контракты в сфере ВТС на сумму более 3 млрд долларов [Shoigu: Russia and China have implemented defense contracts worth more than $3bn during the year]. *Vzglyad*, November 23, 2016, http://www.vz.ru/news/2016/11/23/845346.html.
25. Interview with Rosoboronexport Director General Anatoly Isaykin, *Rossiyskaya Gazeta*, April 11, 2009, http://www.militaryparitet.com/teletype/data/ic_teletype/5066/.
26. Тенденция к росту. Рособоронэкспорт отчитался о результатах 2010ю [Growing trend: Rosoboronexport discloses results for 2010], *National Defense*, no. 1 (2010), http://www.oborona.ru/includes/periodics/armstrade/2011/0317/21515725/detail.shtml.
27. Россия и Китай обсудят проект двигателя для Су-35 [Russia and China to discuss engine for the Su-35], *Aviation Explorer*, November 11, 2014, http://www.aex.ru/news/2014/11/11/126464/.
28. Press conference with Rosoboronexport Chief Anatoly Isaikin, October 10, 2015, https://rg.ru/2015/10/27/orujie-site.html.
29. Китайские дизельные двигатели для малых ракетных кораблей проекта 21631 [Chinese diesel engines for the Project 21631 small missile ships], March 28, 2016, http://vpk.name/news/152235_kitaiskie_dizelnyie_dvigateli_dlya_malyih_raketnyih_korablei_proekta_21631.html.
30. Китай предложил электронику в обмен на ракетные двигатели [China offered to exchange electronics for rocket engines], Lenta.ru, April 19, 2015, https://news.mail.ru/economics/25509290/.
31. ГЛОНАСС и Beidou получат общий сигнал [GLONASS and Beidou will use common signal], *Izvestia*, April 25, 2015, http://izvestia.ru/news/585836.
32. Andrey Ionin, Технологический альянс вместо Североатлантического [Technological alliance instead of the North Atlantic one], Россия в глобальной политике [Russia in global affairs], June 7, 2015, http://www.globalaffairs.ru/number/tekhnologicheskii-alyans-vmesto-severoatlanticheskogo-17502.

33. Russian Electronics Company press release, December 12, 2013, http://www.russianelectronics.ru/leader-r/news/49502/doc/65727/.

34. L. Kiselev, Код Глубины [The code of the depth], Институт проблем морских технологий Дальневосточного отделения РАН. Владивосток 2011 [Institute of the Maritime Technology, Far Eastern Department of the Russian Academy of Sciences, Vladivostok, 2011], 97–98.

35. Шойгу отметил особый характер военного сотрудничества с Китаем [Shoigu noted the special nature of defense cooperation with China], *Vzglyad*, November 19, 2014, http://vz.ru/news/2014/11/19/715958.html.

36. Шойгу: Россия будет расширять военно-техническое сотрудничество с КНР [Russia to expand defense cooperation with China], May 10, 2015, https://rg.ru/2015/05/10/kitay-anons.html.

CONCLUSION

THE LONG-TERM IMPLICATIONS OF FUTURE US STRATEGY FOR CHINA AND CHINESE STRATEGY FOR THE UNITED STATES

Tai Ming Cheung and Thomas Mahnken

The preceding chapters offer evidence that military strategic competition between the United States and China in the defense technological domain is gaining momentum. Whether they are already in a direct arms race is a matter of academic debate, but they appear to be well on their way. What are the long-term implications for future US grand strategy toward China and likewise for Chinese grand strategy toward the United States?

THE EMERGENCE OF A MUSCULAR CHINESE NATIONAL SECURITY STATE

Under Xi Jinping's leadership since 2012, China's low-key, economically focused, and status quo-minded geostrategic posture has steadily evolved to become increasingly muscular, assertive, and revisionist. To be sure, China continues to be cooperative with the United States and the international community on many issues ranging from climate change to maritime piracy. There appears, however, to be a fundamental reorientation in how the Xi Jinping regime perceives the international security environment, the importance of national security in its overall priorities, and China's place in the global order.

China has shifted from being a developmental state to becoming a national security state. Between the late 1970s and the early 2010s, economic development was China's foremost priority, while national security issues were of secondary importance. This contrasted with the fortress-like military-national security state that Mao Zedong had ruled.[1] Deng Xiaoping pressed ahead during the 1980s with economic reforms and integration into the international system. National security challenges regularly intervened and threatened to undermine the economic reform process, most notably in 1989 with the Tiananmen Square protests, and again in the mid-1990s as tensions across the Taiwan Strait threatened to escalate into military conflict. Under the tenures of Jiang Zemin and Hu Jintao between 1990 and 2012, there was an effort to find a more balanced relationship between economic development and national security, although economic issues remained the dominant priority.

For Xi, the balance appears to have tipped decisively in favor of national security considerations. While economic development remains a high on the list of priorities, security concerns are now of even greater importance. Building a robust and expansive national security state is based upon a number of considerations, which include: 1) consolidating China's emergence as a global power; 2) remaking the rules and norms of the US–dominated international order on terms more favorable to Beijing; and 3) fortifying security and expanding control along and well beyond China's land, sea, air, space, and cyber borders, contested areas of sovereignty claims, and the regional neighborhood. This national security state is cemented domestically around an authoritarian leadership structure centered on Xi and the strengthening of tight and pervasive controls on social stability, political and ideological loyalty, and information dissemination designed to thwart any threats or dissent to the continuing rule of the Communist Party.

Xi has put forward a national security strategy that he terms a 'national security path with Chinese characteristics'—a mixture of assertive principles coupled with deep concerns about vulnerabilities.[2] A number of key concepts are behind the shaping of this doctrine:

National security is comprehensive: Xi sees the domestic and external components of national security as overlapping and tightly connected, which is very different from the compartmentalized approach that his predecessors pursued. This is an important reason why Xi decided to establish a new organization, the National Security Commission, to manage this integrated approach.[3]

National security is expansive: Closely connected with the perspective that national security is comprehensive is the notion that it covers many different domains. A new national security law that is being finalized identifies national security as covering 11 categories: political, territorial, military, economic, cultural, social, ecological, science and technology, information, nuclear, and natural resources.

Being proactive and thinking strategically: It is important to identify and address national security challenges and opportunities early, strategically, and decisively rather than being reactive and tactical. This requires extensive and high-level leadership engagement, close coordination across the national security apparatus, and the development of a capable and substantial intelligence system to keep abreast of internal and international developments.

Strongly asserting China's interests: China under Xi is stressing the need to engage in struggle (斗争) in the pursuit of national interests, especially in the military and diplomatic arenas. In describing China's approach to dealing with the United States, Admiral Sun Jiangguo pointed out that

facts have shown that without struggle it will be impossible for the United States to respect our core interests; without struggle it will be impossible to realize cooperation and win-win on the basis of equality; and without struggle it will be impossible to have an excellent situation today.[4]

In other words, China, and especially the People's Liberation Army, needs to take a resilient stance and push hard against the United States in order to win its respect, although the Chinese leadership is also extremely careful not to go too far and spark armed conflict with its more powerful counterpart.

The grave threats that Xi and his leadership think that China faces are a key driver of Xi's efforts to establish a potent national security state. "China now faces the most complicated internal and external factors in [its] history," Xi said at the first meeting of a high-level national security commission that he established in 2014.[5] This is an extraordinary claim, as the People's Republic of China faced severe threats to its very survival between the 1950s and 1970s from the United States and the Soviet Union.

The United States is front and center in China's strategic considerations. However, Beijing does not want to point this out publicly because the United States continues to be far stronger militarily, economically, and technologically. China's defense white papers, including its most recent in 2015, have been circumspect in their treatment of the United States or mention of deepening China–US frictions.

Internally since the mid to late 2000s, however, China's national security policymakers have viewed the United States as a direct military competitor and potential adversary in response to escalating security frictions and competing interests that are deepening US-China strategic distrust. A central reason for this logic is a widely held belief among Chinese strategists that since second half of the last decade the United States has designated China as its main strategic opponent. A 2011 study by analysts from the Chinese Academy of Military Sciences pointed out that "the United States does not want to see big powers like China and Russia grow stronger, and it particularly fears that China's rapid rise would hurt its own status as the hegemon. Therefore, it sees China as its potential strategic opponent." They recommend that "strategic balancing capabilities" be built in nuclear, space, and air deterrence even if this leads to an "intense arms race."[6]

Chinese defense analysts think that the United States has the political, economic, geostrategic, and innovative will and capability to implement the Third Offset Strategy successfully. A prominent analyst in this debate, Tong Zhen of the Academy of Military Sciences, says the United States is pursuing the Third Offset Strategy from a position of superiority compared to its opponents because the US defense and civilian innovation systems have the technological expertise and innovative capacity to implement the strategy. However, Tong also points to challenges faced by the United States, including resource constraints and flat defense budgets; more complex and diverse threats compared to past offset strategies; the ability of adversaries to gain access to technologies that would allow them to compete more effectively; and coordination problems between the White House and US Congress.

Zhang Xiaobin, a defense technology analyst at the State Administration for Science, Technology, and Industry for National Defense, believes that the Third Offset Strategy will have a significant detrimental impact on China's defense science and technology development, making it far more difficult for China to pursue leapfrog-style developments in disruptive innovation successfully. This is because the US defense innovation system, which is spearheaded by the Defense Advanced Research Projects Agency, is far more capable of achieving technological surprises. Stepped-up efforts on the part of the United States to develop lower-cost asymmetric capabilities such as unmanned systems and undersea warfare will put additional pressure on China as it pursues asymmetric technologies.

China's efforts to develop core defense competencies in advanced areas could be undermined by being goaded into an arms race with the United States, forcing China to invest in research and development that it can ill afford and in technologies in which it is ill equipped to compete over the long term. Zhang offers the case of the Reagan "Star Wars" program during the 1980s in which an already economically exhausted Soviet Union wasted enormous resources with little return on its investment, a great example of inducing an adversary to engage in strategically self-defeating behavior. Zhang concludes that China should rely on the long-standing strengths of the Chinese system that were responsible for successes such as the development of the nuclear weapons, ballistic missiles, and manned space programs. This includes the adaptive nature of its authoritarian, top-down management process, especially its ability to concentrate and mobilize resources for specific projects.

Xi appears to share this view, as he has emphasized the importance of China pursuing its own development of asymmetric technological capabilities and not simply following others. At a meeting of the Central Finance and Economics Leading Small Group in August 2014, Xi said that China should "develop its own asymmetric *shashoujian* capabilities and not just do exactly the same as developed countries are doing."[7]

Consequently, the defense technological race between the United States and China can be expected to continue for the foreseeable future, especially during Xi's tenure to at least the early 2020s, and could even intensify depending on the overall direction in US-China relations. While China will watch closely how the United States proceeds with its Third Offset Strategy or whatever other technology development initiatives that emerge in the coming year, Beijing will likely continue to focus on its own priorities and not be drawn too closely into an action-reaction dynamic with a far more able innovation competitor.

US Responses

In Washington, there is growing recognition that the United States is in a long-term competition with China. Four aspects of China's growth stand out as being of particular concern. The first has to do with the Chinese leadership's attention to internal versus external affairs. It is axiomatic that any country's political leadership generally pays greater attention to domestic matters than to international affairs, and that is certainly true with regard to the Chinese Communist Party. Nevertheless, China is becoming increasingly active on the international stage. China has not only become more active in its neighborhood, but also in areas far removed from the Asian continent, to include Africa and the Persian Gulf. This international activism, not only economic investment and attempts to increase political influence, but also increasingly military deployments, raises concern in the United States and among US allies.

The second aspect of China's rise that raises concerns among the United States and its allies has to do with China's geopolitical orientation. Whereas the PLA was long focused on the Asian continent, in recent decades it has increasingly adopted a maritime orientation. The build-up of the PLA Navy as well as other anti-access/area denial (or, in Chinese parlance, counter-intervention) capabilities, such as Beijing's missile and anti-satellite weapons, and not Chinese military spending in the abstract, have stimulated a US and allied response.

A third area of concern involves China's attitude toward the international status quo. China's leadership has increasingly challenged the status quo, whether rhetorically or, increasingly, through action. Nothing illustrates this attitude more tangibly than China's campaign of building and then militarizing new land features in the South China Sea as a means of bolstering Beijing's claim of ownership.

A final area of friction has to do with China's domestic political system. However loudly or quietly the United States and its allies seek to promote democracy abroad, China's authoritarian political system and disregard for human rights and personal freedom is a recurring source of tension with the United States, its allies, and others in the region and beyond.

A strong case can be made that the United States and its allies would be much less concerned about China's overall rise were China to become more internally focused, more supportive of the status quo, more pluralistic, and emphasize the Asian continent over its maritime periphery. Indeed, under these circumstances, China would come more to resemble today's India: a rising power with growing economic strength that is internally focused, continentally focused, supportive of large parts of the international status quo, and pluralistic—indeed, a robust democracy.

As it stands, China's increasing international activism, particularly in maritime Asia, and its opposition to international norms and the status quo, has altered the geopolitical landscape of Asia. First, and foremost, it has triggered a set of responses by China's neighbors as well as those further afield. Both Australia and Japan are increasing their defense budgets at least partially in response to the growth of Chinese military power. Other states are moving closer to the United States as a balancer to China. Vietnam's communist regime, for example, has sought improved ties with the United States.

At the same time, China has been able to use its growing weight to strong-arm smaller regional states, such as forcing Malaysia to backtrack from a condemnatory statement issued on the margins of the 2016 Shangri-La Dialogue in Singapore regarding China's expansion in the South China Sea. Similarly, China has used its political influence to get states to withdraw their recognition of Taiwan and to back China's territorial claims in the South China Sea.

A US response should seek to gain an asymmetric advantage in the areas of geography, alliances, technology, and doctrine. In terms of geography, such a strategy should seek to use Asia's strategic geography—in particular, the barrier formed by Japan, Taiwan, and the Philippines—to constrain China's access to the Western Pacific in time of crisis or war. This could be accomplished by fielding sensor and engagement networks both unilaterally and in cooperation with allies along China's maritime flanks. Associated technologies would include undersea sensors, airborne sensor systems, and land- and sea-based strike systems. Such an approach would capitalize upon the combination of geography, which constrains China's access to the Pacific Ocean, and existing US and allied sensor plans, which promise to give the United States and its allies greater situational awareness of activities in the air and on or under the sea. Japan, for example, is fielding a constellation of reconnaissance satellites, expanding its air- and surface-search radar network, and modernizing its force of land-based anti-ship cruise missiles.

The United States should also deepen its interoperability with allies to bolster their capabilities and strengthen their will. The United States already shares information with its allies, and the case for increasing such cooperation is strong.[8] Washington should consider building on this by establishing an open-architecture intelligence, surveillance, and reconnaissance network in the Western Pacific to complement current bilateral information-sharing agreements. Support for broad information sharing in the Western Pacific is likely to grow in the face of Chinese encroachment. Given the increasing quality and declining cost of both commercial imagery and the sensors that produce it, such an approach will be feasible for a growing number of states.

The United States should deepen cooperation in the areas of theater strike with key allies, to include support to allied air and naval surface strike capabilities. It should work with allies and friends against coercion to make their networks more resilient and to harden key ports and airfields against attack. The goal would be to have a wide variety of facilities that US forces could utilize in time of war. Finally, allies and friends should be provided with counter-invasion capabilities, to include land-based anti-ship cruise missiles, naval mines, and precision-guided rockets and artillery systems.

Undersea warfare, in terms of both submarines and unmanned underwater vehicles, is another area for cooperation. The United States should offer to sell or lease *Virginia*-class nuclear-powered submarines to Australia as either an alternative or supplement to its current submarine modernization program. It should also seek deeper cooperation with Japan in undersea warfare.

In terms of technology, the United States should both develop and deploy countermeasures to hostile precision strike as well as move into the next phase of the precision strike competition. Counters to precision strike include hardening and dispersal of key facilities, countermeasures to precision navigation and timing, and the development of directed energy weapons to destroy precision weapons. The United States should also exploit its dominance in the undersea domain by greatly increasing its subsurface strike capability. At the same time, the United States should develop autonomous systems to mitigate the vulnerabilities inherent in reconnaissance-strike systems (such as the links between sensor, decider, and shooter). Although the United States is pursuing these technologies, such efforts are constrained by both limited budgets and technological feasibility. Finally, although the United States is currently constrained by the Intermediate-Range Nuclear Forces Treaty from developing and deploying land-based ballistic and cruise missiles with a range of between 500 and 5,500 kilometers, no such constraint exists on sea-based systems.

The United States should also safeguard its technological edge by redoubling efforts to deny China access to strategic technologies. China has proven adept at pursuing a fast-follower strategy of acquisition, buying or stealing technology and the underlying intellectual property from both the United States and Russia. Efforts to deny China easy access to US military technology and intellectual property will, at the least, drive up the cost in terms of time and effort that China is forced to expend to acquire it. In other cases, such efforts may force China to seek less capable substitutes for US technology.

Technology transfer restrictions need to be updated, both to reflect the current international technology market as well as to maximize their effectiveness. It is in the national interest for the US government and private industry to work cooperatively to develop best practices and share threat information. To be effective, however, such measures should prioritize the technologies that are likely to provide the greatest battlefield edge in the future. These include space and cyber capabilities, unmanned systems, high-speed propulsion, advanced aeronautics, autonomous systems, electromagnetic rail guns, and directed-energy systems.

In terms of doctrine, the United States should exploit the weaknesses inherent in a centralized approach to warfare, including the need to gather and process large volumes of information. Chinese military doctrine displays a strong belief that strategy is a science rather than an art and maintains great confidence in its ability to predict the outcome of conflicts.[9] To bolster deterrence, the United States and its allies should work to reduce the confidence of the Chinese leadership in its ability to control the course and outcome of a future conflict.

Such a strategy, if implemented consistently over time, holds the promise of influencing Chinese actions at the tactical, operational, and strategic level. Tactically, it would erode the effectiveness of Chinese counter-intervention systems. Operationally, it would deny the PLA leadership the type of war it has been planning for decades, forcing it to either double down on its investment in anti-access capabilities or seek a new approach. Its greatest promise is likely to be strategic: such an approach holds the potential to alter the decision-making calculus of the leadership of the Chinese Communist Party. A strategy of this type could markedly increase the cost of pursuing a strategy of maritime expansion and potentially divert Chinese attention away from its maritime flanks and toward the Asian continent. It would increase the cost of challenging international norms and possibly give the Chinese leadership greater incentives to accept significant elements of the existing international order.

NOTES

1. See Xuezhi Guo, *China's Security State: Philosophy, Evolution, and Politics* (Cambridge: Cambridge University Press, 2012).
2. "China to Follow Specific National Security Strategy," Xinhua, April 16, 2014.
3. See David Lampton, "Xi Jinping and the National Security Commission: Policy Coordination and Political Power," *Journal of Contemporary China* 24 (1995); You Ji, "China's National Security Commission: Theory, Evolution and Operations," *Journal of Contemporary China* 25 (1998); Joel Wuthnow, "China's Much-Heralded National Security Commission Has Disappeared," *Foreign Policy*, June 30, 2016.
4. "Unwaveringly Take the National Security Path with Chinese Characteristics: Study General Secretary Xi Jinping's Major Strategic Thinking on Overall National Security Concept," Qiushi, March 1, 2015.
5. "National Security Matter of Prime Importance: President Xi," Xinhua, April 15, 2014.
6. Wang Faan, ed., *Zhongguo heping fazhan zhong de qiangjun zhanlue* 中国和平发展中的强军战略 [China's strategy for invigorating the armed forces amid peaceful development] (Beijing: Military Science Press, 2011).
7. Chinese Communist Party Literature Research Office, *Xi Jinping guanyu keji chuangxin lunshu zhaobian* 习近平关于科技创新论述摘编 [Selection of Xi Jinping's comments on science, technology and innovation] (Beijing: Central Party Literature Press, 2016), 48–49.
8. See, for example, Patrick M. Cronin and Paul S. Giarra, *Robotic Skies: Intelligence, Surveillance, Reconnaissance, and the Strategic Defense of Japan* (Washington, DC: Center for a New American Security, 2010).
9. Thomas G. Mahnken, *Secrecy and Stratagem: Understanding Chinese Strategic Culture* (Sydney: Lowy Institute, 2011).

SELECTED BIBLIOGRAPHY

Abramovitz, Moses. "Catching Up, Forging Ahead, and Falling Behind." *Journal of Economic History* 46, no. 386 (1986).

Achasov, O. B., and G. N. Vylegzhanin. Проблемы обеспечения эффективного решения задач силами общего назначения в современных условиях [The problems of ensuring the effective implementation of combat missions by conventional forces under current conditions]. Вооружения и Экономика [Arms and economics] 1 (2014).

Anin, A. Влияние стратегических наступательных вооружений в неядерном оснащении на стратегическую стабильность [The influence of non-nuclear strategic offensive weapons on strategic stability]. Мировая экономика и международные отношения [International economy and international relations] 6 (2011). http://www.ebiblioteka.ru/browse/doc/25256650.

Barrass, Gordon S. "US Competitive Strategy during the Cold War." In *Competitive Strategies for the 21st Century: Theory, History, and Practice,* edited by Thomas G. Mahnken. Palo Alto, CA: Stanford University Press, 2012.

Bi, Xinglin, ed. *Campaign Theory Study Guide.* Beijing: National Defense University Press, 2002.

Brown, Harold, Joseph W. Prueher, and Adam Segal. *Chinese Military Power.* New York: Council on Foreign Relations Press, 2003.

Campbell, Caitlin. "Highlights from China's New Defense White Paper, 'China's Military Strategy,'" US-China Economic and Security Review Commission Issue Brief, June 1, 2015.

Campbell, Caitlin, Ethan Meick, Kimberly Hsu, and Craig Murray. "China's 'Core Interests' and the East China Sea." US-China Economic and Security Review Commission Staff Research Backgrounder, May

10, 2013. https://www.uscc.gov/sites/default/files/Research/China's %20Core%20Interests%20and%20the%20East%20China%20Sea.pdf.

Carlsson, Märta, Susanne Oxenstierna, and Mikael Weissmann. "China and Russia: A Study on Cooperation, Competition and Distrust." FOI Research Report, June 2015.

Channer, Hayley. "Steadying the US Rebalance to Asia: The Role of Australia, Japan and South Korea." *ASPI Strategic Insights,* November 2014.

Chase, Michael, Jeffrey Engstrom, Tai Ming Cheung, Kristen A. Gunness, Scott Warren Harold, Susan Puska, and Samuel K. Berkowitz. *China's Incomplete Military Transformation: Assessing the Weaknesses of the People's Liberation Army (PLA).* Washington, DC: RAND, 2015.

Chase, Michael S., and Cristina L. Garafola. "China's Search for a 'Strategic Air Force.'" *Journal of Strategic Studies* 39, no. 1 (2016): 4–28.

Chen, Zhou. "Meiguo dui Hua zhanlü e yanbian yu Zhongguo heping fazhan" 美国对华战略演变与中国和平发展 [Evolution of the US strategy toward China and China's peaceful development] 和平与发展 [Peace and development] 4 (2008).

Cheung, Tai Ming. *Fortifying China: The Struggle to Build a Modern Defense Economy.* Ithaca, NY: Cornell University Press, 2008.

Cheung, Tai Ming. "The Chinese Defense Economy's Long March from Imitation to Innovation." *Journal of Strategic Studies* 34, no. 3 (2011).

Cheung, Tai Ming, Thomas Mahnken, Kevin Pollpeter, Deborah Seligsohn, Eric Anderson, and Fan Yang. *Planning for Innovation: Understanding China's Plans for Technological, Energy, Industrial, and Defense Development.* La Jolla, CA: IGCC, 2016.

Chief of Naval Operations. Undersea Warfare Directorate. "Report to Congress: Autonomous Undersea Vehicle Requirement for 2025." February 2016.

China Civil-Military Integration Development Report 2015. Beijing: National Defense University Press, 2015.

China International Strategy Association. *International Strategic Studies,* no. 2 (2015).

China National Defense Science and Technology Information Center. *Weapons and Equipment 2030*. Beijing: National Defense Industry Press, 2014.

China Strategic Culture Promotion Association. "Report on US Military Power 2013." July 2014.

Chinese Communist Party Literature Research Office. *Xi Jinping guanyu keji chuangxin luntan zhaibian* 习近平关于科技创新论述摘编 [Selection of Xi Jinping's comments on science, technology and innovation]. Beijing: Central Party Literature Press, 2016.

Chu, Shulong, and Tao Shasha. "Responding to Our Peripheral Security Challenges." *Journal of Contemporary International Relations* (November/December 2013).

Cliff, Roger. *Shaking the Heavens and Splitting the Earth*. Santa Monica, CA: RAND Corporation, 2011.

Cole, Bernard D. *China's Quest for Great Power: Ships, Oil, and Foreign Policy*. Annapolis, MD: Naval Institute Press, 2016.

Cole, Bernard D. *The Great Wall at Sea: China's Navy in the Twenty-First Century*. Annapolis, MD: Naval Institute Press, 2010.

Cordesman, Anthony H., Steven Colley, and Michael Wang. *Chinese Strategy and Military Modernization in 2015: A Comparative Analysis*. Lanham, MD: Rowman and Littlefield, 2015.

Cordesman, Anthony H., Ashley Hess, and Nicholas S. Yarosh. *Chinese Military Modernization and Force Development: A Western Perspective*. Lanham, MD: Rowman and Littlefield, 2013.

Cronin, Patrick M., and Paul S. Giarra. *Robotic Skies: Intelligence, Surveillance, Reconnaissance, and the Strategic Defense of Japan*. Washington, DC: Center for a New American Security, 2010.

Donnelly, Thomas, and Phillip Lohaus. *Mass and Supremacy: A Comprehensive Case for the F-35*. Washington, DC: American Enterprise Institute, 2013.

Dutton, Peter. "A Maritime or Continental Order for Southeast Asia and the South China Sea?" *Naval War College Review* 69, no. 3 (2016).

Ehrhard, Thomas P. *An Air Force Strategy for the Long Haul.* Washington, DC: Center for Strategic and Budgetary Assessments, 2009.

Ekman, Kenneth P. *Winning the Peace through Cost Imposition.* Washington, DC: Brookings Institution, 2014.

Ekmektsioglou, Eleni. "Hypersonic Weapons and Escalation Control in East Asia." *Strategic Studies Quarterly* 9, no. 2 (2015).

Engerman, David C. *Know Your Enemy: The Rise and Fall of America's Soviet Experts.* Oxford: Oxford University Press, 2009.

Erickson, Andrew S. "China's Blueprint for Sea Power." *China Brief* 16, no. 11 (2016).

Erickson, Andrew S. *Chinese Anti-Ship Ballistic Missile Development: Drivers, Trajectories, and Strategic Implications.* Washington, DC: Jamestown Foundation, 2012.

Erickson, Andrew S., and Adam P. Liff. "Demystifying China's Defense Spending: Less Mysterious in the Aggregate." *China Quarterly* 216 (2013).

Erickson, Andrew S., and Joel Wuthnow. "Barriers, Springboards and Benchmarks: China Conceptualizes the Pacific 'Island Chains.'" *China Quarterly* 225 (2016).

Ford, Christopher, and David Rosenberg. *The Admirals' Advantage: US Navy Operational Intelligence in World War II and the Cold War.* Annapolis, MD: US Naval Institute Press, 2005.

Fravel, M. Taylor. "China's New Military Strategy: 'Winning Informationized Local Wars.'" *China Brief* 15, no. 13 (2015).

Friedberg, Aaron L. *A Contest for Supremacy: China, America, and the Struggle for Mastery in Asia.* New York: W.W. Norton, 2011.

Gormley, Dennis M., Andrew S. Erickson, and Jingdong Yuan. *A Low-Visibility Force Multiplier: Assessing China's Cruise Missile Ambitions.* Washington, DC: National Defense University Press, 2014.

Gouré, Daniel I. "Overview of the Competitive Strategies Initiative." In *Competitive Strategies for the 21st Century: Theory, History, and Practice,* edited by Thomas G. Mahnken. Palo Alto, CA: Stanford University Press, 2012.

Green, Michael, Kathleen Hicks, and Mark Cancian. *Asia-Pacific Rebalance 2025: Capabilities, Presence, and Partnerships*. Lanham, MD: Rowman and Littlefield, 2016.

Greenert, Jonathan, James Amos, and Paul Zunkuft. *A Cooperative Strategy for 21st Century Seapower*. Washington, DC: US Department of the Navy, 2015.

Grossman, Elaine M. "Top Commander: Chinese Interference with US Satellites Uncertain." *World Politics Review,* October 18, 2006.

Gunziger, Mark, and Bryan Clark. *Winning the Salvo Competition: Rebalancing America's Air and Missile Defenses*. Washington, DC: Center for Strategic and Budgetary Assessment, 2016.

Guo, Xuezhi. *China's Security State: Philosophy, Evolution, and Politics*. Cambridge: Cambridge University Press, 2012.

Hadley, Stephen J., and William J. Perry, co-chairs. *The QDR in Perspective: Meeting America's National Security Needs in the 21st Century*. Washington, DC: US Institute of Peace, 2010.

He, Wen, Kai Hwang, and Deyi Li. "Intelligent Carpool Routing for Urban Ridesharing by Mining GPS Trajectories." *IEEE Transactions on Intelligent Transportation Systems* 15, no. 5 (2014): 2286–2296.

Heginbotham, Eric. *The US-China Military Scorecard: Forces, Geography, and the Evolving Balance of Power, 1996–2017*. Santa Monica, CA: RAND Corporation, 2015.

Hoffman, David E. *The Dead Hand*. New York: Doubleday, 2009.

Holmes, James R. "The State of the US-China Competition." In *Competitive Strategies for the 21st Century: Theory, History, and Practice,* edited by Thomas G. Mahnken. Palo Alto, CA: Stanford University Press, 2012.

Howard, Michael. "Military Science in an Age of Peace." *Journal of the Royal United Services Institute for Defense Studies* 119, no. 1 (March 1974).

Hughes, Wayne P. *Fleet Tactics and Coastal Combat*. Annapolis, MD: Naval Institute Press, 2000.

International Institute for Strategic Studies. *The Military Balance 2016.* London: Routledge, 2016.

Ionin, Andrey. Технологический альянс вместо Североатлантического ["Technological alliance instead of the North Atlantic one". Россия в глобальной политике [Russia in global affairs], June 7, 2015. http://www.globalaffairs.ru/number/ tekhnologicheskii-alyans-vmesto-severoatlanticheskogo-17502.

Jervis, Robert. "Cooperation under the Security Dilemma." *World Politics* 30, no. 2 (1978).

Johnston, Alastair Iain. "The Evolution of Interstate Security Crisis Management Theory and Practice in China." *Naval War College Review* 69, no. 1 (2016).

Kamphausen, Roy. "Asia as a Warfighting Environment." In *Strategy in Asia: The Past, Present, and Future of Regional Security,* edited by Thomas G. Mahnken and Dan Blumenthal. Palo Alto, CA: Stanford University Press, 2014.

Kazianis, Harry J. "America's Air-Sea Battle Concept: An Attempt to Weaken China's A2/AD Strategy," China Policy Institute Policy Paper 2014, no. 4.

Kiselev, L. Код Глубины [The code of the depth]. Институт проблем морских технологий Дальневосточного отделения РАН. Владивосток 2011 [Institute of the Maritime Technology, Far Eastern Department of the Russian Academy of Sciences, Vladivostok, 2011].

Kokoshin, A. A., V. I. Bartenev, and V. A. Veselov. Подготовка революции в военном деле в условиях бюджетных ограничений. Новые инициативы министерства обороны США [The preparation of a revolution in military affairs at a time of budgetary limitations: New initiatives of the US Ministry of Defense]. США и Канада: экономика, политика и культура [US and Canada: Politics, economy, and culture] 11 (2015).

Kostecka, Daniel J. "From the Sea: PLA Doctrine and the Employment of Sea-Based Airpower." *US Naval War College Review* 64, no. 3 (2011).

Kotkin, Stephen. "The Unbalanced Triangle." *Foreign Affairs* (September/October 2009).

Krepinevich, Andrew F. *Why AirSea Battle?* Washington, DC: Center for Strategic and Budgetary Assessments, 2010.

Krepinevich, Andrew F., and Robert C. Martinage. *Dissuasion Strategy.* Washington, DC: Center for Strategic and Budgetary Assessments, 2008.

Lacey, James, ed. *Great Strategic Rivalries from the Classical World to the Cold War.* Oxford: Oxford University Press, 2016.

Lampton, David, ed. *Policy Implementation in Post-Mao China.* Berkeley: University of California Press, 1987.

Lampton, David. "Xi Jinping and the National Security Commission: Policy Coordination and Political Power." *Journal of Contemporary China* 24 (1995).

Lee, Bradford A. "Strategic Interaction: Theory and History for Practitioners." In *Competitive Strategies for the 21st Century: Theory, History, and Practice,* edited by Thomas G. Mahnken. Palo Alto, CA: Stanford University Press, 2012.

Li, Jian. "Xin dixiao zhanlüe: Meiguo yi jishu youshi mouqiu chixu junshi youshi de lao taolu he xin sikao" 新抵消战略：美国以技术优势谋求持续军事优势的老套路和新思考 [New offset strategy: An old means with new thinking for the US to maintain military dominance], 空天力量杂志 [Air and space power] 9, no. 2 (2015): 92–94.

Li, Jian, and Lu Dehong. "The Third Offset Strategy: The US Competition Strategy to Seek Military Monopoly." *World Military Review* 5 (2015): 9–10.

Li, Nan. "Evolution of Strategy: From 'Near Coast' to 'Far Seas.'" In *The Chinese Navy: Expanding Capabilities, Evolving Roles,* edited by Phillip C. Saunders, Christopher Yung, Michael Swain, and Andrew Nien-Dzu Yang. Washington, DC: National Defense University, 2011.

Lieberthal, Kenneth, and Wang Jisi. *Addressing US–China Strategic Distrust.* Washington, DC: Brookings Institution, 2012.

Lieberthal, Kenneth, and David Lampton, eds. *Bureaucracy, Politics, and Decision Making in Post-Mao China.* Berkeley: University of California Press, 1992.

Lieberthal, Kenneth, and Michel Oksenberg. *Policy Making in China: Leaders, Structures, and Processes.* Princeton, NJ: Princeton University Press, 1988.

Lin, Limin. "2012 nian guoji zhanlüe xingshi pingxi" 2012年国际战略形势评析 [A review of the international strategic situation in 2012]. 现代国际关系 [Contemporary international relations], December 2012.

Liu, Ming. "Aobama zhengfu dongya zhanlüe tiaozheng ji qi dui Zhongguo de yingxiang" 奥巴马政府东亚战略调整及其对中国的影响 [Obama administration's adjustment of East Asia policy and its impact on China]. 现代国际关系 [Contemporary international relations], February 2011.

Liu, Yonghong. "Strategic Consideration on the Transformation of the PLA Navy under the New Situation." *China Military Science,* November 30, 2012.

Mahnken, Thomas G. "Arms Races and Long-Term Competition." In *Strategy in Asia: The Past, Present, and Future of Regional Security,* edited by Thomas G. Mahnken and Dan Blumenthal. Palo Alto, CA: Stanford University Press, 2014.

Mahnken, Thomas G. "Competitive Strategies for Small States." In *Frontline Allies: War and Change in Central Europe,* edited by A. Wess Mitchell, Edward Lucas, Jakub Grygiel, and Marcin Zaborowski. Washington, DC: Center for European Policy Analysis, 2015.

Mahnken, Thomas G., ed. *Competitive Strategies for the 21st Century: Theory, History, and Practice.* Palo Alto, CA: Stanford University Press, 2012.

Mahnken, Thomas G. *Cost-Imposing Strategies: A Brief Primer.* Washington, DC: Center for a New American Security, 2014.

Mahnken, Thomas G. *Secrecy and Stratagem: Understanding Chinese Strategic Culture.* Sydney: Lowy Institute, 2011.

Mahnken, Thomas G. "The Reagan Administration's Strategy toward the Soviet Union." In *Successful Strategies: Triumphing in War and Peace from Antiquity to the Present*, edited by Williamson Murray and Richard Hart Sinnreich, 403–431. Cambridge: Cambridge University Press, 2014.

Mahnken, Thomas G. *Technology and the American Way of War Since 1945*. New York: Columbia University Press, 2008.

Mahnken, Thomas G. "Thinking About Competitive Strategies." In *Competitive Strategies for the 21st Century: Theory, History, and Practice*, edited by Thomas G. Mahnken. Palo Alto, CA: Stanford University Press, 2012.

Mahnken, Thomas G. "Weapons: The Growth and Spread of the Precision Strike Regime." *Daedalus* 140, no. 3 (Summer 2011): 45–57.

Mahnken, Thomas G., and Dan Blumenthal, eds. *Strategy in Asia: The Past, Present, and Future of Regional Security*. Palo Alto, CA: Stanford University Press, 2014.

Marshall, A. W. "Long-Term Competition with the Soviets: A Framework for Strategic Analysis." R-862-PR. Santa Monica, CA: RAND Corporation, 1972.

Martinage, Robert. *Toward a New Offset Strategy: Exploiting US Long-Term Advantages to Restore U.S. Global Power Projection Capability*. Washington, DC: Center for Strategic and Budgetary Assessments, 2014.

Mastro, Oriana Skylar, and Ian Easton. "Risk and Resiliency: China's Emerging Air Base Strike Threat." Project 2049 Institute Report, November 8, 2017.

Mazarr, Michael J. *Mastering the Gray Zone: Understanding a Changing Era of Conflict*. Carlisle, PA: Strategic Studies Institute, 2015.

McDeavitt, Michael. "China's Far Sea's Navy: The Implications of the 'Open Seas Protection' Mission." Paper presented at the "China as a Maritime Power" conference, Center for Naval Analyses, Arlington, Virginia, April 2016.

McDeavitt, Michael. *Becoming a Great 'Maritime Power': A Chinese Dream.* Arlington, VA: Center for Naval Analyses, 2016.

Mulvenon, James, and Rebecca Samm Tyroler-Cooper. "China's Defense Industry on the Path of Reform." Report prepared for the US-China Economic and Security Review Commission, October 2009.

Murray, Craig, Andrew Berglund, and Kimberly Hsu. "China's Naval Modernization and Implications for the United States." US-China Economic and Security Review Commission Staff Research Backgrounder, August 26, 2013.

Murray, William S. "Revisiting Taiwan's Defense Strategy." *Naval War College Review* 61, no. 3 (Summer 2008), 13–38.

National Institute for Defense Studies (Japan). *NIDS China Security Report 2016: The Expanding Scope of PLA Activities and the PLA Strategy,* trans. Japan Times. Tokyo: National Institute for Defense Studies, 2016.

Office of the Secretary of Defense. *Annual Report to Congress: Military and Security Developments Involving the People's Republic of China.* Washington, DC: US Department of Defense, various years.

O'Rourke, Ronald. "China Naval Modernization: Implications for US Navy Capabilities—Background and Issues for Congress," Congressional Research Service Report, May 31, 2016.

O'Rourke, Ronald. *Navy Lasers, Railgun, and Hypervelocity Projectile: Background and Issues for Congress,* Congressional Research Service Report, May 27, 2016.

O'Rourke, Ronald. "PLAN Force Structure: Submarines, Ships, and Aircraft." In *The Chinese Navy: Expanding Capabilities, Evolving Roles,* edited by Phillip C. Saunders, Christopher Yung, Michael Swain, and Andrew Nien-Dzu Yang. Washington, DC: National Defense University, 2011.

Pankova, L. V. Стратегическая стабильность и новая американская стратегия компенсации [Statement on strategic stability and the new American offset strategy]. Международные отношения и мировая политика [Bulletin of the Moscow University] 3 (2015).

Perry, William J., and John P. Abizaid, co-chairs. *Ensuring a Strong US Defense for the Future: The National Defense Panel Review of the 2014 Quadrennial Defense Review.* Washington, DC: US Institute of Peace, 2014.

Pilger, Michael. "China's New YJ-18 Antiship Cruise Missile: Capabilities and Implications for US Forces in the Western Pacific." US-China Economic and Security Review Commission Staff Research Report, October 28, 2015.

Pillsbury, Michael. "The Sixteen Fears: China's Strategic Psychology," *Survival* 54, no. 5 (October-November 2012), 149–182.

PLA Academy of Military Science. Military Strategy Research Department. 战略学 (2013年半) [The science of military strategy 2013]. Beijing: Military Science Press, 2013.

Porter, Michael E. "The Competitive Advantage of Nations." *Harvard Business Review* (May-June 1990): 73–93.

Pradun,Vitaliy O. "From Bottle Rockets to Lightning Bolts." *Naval War College Review* 64, no. 2 (2010): 29–30.

Richardson, John. *Design for Maritime Superiority.* Washington, DC: US Department of the Navy, 2016.

Rosen, Stephen Peter. "Competitive Strategies: Theoretical Foundations, Limits and Extensions." In *Competitive Strategies for the 21st Century: Theory, History, and Practice,* edited by Thomas G. Mahnken. Palo Alto, CA: Stanford University Press, 2012.

Ross, Dylan B., and Jimmy A. Harmon. *New Navy Fighting Machine in the South China Sea.* Master's thesis, Naval Postgraduate School, June 2012.

Ross, Robert S. "The Rise of the Chinese Navy: From Regional Power to Global Naval Power." In *China's Global Engagement: Cooperation, Competition, and Influence in the 21st Century,* edited by Jacques Delisle and Avery Goldstein. Washington, DC: Brookings Institution Press, 2017.

Saunders, Phillip C., Christopher Yung, Michael Swain, and Andrew Nien-Dzu Yang, eds. *The Chinese Navy: Expanding Capabilities, Evolving Roles.* Washington, DC: National Defense University, 2011.

Sayers, Eric. "Military Dissuasion: A Framework for Influencing PLA Procurement Trends." *Joint Force Quarterly* 58 (2010): 89–93.

Schelling, Thomas C. "The Strategy of Inflicting Costs." In *Issues in Defense Economics,* edited by Roland N. McKean. Cambridge, MA: National Bureau of Economic Research, 1967.

Seligmann, Matthew S. "The Anglo-German Naval Race, 1898–1914." In *Arms Races in International Politics,* edited by Thomas G. Mahnken, Joseph A. Maiolo, and David Stevenson. Oxford: Oxford University Press, 2016.

Sharman, Christopher H. *China Moves Out: Stepping Stones toward a New Maritime Strategy.* Washington, DC: National Defense University Press, 2015.

Sidorenko, A. A. *The Offensive: A Soviet View.* Washington, DC: US Government Printing Office, 1970.

Swaine, Michael. "Chinese Leadership and Elite Responses to the US Pacific Pivot." *China Leadership Monitor* no. 38 (Summer 2012).

Swartz, Peter M. "Rising Powers and Naval Power." In *The Chinese Navy: Expanding Capabilities, Evolving Roles,* edited by Phillip C. Saunders, Christopher Yung, Michael Swain, and Andrew Nien-Dzu Yang. Washington, DC: National Defense University, 2011.

Tang, Xiaohua, and Dan Shijun. "Calm Thinking about the Third Offset Strategy: Reflection of Hegemonic Mentality and Strategic Anxiety." *World Military Review* 5 (2015): 21.

Tong, Zhen, and Zhang Maolin. "Contents and Prospect of the Third Offset Strategy." *World Military Review* 5 (2015).

US Department of Defense. *Quadrennial Defense Review 2014.* Washington, DC: US Department of Defense, 2014.

US Department of Defense. *Quadrennial Defense Review Report.* Washington, DC: Department of Defense, 2001.

US Office of Naval Intelligence. *The PLA Navy: New Capabilities and Missions for the 21st Century.* Washington, DC: Office of Naval Intelligence, 2015.

Van Tol, Jan. *AirSea Battle: A Point-of-Departure Operational Concept.* Washington, DC: Center for Strategic and Budgetary Assessment, 2010.

Von Clausewitz, Carl. *On War.* Edited and translated by Michael Howard and Peter Paret. Princeton, NJ: Princeton University Press, 1989.

Wang, Faan, ed. *Zhongguo Heping Fazhan Zhong De Qiangjun Zhanlue* 中国和平发展中的强军战略 [China's strategy for invigorating the armed forces amid peaceful development]. Beijing: Military Science Press, 2011.

Watts, Barry D. "Barriers to Acting Strategically: Why Strategy Is So Difficult." In *Competitive Strategies for the 21st Century: Theory, History, and Practice,* edited by Thomas G. Mahnken. Palo Alto, CA: Stanford University Press, 2012.

Watts, Barry D. *The Maturing Revolution in Military Affairs.* Washington, DC: Center for Strategic and Budgetary Assessments, 2011.

Wilson, Jordan. "China's Expanding Ability to Conduct Conventional Missile Strikes on Guam." US-China Economic and Security Review Commission Staff Research Report, May 10, 2016.

Wu, Ji, Shen Xushi, Zhao Haiyang, and Xu Xiaoping. "Dianfu xing jishu de fazhan yu qiangzhan xin 'san da geming' zhanlue zhigaodian" 颠覆性技术的发展与抢占新"三大革命"战略制高点[Grasping developping [*sic*] opportunities of disruptive technologies and surging to strategic highland of new 'tri-revolution']. 国防科技 [National defense science and technology] 36, no. 3 (2015).

Wu, Zhengyu. "The Crowe Memorandum, the Rebalance to Asia, and Sino-US Relations." *Journal of Strategic Studies* 39, no. 3 (2016).

Wuthnow, Joel. "China's Much-Heralded National Security Commission Has Disappeared." *Foreign Policy,* June 30, 2016.

Yang, Zhen, Zhao Juan, and Bian Hongjin. "Lun haiquan yu hangkong mujian shidai de Zhongguo haijun jianshe" 论海权与航空母舰时代

的中国海军建设 [On the development of [the] Chinese Navy in the era of sea power and aircraft carriers]. 世界地理研究 [World regional studies] no. 4 (2013).

Yoshihara, Toshi. "Chinese Missile Strategy and the US Naval Presence in Japan: The Operational View from Beijing." *Naval War College Review* 63, no. 3 (Summer 2010).

Yoshihara, Toshi. "Japanese Bases and Chinese Missiles." In *Rebalancing US Forces: Basing and Forward Presence in the Asia-Pacific,* edited by Andrew S. Erickson and Carnes Lord, 45. Annapolis MD: Naval Institute Press, 2014.

Yoshihara, Toshi. "Japan's Competitive Strategies at Sea: A Preliminary Assessment." In *Competitive Strategies for the 21st Century: Theory, History, and Practice,* edited by Thomas G. Mahnken. Palo Alto, CA: Stanford University Press, 2012.

Yoshihara, Toshi, and James R. Holmes. *Red Star over the Pacific: China's Rise and the Challenge to US Maritime Strategy.* Annapolis, MD: Naval Institute Press, 2010.

You, Ji. "China's National Security Commission: Theory, Evolution and Operations." *Journal of Contemporary China* 25 (1998).

Yu, Jixun, ed. *The Science of Second Artillery Campaigns.* Beijing: PLA Press, 2004.

Zhang, Feng. "Zhongguo de changzheng wu hao yunzai huojian" 中国的长征五号运载火箭 [China's long march 5 launch vehicle]. 卫星应用 [Satellite application] 2012/5.

Zhang, Ming. "'Quanqiu gongdi' anquan zhili yu Zhongguo de xuanze" "全球公地" 安全治理与中国的选择 [Security governance of the 'global commons' and China's choice] 现代国际关系 [Contemporary international relations], May 2012.

Zhang, Xiaobin. "Meiguo 'di san ci dixiao zhanlüe' dui guofang keji gongye de tiaozhan yu yingdui" 美国"第三次抵消战略" 对国防科技工业的挑战与应对 [The challenge imposed by the third US offset strategy on the development of defense science and technology industry and contermeasures [*sic*]]. 国防科技 [National defense science and technology] 36, no. 6 (2015): 74–76.

Zhang, Yuliang, ed. *The Science of Campaigns.* Beijing: National Defense University Press, 2006.

Zhao, Qinghai. "US Maritime Threats to China and Thoughts on China's Countermeasures." *China International Studies* (English) (March/April 2015).

Zhen, Bingxi. 21世纪初美国经济实力走势 [Trends of US economic strength in the early 21st century]. *Research on International Challenges*, October 19, 2000. http://www.cqvip.com/read/read.aspx?id=11790348.

Zhou, Yunheng, and Yu Jiahao. "Haishang nengyuan tongdao anquan yu Zhongguo haiquan fazhan" 海上能源通道安全与中国海权发展 [Security of maritime energy channels and the development of China's sea power]. 太平洋学报 [Pacific journal] no. 3 (2014).

Zhu, Hui, ed., *Strategic Air Force.* Beijing: Blue Sky Press, 2009.

About the Contributors

Daniel Alderman is the operations manager of SOS International's (SOSi) Special Programs Division (SPD), formerly the Defense Group Inc. (DGI). He holds an MA from the Elliott School of International Affairs at the George Washington University, and a BA from Presbyterian College. Alderman previously served as an assistant director at the National Bureau of Asian Research.

Eric Anderson is a research analyst at the UC Institute on Global Conflict and Cooperation. He holds an MPIA from the School of Global Policy and Strategy at the University of California San Diego. He is fluent in Mandarin Chinese.

Michael S. Chase is a senior political scientist at the RAND Corporation. He holds a PhD and MA from SAIS and a BA from Brandeis University. Dr. Chase is the author of the book *Taiwan's Security Policy* and numerous chapters and articles on China and Asia-Pacific security issues. His work has appeared in journals such as *Asia Policy, Asian Security, China Brief, Survival,* and the *Journal of Strategic Studies.*

Tai Ming Cheung is director of the UC Institute on Global Conflict and Cooperation and a professor at the School of Global Policy and Strategy at UC San Diego. He holds a PhD from King's College, London University and a BA from Sussex University. Dr. Cheung's previous publications include *Fortifying China: The Struggle to Build a Modern Defense Economy* and many edited volumes, book chapters, and journal articles. Dr. Cheung is a long-time analyst of Chinese and East Asian defense and national security affairs.

Bryan Clark is a senior fellow at the Center for Strategic and Budgetary Assessments. He holds an MS from the National War College and a BS from the University of Idaho. Previously, Clark was special assistant to the Chief of Naval Operations and director of his Commander's Action Group, where he led development of Navy strategy and implemented new initiatives in electromagnetic spectrum operations, undersea warfare, expeditionary operations, and personnel and readiness management. He is the recipient of the Department of the Navy Superior Service Medal and the Legion of Merit.

Senior Colonel (ret.) **Fan Gaoyue**, former director and researcher at the PLA Academy of Military Science, is now a guest professor at the Collaborative Innovation Center for Security and Development of Western Frontier China, Sichuan University.

Vasily Kashin is a senior researcher at the National Research University Higher School of Economics, Moscow, Russia, and at the Russian Academy of Sciences Institute of Far Eastern Studies (IFES) North-East Asia Center. He holds a PhD from the Institute of Far Eastern Studies. Previously he worked in the Institute for Far Eastern Studies in the Russian Academy of Sciences, for the Vedomosti business newspaper, as deputy chief of the Beijing office of RIA Novosti, and as a senior research fellow at the Center for Analysis of Strategies and Technologies (CAST), a Moscow-based defense industry consultancy.

Thomas G. Mahnken is president and chief executive officer of the Center for Strategic and Budgetary Assessments and a senior research professor at the Philip Merrill Center for Strategic Studies at the Johns Hopkins University's Paul H. Nitze School of Advanced International Studies (SAIS). He holds a PhD and MA from SAIS and a BA from the University of Southern California. Dr. Mahnken is the author of *Strategy in Asia: The Past, Present and Future of Regional Security, Competitive Strategies for the 21st Century: Theory, History, and Practice, Technology and the American Way of War Since 1945*, and *Uncovering Ways of War: U.S. Intelligence and Foreign Military Innovation, 1918–1941*, among other works.

Oriana Skylar Mastro is an assistant professor of security studies at the Edmund A. Walsh School of Foreign Service at Georgetown University.

She holds a PhD and an MA from Princeton University and a BA from Stanford University. Dr. Mastro is currently a 2017–2019 Jeane Kirkpatrick Scholar at the American Enterprise Institute. She has served as an officer in the US Air Force Reserve since 2009, currently as a political-military affairs strategist. Her work has appeared in journals such as *Foreign Affairs, Asia Policy, Asian Security, Survival, Journal of Strategic Studies, Washington Quarterly,* and *International Studies Review.*

Kevin Pollpeter is a research scientist at the Center for Naval Analysis in Washington, DC. He holds an MA from the Monterey Institute of International Studies. Pollpeter is widely published on China national security issues, with a focus on China's space program and information warfare issues. Previously, he was a was deputy director of IGCC's project on the Study of Innovation and Technology in China, the deputy director of the East Asia program at Defense Group, Inc., and a researcher at RAND.

Jonathan Ray is the chief of analysis for SOS International's (SOSi) Special Programs Division (SPD), formerly Defense Group Inc. (DGI). He holds an MA from the Monterey Institute of International Studies and a BA from Cornell University. Ray has written and published on the PRC's research and development of advanced technologies, including artificial intelligence, semiconductors, unmanned systems, nuclear weapons, and outer space systems. In 2017 Ray testified before the US-China Economic and Security Review Commission on China's pursuit of next generation technologies.

Jordan Wilson is a former security and foreign affairs policy analyst at the US-China Economic and Security Review Commission, where he contributed to reports for Congress on US national security and foreign affairs policy issues involving China and the Asia-Pacific region. He holds an MIA from the School of Global Policy and Strategy at the University of California San Diego and a BS from Thomas Edison State College.

Fan (Emily) Yang is a JD candidate at the University of California Berkeley School of Law, with a focus on intellectual property law. She holds an MPIA from the School of Global Policy and Strategy at the University of California San Diego. Previously, she was a research analyst at the UC Institute on Global Conflict and Cooperation.

INDEX

absorption, 55, 59, 67
acquisition, 3, 6, 19, 22, 42, 44, 49,
    57–59, 62, 72, 77, 97, 113, 130,
    144, 179, 184–185, 190, 195, 198,
    201, 204, 226, 248
Advanced Research Foundation
    (ARF), 220–222, 236
aerospace industry, 22, 215
Afghanistan, 2, 36, 125
air and missile defense (AMD), 38,
    44, 152
air-to-surface missile (ASM), 22,
    83–85, 100, 102–103, 105
aircraft engines, 222–223, 225
AirLand Battle, 17, 23
AirSea Battle, 2, 131, 169, 172, 174,
    176–177
    Joint Concept for Access and
        Maneuver in the Global
        Commons, 45, 128, 164
anti-access/area denial (A2/AD),
    2, 4, 16, 23, 26, 38, 42, 122,
    126–128, 131, 143, 146, 150, 153,
    155, 166, 169, 183, 212, 245, 249
    "counter-intervention"
        capabilities, 18
anti-satellite weaponry, 18
anti-ship missile (ASM), 22, 83–85,
    100–103, 105, 108, 172
anti-ship cruise missile (ASCM),
    85–86, 95, 97–98, 101, 159, 247
antisubmarine warfare (ASW), 145,
    151–152
artificial intelligence (AI), 6–7, 11,
    40, 179–185, 187, 189–197, 199,

artificial intelligence (AI)
    (*continued*), 201–208, 212
asymmetric competition, 5, 139
aviation, 10–11, 42, 60, 70, 73,
    111–114, 116, 120–123, 125,
    129–131, 135–137, 237
B-1 bomber, 22
B-2 bomber, 22
B-21 bomber, 127, 136
ballistic missiles, 6, 85, 95, 97–99,
    103, 108, 151, 162, 218, 244
    anti-ship ballistic missiles, 18
    conventional ballistic missiles,
        18
"Better Buying Power" program, 44
capital market, 10, 56, 58, 61, 71–73,
    81, 191
Central Military Commission
    (CMC), 65–67, 70, 78, 113, 134,
    229
Central Commission for
    Integrated Military and Civilian
    Development, 69, 229
C4ISR (command, control,
    communications, computers,
    intelligence, surveillance, and
    reconnaissance), 29, 84–86, 92,
    103–104, 128
civil-military integration (CMI), 10,
    56, 58, 60, 66–67, 69–72, 75, 77,
    79–80, 82, 184–185, 195
China Aerospace Science and
    Industry Corporation (CASIC),
    71

CAMBRIA RAPID COMMUNICATIONS IN CONFLICT AND SECURITY (RCCS) SERIES

General Editor: Geoffrey R. H. Burn

The aim of the RCCS series is to provide policy makers, practitioners, analysts, and academics with in-depth analysis of fast-moving topics that require urgent yet informed debate.

Since its launch in October 2015, the RCCS series has the following book publications:

For more information, visit www.cambriapress.com.

CPSIA information can be obtained
at www.ICGtesting.com
Printed in the USA
FFHW022114150719
53665607-59327FF